BEST OF CFW ——————— VOL. 1
MARTIAL ARTS

EDITED & COMPILED
JOSE M. FRAGUAS

EMPIRE BOOK/AWP LLC
Los Angeles, CA.

Disclaimer

Please note that the author and publisher of this book are NOT RESPONSIBLE in any manner whatsoever for any injury that may result from practicing the techniques and/or following the instructions given within. Since the physical activities described herein may be too strenuous in nature for some readers to engage in safely, it is essential that a physician be consulted prior to training.

Revised Edition published in 2024 by AWP LLC/Empire Books. Copyright (c) 2024 by Jose M. Fraguas.

All rights reserved. No part of this publication may be reproduced or utilized in any form or by any means, electronic or mechanical, including photo-copying, recording, or by any information storage and retrieval system, without prior written permission from Jose M. Fraguas.

ISBN-13: 978-1-949753-74-5

24 23 22 21 20 19 18 17 16 15 14 13 12

Library of Congress Cataloging-in-Publication Data

Best of CFW Martial Arts. Edited and Compiled by Fraguas, Jose M. -- ed. p. cm.

ISBN 978-1-949753-73-8 (pbk. : alk. paper) 1. Martial arts-- philosophy. 3. Large type books. I. Title. GV1114.3.F715

20741261.815'3--dc22

20069892492

Printed in the United States of America.

BEST OF CFW ——————— VOL.1
MARTIAL ARTS

Dedication

To all of you—those who deserve the most of the credit, the writers who supply us with an enormous amount of material every year to fill the pages of our magazines.

Acknowledgements

Our special thanks go out to the usual suspects, our staff editors, for taking time and effort to make every article better and comprehensive for the reader.

BEST OF CFW — VOL. 1
MARTIAL ARTS

Contents

Foreword 10
  Jose M. Fraguas

An Uphill Battle 12
  Doug Jeffrey

Finally! Something to Crow About 18
  Dave Cater

Everyday Tools, Extraordinary Weapons 26
  Jane Hallander

Teaching Taiji's New Generation 32
  Lawrence Huang, photos by Lo Hong Yuan

Hand Techniques 101 36
  Justin Iverson

The Secret Is Out 46
  Stephan Berwick, photos courtesy of Donnie Yen

Jade Leung: Black Cat Rising 52
  Ric Meyers

Wang Hui-Juin's 7 Principles of Tai Chi 58
  Dr. Peter Uhlmann

Chance Action Fighting 64
  Gregory E. LeBlanc, M.S., L.Ac.

Stick Attack 68
  Doug Jeffrey

Make Your Defense OFFENSIVE 74
  Eric Oram

Warrior Training with Baguazhang 82
  Dr. John P. Painter

The Perfect Warrior 88
  Doug Jeffrey

The Best of Both Worlds 94
  Dave Cater

The Mechanics of Spiral Throws 100
  Tim Cartmell, photos by Matt Huang

The Secret Behind Baji Basics 106
  Neil Thomas, with Jason Tsou

Martial Science 120
  Doug Jeffrey

Choy Lay Fut's Renaissance Man 126
  David Tadman

Extreme Hwa Rang Do 134
  Hyung-Min Jung

Liangong, the Chinese Way to Better Health 144
  Wen Mei Yu

BEST OF CFW — VOL. 1
MARTIAL ARTS

Big "D" *152*
  Doug Jeffrey
Classic Jackie—10 Chantastics That Will Never Die *158*
  Ric Meyers
What's in a Xing Ming *166*
  Peter Gryffin
Chin Na—The Art of Fighting Without Fighting *172*
  Brian M. Brinkman
Planting the Seeds of Hung Gar *178*
  Donald Hamby
Gut-Wrenching Plyometrics *184*
  Doug Jeffrey
Vision-Airy *190*
  David Tadman
Shin Lin, Warrior-Scholar for the 21st Century *196*
  Ric Meyers
Strike First *202*
  Bill Lasiter
Ready for Battle *208*
  Thomas J. Nardi, Ph.D.
Versatile Taekwondo *212*
  Terry L. Wilson
Defense Against a Punch *218*
  Dan Ivan
Zhuang Gung—Back to Basics *224*
  Kenny Perez
The Next Generation *230*
  Doug Jeffrey
Bringing the Past to Life *234*
  Brian Kennedy
Fundamentally Sound *240*
  Jose Fraguas
The 3 Doors of Raymond Wong *252*
  Ron Quan
Andy Kimura—The Sum of All Parts *258*
  David Tadman
Internal Power: How to cultivate Ki in Aikido *264*
  Rev. Kensho Furuya
The Secret Behind Tiger Iron Palm *270*
  Wing Lam and Chet Braun
Karate Hand Strikes *278*
  Doug Jeffrey

Foreword

To say we get a lot of mail at CFW Enterprises would be quite an understatement. Every year we receive literally hundreds and hundreds of story submissions for all of our various magazines. These manila envelopes contain works ranging from fascinating to—well, to put it diplomatically, "fanciful." Yet we open nearly each and every piece of mail to separate contents from the envelope while doing our best not to commit an eco-crime.

Kidding aside, what we look for in the mail is the best martial arts writing in existence. To be considered "the best" there are some basic criteria which must be met. The editors at CFW Enterprises carefully evaluate the articles they receive to finally decide those which will be published. It is not an easy task since many variables are involved in the process.

Needless to say, while we receive a lot of good submissions we also, as an occupational hazard, have to read a lot of "really bad stuff." Fortunately, after years of working as an editor you develop an instinct and can quickly identify an unusable submission.

That's what this series is all about: bringing you the "Best of CFW" for each year, without prejudice in terms of the writer, the source, or the subject. Our aim is to provide the readers with a wide selection of styles and systems. The collection includes many different authors who offer their own perspectives of the arts and the influences of their respective arts in the field. All of them have expressed their ideas in a very different way. But whether expressed in the language of the teachers, the language of the students, or the language of the thinker, there is truth in concepts, philosophies and techniques that so many martial artists have believed and lived by for decades.

Here at CFW, we have made every effort to present each article and work as accurately as possible within the limitations of the book format. In addition to being a resource for researches, writers, students and teachers, we hope this collection of works will provide comfort and inspiration for all those who love the martial arts. There are many excellent books about the martial arts with more on the way. My hope is that this book of collective works and articles will prove a worthy companion to them in two main ways: first, in its size and scope; second in its practicality and ease of use.

There have been many changes in the martial arts but some things are still the same. A well-written article is one of them. Our job and responsibility at CFW as the world leaders in the publication of martial arts magazines, videos, and books is to inform and educate the reader, promoting all the styles and approaches without being limited by any of them.

MARTIAL ARTS
BEST OF CFW — VOL. 1

As early as I can remember. My house was filled with martial arts magazines from around the world. For many years, I gathered publications and became curious about many of the authors who wrote for them. The more I researched, the more I realized that those "great people" were a lot more like you and me than they were different. Today I have written hundreds of articles in magazines around the world, more than a dozen of books under my own name and a couple under some else's. At CFW, our editors have read, written, edited and re-written more articles and books than one could possibly imagine. Although it is unlikely any of us will ever be awarded the Nobel Prize, the writing that we like is the writing that we like. Nothing can change that.

I bring all this up because I believe all the writers who have submitted material to be published in the different magazines owned by CFW Enterprises have followed similar paths.

Walk on!

—**Jose Fraguas**
General Manager
CFW Enterprises

An Uphill Battle

Willy Cahill Overcame Polio and a Lack of Confidence To Become One of the Greatest Judo Coaches in History

Doug Jeffrey

On the way home from work some day, think back to when you were eight years old. You remember ... the third grade. If you were going to buy lunch, the teacher had you stand so the cafeteria workers would have an accurate count of the number of meals they needed to prepare. At about 10:15 every morning, the bell echoed through the halls. You weren't supposed to, but it seems like you and everyone else ran to the yard so you could throw a dodge ball or slam a handball against those huge wooden backboards with the circles on them.

On the way home from school, you and your friends pushed, shoved and kicked just about everything in sight. When you pushed the front door of your home open, you immediately went to the cupboard and refrigerator for graham crackers and milk. Then, as soon as the homework was done, you were outside with your friends, throwing a baseball, chasing butterflies or running with your dog. Pretty normal stuff.

Now, imagine you can't move your legs. Not an inch. Forget about standing, throwing a baseball or chasing a butterfly. You're confined to a hospital bed with polio. While most of us enjoyed life's simple pleasures, Willy Cahill could not. He experienced that nightmare. He had polio.

"I was about eight years old at the time, and the doctor said I would never walk again," says Cahill, who has coached extensively throughout his career, including the U.S. Blind Judo Team in the 2000 Olympics. "It was pretty devastating because I could not walk. I don't think I realized how serious it was until they put me in the hospital. I could not even get out of bed."

In addition to the medical care he received to combat the viral disease that inflames the brainstem and spinal cord, Cahill also got some help from his father's judo instructor. He used to put herbs on Cahill's legs and give him a massage while he was confined to the bed. About a year later Cahill was out of the hospital and free of polio.

"I was pretty nervous when I could not walk without a brace," says the 65-year-old owner of Cahill's Judo

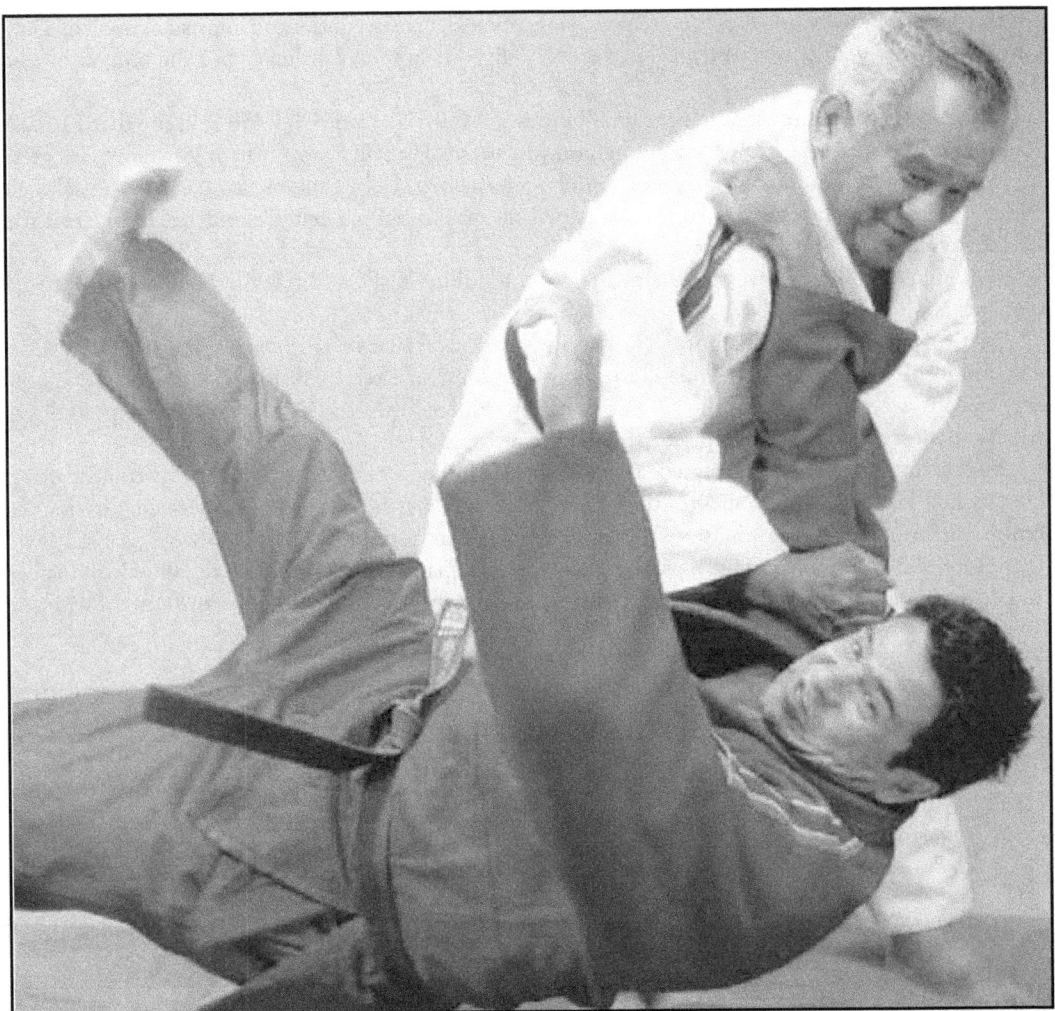

Academy in San Bruno, California. "I knew I wanted to play football. I also started judo about the same time. It was pretty depressing. Somehow, however, I knew I would walk again."

The youngster was optimistic because he just felt he was too young not to be able to walk again. That is the mentality he had. And that determination has stayed with him throughout his life.

WAVES, FOOTBALL, JUDO

Growing up in Hawaii, you might imagine that the crystal blue waves of the Pacific would be too strong to resist. Not for Cahill. He particularly loved the gridiron, and he also had a fairly strong interest in the martial arts, especially since his dad was teaching judo and *jujutsu*.

"Although he was teaching, he did not pressure us to participate," says Cahill. "He was not like that. We (his brothers) wanted to play football, and he said we would have to learn how to fall, [which we would learn in the martial arts]. He was also not the kind of coach or father who expected us to win. He just wanted us to go out and participate."

And that he did. Cahill got into both sports, big time. Everything was great until the Army drafted him right out of high school. He spent the next two years in the service and then his family moved to the mainland in 1947. They settled in San Francisco.

BEST OF CFW — VOL. 1
MARTIAL ARTS

His father, John, worked as a machinist and opened his first judo and jujutsu school in Daly City. In 1962, when he was just 50, John died. Willy was supposed to take over the school, but he was reluctant.

"Initially, I even dropped out," he says. "However, Wally Jay came over and told me that I had to teach. He suggested that I quit competing and just teach. He said I owe it to my parents. He grew up with my dad and offered to help me. Another gentlemen, Bill Montera, my dad's first black belt student from Hawaii, also came out and helped me teach. Soon I felt I could teach and run the school myself."

Although Cahill took over the helm in 1962, he didn't feel like he really belonged for several more years.

"Things started to look good in 1965," he says. "I took some kids to the U.S. Judo Championships, and one of the kids did really well. One year later, he finished second and two others placed. I was now on a roll. In 1968, one of my students won the U.S. Championships and was voted the most outstanding competitor. That gave me confidence."

That early success led to later success and soon he had more offers to coach than he could handle. He coached his first international team in 1976 when he took the U.S. team to Mexico City for the Junior Pan American Championships. After that, there was Stanford University, San Francisco State University, the World Championships, the Pan American Games, the Olympics, the Goodwill Games and on and on. Along the way, he's produced more than 900 national and international medal winners.

The combatants square off (1). When his opponent throws a punch, Cahill steps back slightly (2) and pushes Matt Midyette's punching hand in while throwing a shot to the elbow (3 and 4). Cahill then takes his opponent to the ground (5) and drops a knee onto Midyette's neck as he twists his arm (6).

MARTIAL ARTS

U.S. JUDO IS STRUGGLING

While Cahill and his teams have enjoyed an unprecedented amount of success throughout the years, the same really can't be said for the current U.S. Judo teams.

"I believe that the U.S. has to start all over again," he says. "There were eight people in the last world championships, and they all lost in less than a minute. Six of them lost in less than 30 seconds. Instead of getting better, we're getting worse. I don't want to be critical of the people who are running the program, but it just seems as if we are going backward instead of forward. It seems like the United States feels lucky when we place someone in the Olympics or the World Championships. It shouldn't be that way."

Despite the slump, Cahill sees a glimmer of hope.

"There is now a young kid named Tom Dyer, who is the new director of development," he says. "He's a former competitor, and I think we need guys who have been there before. In the past, I'm not sure things were always done in the best interest of the athletes. But I believe he will make changes, and he can make a difference."

To succeed, Dyer is going to need some help, says Cahill.

"We need to let him know that we are all behind him, and we need to ask him what we can do to make it easier for him to continue with his program and help put it in the

Matthew Midyette (right) attacks Willy Cahill with a right punch, which he blocks with his forearm (1). While Cahill pulls his right hand back, he pushes his attacker's right arm away with his left hand (2) and throws a right to Midyette's ribs (3). Cahill then pulls his opponent's right arm down (not visible) and simultaneously grabs him across the neck (4). Meanwhile, Cahill steps forward with his right leg as he prepares to sweep his opponent to the ground (5).

Willy Cahill Up Close

Age: 65, **Born:** Honolulu, Hawaii, **Residence:** Foster City, California
Occupation: Owner of Cahill Judo Academy in San Bruno
Students: 180-200, **Opened:** 1948

Accomplishments
Following are some of Willy Cahill's accomplishments throughout the years.
- 7th-degree black belt in judo
- 10th-degree black belt in jujutsu
- Produced more than 900 national and international medal winners
- Judo coach at San Francisco State University, 1981-1993
- Judo coach at Stanford University, 1980-1994
- U.S. coach Junior Pan American championships, 1976
- U.S. coach at world championships, 1981, 1985, 1987, 1989, 1991
- U.S. coach Pan American Games, 1983, 1987
- U.S. Olympic Games assistant coach, 1984, 1988
- Coach of the 2000 Paralympic Judo Team

right direction so we can get better results," he notes. "In the past, I think there were some people who were more interested in what they could get out of it. Their attitude was pretty much, 'What's in it for me?' Those in control should control the sport and help it along. The decisions that are made should be in the best interests of everyone."

THE RIGHT DIRECTION

While it's easy to sit back from a distance and criticize, Cahill is careful not to do that. He carefully chooses his words and gently makes observations that may help to get the teams back on track.

"We won our first championship in 1953," he notes. "Here we are down the line, and we've only got four world champions. Therefore, the first thing we need to do is make sure all of the coaches are certified. All the coaches need to know and understand the sport. Too many coaches come in and start to teach without any background."

Next, the coaches have to know the players, he says. During the Pacific Rim championships in Los Angeles last summer, one of the coaches did not know all of the player's names.

"That's embarrassing," he says.

Next, there should be more training done in Europe and with the countries in the Pan American Union, Brazil, Cuba, Mexico, Argentina, Venezuela, etc. take advantage of the progress others are making. Cahill also feels it's wrong for the elite U.S. athletes to train by themselves because they often make up their own programs.

"A lot of it is still guesswork," he says. "Our first national judo championships were held at San Jose Sate in 1953, and now, almost 50 years later, we are still struggling to stay afloat in the international arena."

To remedy this problem, American coaches

Midyette reaches over Cahill's shoulder to apply a choke (1). Before his adversary has a chance to apply any pressure, Cahill turns his head to the right, grabs his arm close to the shoulder and pulls downward (2). As Cahill continues to pull downward, he moves his right leg closer to Midyette so he can execute a throw (3). When his opponent is on the ground, Cahill can execute an armbar and/or strike him in the ribs (4 and 5).

need to look at other sports such as football and baseball, he says.

"They need to look at how they train," he says. "There are a lot of judo guys who work out, but they do not train. And that is a big difference. When you train, that should include weights, running, sprints, nutrition, sports psychology and a lot of drills."

The players also need to take a break, so they do not burn out and plan the season, he says.

"These guys should be making a graph of the whole year and set five different goals," he says. "You can then strive for those and peak at the right time."

> ## Can Anyone Catch the Russians?
>
> **Martial Arts & Combat Sports:** How would you rate the quality of the Russian athletes?
> **Willy Cahill:** The Russians have techniques that are different than those of standard judo. They grab you differently and throw differently. As you know, everyone in judo performs hip, shoulder and leg throws. They have variations of these that have really helped their style.
> **MACS:** Would you say that the Russians are tougher than the rest of the judo players throughout the world, including the United States?
> **Cahill:** Mentally? Yes. There wasn't one U.S. athlete who won at the world championships.
> **MACS:** How far ahead of everyone are they?
> **Cahill:** I'd say they have really pulled away.
> **MACS:** Can anyone catch them?
> **Cahill:** Oh, yeah. Japan and Korea will come back. Interestingly, however, judo is not as big as it used to be in Japan. In the past, everyone took it through the school system. Now, that doesn't occur as much.

After pausing for a moment, Cahill sits up and recounts an incident in Venezuela that exemplifies the problems the U.S. is having.

"I was the coach of the U.S. Judo Team, and we were housed along with the U.S. men's and women's swim team," he says. "Both teams were scheduled to compete the following day. The only thing that separated our dorm from theirs was a glass door. The coach asked me if we could keep the noise down because his team would be going to bed at 8 p.m. On the other hand, the judo team didn't want to go to bed until they were tired. They wanted to stay up and play cards. In essence, the swim team, which always wins a lot of medals, came to win, and the judo players were hoping to win."

GOALS, BLIND JUDO

In 2000, the members of the Blind Judo Team certainly did not go into the competition hoping to win. They were expecting to win. And it was extremely refreshing, says Cahill.

"They were all eager to learn and try things," he says. "It was a great high. The players really had the enthusiasm. They wanted to be the first to get gold for the United States."

Although the players already had an abundance of confidence, he tried to instill more in them.

"I used to them that the last thing they do before they fall asleep is see themselves on the victory stand with that medal," he says. "Every night. Every morning. That is all they thought about for eight months."

It also helped that he had them set some attainable goals along the way.

"Setting goals is the most important thing, and that is what I always tell my students right in the beginning," he says. "You have to set a reachable goal. For example, I tell the white belts to strive for yellow. I tell the athletes the same thing. Making the Olympic team might be unreachable at first, but winning a national championship is certainly reasonable."

STANDING AND CHEERING

It's certainly reasonable to expect that U.S. Judo will get untracked fast. Some recent results show they might be headed in the right direction.

They won't be all the way back, however, until someone from the U.S. Judo team lands a gold in the Olympics. That's when we'll really know they're back. When that happens, you can bet that Willy Cahill will be standing firmly on both feet, loudly applauding.

Finally! Something to Crow About

After spending a year in self-imposed seclusion, Mark Dacascos is ready to tackle the world.

Dave Cater

This is a wondrous time to be Mark Dacascos.
- He's carrying around a bouncing brand new baby boy.
- A six-month acting stint in France has produced what many industry insiders are calling a "can't-miss" classic.
- Several other films in different stages of post-production will only add to his acting stock.
- There's excitement about an upcoming opportunity to work with a great director, even if it means an extended stay in South America.
- For the first time in years he's relaxing at home with wife, Julie.
- Why, he even coaxed the martial arts' poster child for humility—father Al—to appear with him on a magazine cover.

Could life get any better? For the moment at least, the world is treating the 38-year-old son of won hop kuen do grandmaster Al Dacascos and Malia Bernal with all the pomp and circumstance of royalty.

• • •

Young Makoalani (Makoa for short), born Dec. 31, 2000, is brimming with the kind of childlike wonderment reserved those seeing the world for the first time. He looks up and Mark meets the gaze halfway. They smile. Two chairs away, mom and grandpa admire the newest member of the Dacascos dynasty. In a few minutes, the youngest member of one of martial arts' greatest families will don a specially made martial arts uniform and pose (as well as babies can) for his first cover shot. There are perks to being the son of the son of the king, after all, especially when you're born in the Year of the Dragon.

Mark Dacascos has never seemed more at peace with himself or his surroundings. He's worked hard to get to this place in his life. If any martial artist has paid his dues and earned the right to be called a survivor, it is Mark Dacascos.

Long before he made his mark in Hollywood, Mark Dacascos was one of the most respected martial artists in the country. But he also was among its most humble, a trait he says he got at an early age from his father.

Although papa Al trained as a youth in Hawaii with the great William Kwai Sun Chow and can

Scenes from Brotherhood of the Wolf, an 18th-century period epic which Mark shot over six months in Europe. Dacascos prepped for the assignment by learning to ride a horse, studying Mohawk Indian culture, and becoming fluent in French.

"I've never seen anything like this movie; it has a beast, it has action, it has romance, it has horses and Indians and French soldiers."

call among his martial arts brothers such incredible figures as Ed Parker, Ralph Castro and Adriano Emperado, his humbleness sometimes defies even traditional description.

Mark finally popped up on the radar screen in 1987 when he played in the Universal Studios stage show of "Conan the Barbarian." His partner in those days was former forms great Karen Sheperd, who like Dacascos had a Hollywood dream.

Dacascos left the four-to-ten-shows-a-day grind in 1991 to pursue acting full time. Taking several months off to shoot *American Samurai* in Israel only whetted his appetite for the possibilities.

"I've come a long way from my days at Universal, yet at that time in my life Universal was 100 percent necessary," he admits. "I was working five days a week, playing two characters, it was a live show and it was very physical. This was the first time I had to do something as far as being a performer long-term. It prepped me for spending six months on a movie set or doing nine months on a television show. It was a great learning experience."

Dacascos talks and walks with the bounce of a man on the verge of something great. Like he can't wait for the next step, the next phone call, the next assignment. Confidence. Resolve. Grittiness. An inner tranquility that translates into an outer serenity.

• • •

It all seems so easy now, so worth it. But there was a time in the not-so-distant past when Mark Dacascos was mired in such a deep and personal malaise you wondered if he'd ever see the surface a second time. Kind of like a veteran Pipeline surfer who gets dumped by a 50-footer, is violently trashed against the rugged bottom and thinks this time the wave has finally exacted revenge.

Four years ago, Dacascos accepted what many in the industry considered an instant ticket to stardom—the lead in the syndicated television series "The Crow." What a break for the young star, what a chance to show the breadth and depth of his talents.

The film version of *The Crow* cost Brandon Lee his life. And the television series—although it only lasted a year—almost cost Mark Dacascos his sanity. He played the character of Eric Draven, a murdered musician who comes back in the form of a crow to avenge his death. Lee, who was accidentally killed by a shell casing from a prop gun, became a cult hero when the movie was released. Dacascos almost became a tragic hero; 17-hour days followed by sleepless nights spent in the editing trailer turning his world upside down.

"It was really, really difficult," admitted Dacascos, who was married just weeks before the crew set up shop in Vancouver. "I mean it put a strain on not just my physical body, but on my heart and soul and my personal life. I had just gotten married and we had a house in California but here I was working 60-to-70 hours a week in Canada in a place where everything was so dramatic, so traumatic.

"You know it wasn't one of those happy shows," he adds, his face now dour and sullen. "It was just death and life and everything was just so very, very serious. I found myself physically and spiritually exhausted. During the last couple of episodes I had some very sensitive scenes. As an actor you know the more experiences you have in your life the more you can draw upon."

Playing Conan to a bunch of tourists didn't provide Dacascos with the reserve he needed.

"My soul was like a sponge and it was squeezed dry by the substance of the scenes," he related. "I was trying to put everything I had into it but I didn't know how to let go."

He couldn't sleep, couldn't eat, couldn't rest. He was drained, spent, an actor running on empty. The mental turmoil was heightened to a fever pitch when the "curse" of "The Crow," a familiar refrain heard 'round the movie set, hit the series as well. Six shows into the run, well-known stuntman Mark Ackerstream was killed when he was struck by a piece of flying metal during the shooting of a boat explosion. Making things all the more bizarre is that no stuntman—Ackerstream included—was being used during the fateful scene.

"We were all—maybe 50 or 60 cast and crewmembers—sitting behind the camera watching the monitors and watching this boat from afar," Dacascos remembers. "The explosion happens and

everything seemed fine. A second or two later we heard this whistling through the trees and the next thing you know we hear this thunk and somebody screamed and I saw Mark lying down. Some debris flew up from the explosion, traveled that far a distance and hit him in the head. It could have been anybody, because we were all within 15-to-20 feet from each other."

There was talk of shutting the show down for good, of sending everyone home, of the curse and how it would strike next. The cast and crew felt they owed to themselves, to Ackerstream, to continue. Even if it felt like a dark cloud was hanging over a set punctuated by rainy days, dark sets and gloomy subject matter.

"I personally don't feel like the show or the subject matter was cursed," Dacascos uneasily admits. "But you know, if you take Mark's death into account…you know it depends on how you look at it…it certainly did bring a certain feel to the show."

• • •

Although ratings were good, the show's cancellation after one season came as bittersweet news to Dacascos. On one hand, his heart and soul lay on the Vancouver set; on the other hand, he had nothing left to give.

"I may have been able to do another year, but I don't think I would have been a happy person doing it," he explains. "And that's not worth it."

MARTIAL ARTS

Sifu Al Dacascos shows the reaction against a right roundhouse, sidekick or front straight kick. These movements would apply with minor adjustments. Dacascos moves toward his safe zone (1). He shifts to the 1 o'clock position to defend against a roundhouse kick (2). He applies a left elbow strike to his opponent's left inner thigh. From there, he weaves under to strike the opponent's groin area with his right shoulder (3) and then lifts (4). He then redirects the opponent head first to the surface (5).

Instead, Mark knew his life wouldn't be worth much to himself or his new wife unless he regained his personal balance. So he spent much of the next year in his birthplace of Hawaii—surfing, rekindling, rediscovering the energy lost in a year of hardship and heartbreak.

"I needed it, I needed the time away to get my energy back."

It was time well-spent. Since "The Crow," Dacascos has made four movies—including one which kept him on location in France for six months—*China Strike Force* in Shanghai, China, with Hong Kong director Stanley Tong of *Rumble in the Bronx* fame; *Instinct to Kill*, based on the novel *Perfect Husband*; and *Scorcher*, with John Rhys-Davies. He also will leave later this year for French Guyana and Brazil where he'll film *Shaman*.

Mark, with son Makoa and father Al.

The eyes of the world, however, will be on Dacascos' performance in *Le Pacte des Loups* or *Brotherhood of the Wolf*, which was scheduled to be released in November. By far his biggest acting challenge, the film directed by Christophe Gans (who also helmed the Dacascos' film *Crying Freeman*) is a grand period epic with action, religion, romance and politics set against the rugged 18th-century European countryside. A cast of 250 was complemented by 300 extras and 50 horses.

"It has one of the most unbelievable opening scenes since *Jaws*," notes Dacascos, who plays a Mohawk Indian in the film. "I've never seen anything like this movie; it has a beast, it has action, it has romance, it has horses and Indians and French soldiers."

Playing the part of an Indian required Dacascos to ride a horse. Horse stances? No problem. Riding a horse? That was another matter entirely for this self-described "surfer dude." He was brought over to France several weeks before the beginning of filming and given formal riding lessons.

"I told the trainer I basically knew nothing," Mark relates, laughing, "so he got me on the horse, made sure my back was straight and my hips were relaxed and then told me to drop the reins and pull my feet out of the stirrups. Then he whistled and the horse just took off on a gallop. Listening to what he said and using my instincts, along with my body wanting to survive this thing, I was able to ride without hanging on at a gallop. By the end of the shoot I felt pretty comfortable on a horse."

The same could be said for his French and Mohawk dialect. Although he took French in high school, repeating sil vous plait to your teacher and speaking well enough to make yourself believable to foreign audiences is quite a challenge. A two-month crash course in French courtesy of Berlitz followed by lessons on the set helped bridge the gap. But even Berlitz came up empty when it came to speaking Mohawk.

"Prior to leaving I had to take Mohawk cultural lessons from a lady in Eastern Canada named Alice Rice," Dacascos explained. "She taught me what she could in the limited amount of time about Mohawk culture and language and songs so that I had some substance to work with and bring reality to my character."

By the end of the shoot, Dacascos felt comfortable—period. Three months turned into four months, which eventually became six months. In the interim, he read three biographies—two about Napoleon and a 500-pager about the Romanoff's—played guitar and practiced his French.

So far removed from martial arts, yet so close, Dacascos maintains.

"My martial arts training helped with my balance, my confidence and just not wanting to give up," he relates. "Actually, everything I did was helped my by martial arts because everything was so new. I use martial arts every day of my life."

The objective here is to dislocate the opponent's knee.
From an on-guard position (1), Al Dacascos moves to the 1 o'clock position with his left leg. He blocks the kick with his left hand (2) and strikes to the groin area. His right leg is flush against his opponent's knee area. Note that his right heel is not planted. As the opponent's momentum is about to pass Dacascos' central point, he immediately plants his heel and stiffens his leg (3), causing the opponent to fall backward or suffer the consequences of a dislocated left knee (4).

MARTIAL ARTS

• • •

Tiny Makoa is a can't-miss in the ham department. At six months and a hefty 17 pounds, he steals the show from his famous family tree.

Garbed in an outfit straight out of *The Last Emperor*, he poses like a pro and then goes with mom for a wardrobe and diaper change. Then father and son have a go at a few techniques. They play like old friends, until Al deftly turns a wrist and has Mark writhing in pain. Talk about your Kodak moments.

"I think the last time we got to train and play around together was about three years ago," Mark mentions later. "I miss being able to get kicked and tossed around by my dad. I really miss it."

Soon, Mark and Makoa will be able to share that same feeling of playing at something so close to the family's raison e'tre.

"I will always do martial arts and at least for the first years my son will do martial arts," Mark promises. "Whether or not I act I will always do martial arts. Because martial arts is in our family, like eating and sleeping, it's part of our lifestyle. I didn't do martial arts to get into acting; it's two completely different things, two parts of my life that on a good day come together and make me really, really happy. Today is one of those days."

It's a wondrous time to be Mark Dacascos.

MARTIAL ARTS

Everyday Tools, Extraordinary Weapons

Ancient Chinese turned the common horse bench and hoe into uncommon self-defense tools.

Jane Hallander

Traditional Chinese martial arts weapons, such as swords and spears, were almost always the property of professional fighters or armed robbers in ancient China. Monks, farmers and other workers had to rely solely on their everyday tools for self-defense. Buddhist monks used their spades and canes as powerful weapons against armed robbers, while farmers turned to their hoes, rakes, staffs and horse benches for personal protection.

Choy li fut, one of the largest martial arts in Southern China, contains as many, if not more, different weapons than any other Chinese style. Among choy li fut's weapons' arsenal is the horse bench and farmer's hoe.

Choy li fut grandmaster, Doc Fai Wong, views all weapons as indispensable, including the horse bench and hoe. Wong, whose Doc Fai Wong Martial Arts Center is headquartered in San Francisco, Calif., teaches those once-humble farmers' weapons to his most promising students.

"Although considered lowly farmers' weapons, the horse bench and hoe are just as effective as the professional martial artists' sword and spear," explains Wong.

Horse Bench

Often considered no more than a resting place for the tired, the Chinese horse bench, or cheong kiu dang, is actually a powerful weapon that even has applications in today's sometimes-dangerous society.

The horse bench was shaped like the common sawhorse. It had a flat board on top where it was used as a seat. The bench was approximately two feet tall and four-to-five feet in length—longer than today's sawhorse. The flat top board was between six-to-eight inches wide.

Horse benches were used in everyday restaurants and homes,

in place of more expensive chairs. Of course, when fights broke out at eating and drinking establishments, horse benches were among the first items used as weapons.

Although not as long as a staff or spear, the horse bench is still classified as a long weapon in Chinese martial arts, because the heavy bench is usually held with both hands. Also, most of the techniques are double-ended staff movements, caused by twisting the waist and generating striking power alternately with both ends of the bench.

There are also overhead strikes that use the bench as a downward striking or pressing weapon. Featured are low sweeping actions that instantly take the opponent off balance and down to the ground, where he falls prey to the horse bench's downward hammer-like blow.

Working the Bench

Common bench techniques are left and right jabs made with either end. Again, the weapon is held with both hands while making these attacks to steady its weight and somewhat spread-out construction. Sometimes the leg portion of one end can be used either to trap other weapons or as an uppercut blow to an opponent.

Some horse bench techniques feature the weapon being held in only one hand. In one instance, the choy li fut practitioner holds the upper part of one of the bench's legs and either swings the bench above his head to block other attacking weapons, or sweeps the bench low to attack an opponent's legs in a sweeping motion.

As a defensive weapon, the horse bench could be used for overhead blocks, lower bocks and side-to-side blocking actions. There are even horse bench techniques that mimic human kicks, where the stylist holds one leg of the weapon in one hand and strikes forward with an underhand blow to the opponent's midsection.

In today's world, an altercation in a restaurant or bar might lead someone to defend himself with a chair using horse bench techniques. However, the horse bench's real value is as a training weapon. Since it is a heavy weapon (15-to-20 pounds), it is often used in Wong's schools to build strength

"The horse bench and hoe are just as effective as the professional martial artists' sword and spear."

and stamina through weight training as students practice the horse bench form. At the same time its use improves the practitioner's balance and coordination.

Wong maintains that before attempting serious horse bench practice, you should strengthen your wrists and fingers. If they are not strong enough you can easily sprain or strain them. Lifting exercises, where you lift weights or even jars filled with sand or dirt, are excellent ways to condition your wrists and hands.

The Hoe

One of the most practical weapons among Southern China's farmers was the hoe, a weapon that could be used double-ended, like the staff, for blocking and striking, or as a bladed weapon for chopping and slicing. And, of course, it was easily available, since every farmer had a hoe and was well-versed in its use.

The choy li fut hoe form contains more than just fighting applications. It also has drama.

"In the old days, Southern Chinese martial arts weapons' forms displayed many flowery movements that appeared unlikely practical actions," Doc Fai Wong explains. "This was designed to draw the public's interest to the martial art, a common method of recruiting students. Martial arts schools

performed during village festivals and celebrations, often celebrating harvests and seasonal plantings in farming villages.

"Since many of the weapons taught in the old days were originally farm implements, to liven demonstrations kung-fu practitioners added some acting to the form," he adds. "For instance, traditional hoe forms begin with the martial artist rolling up his sleeves and mimicking hoeing the field. He stops to wipe the sweat from his brow and looks at the sun's position to check the time of day. The martial artist rubs his aching back and slings the hoe over his shoulder, as if trudging home after a long day's work. Then the fighting action begins."

Staff and Blade

Most traditional Chinese martial art hoe forms have a beginning similar to what Wong describes. This makes the form more interesting to watch and explains the weapon's background.

The Chinese hoe is similar to the variety you find in today's garden centers. The blade was a little longer (approximately ten inches) and about six inches wide. The hoe was a relatively heavy weapon, weighing about six-to-eight pounds. A sturdy tool and weapon, the handle was constructed from Chinese hardwood. As with the horse bench, the hoe form is taught today as a means of weight training to strengthen and condition a student's forearms and wrists, as well as improve balance and power.

The farmer's hoe was both a long staff-like weapon and a bladed weapon, using many techniques similar to the staff and long-bladed weapons, such as the kwan do. It is always held with the right hand forward, placed approximately two-thirds down the length of the handle. The hoe practitioner's left hand grips the center of the weapon. This allows the stylist to move quickly in any direction. He can also use the center portion of the handle for blocking an attacker's weapon. At the same time, he can quickly pull the hoe back to thrust forward or scoop upward with the bladed end.

The bladed end is used to either chop downward or thrust forward at an opponent. It is heavy and sharp, requiring little force to make an effective strike. When thrust forward, the flat side of the blade makes contact in a poking motion.

The horse bench and hoe are excellent representatives of the creativity and resourcefulness of Chinese martial artists, who developed effective fighting techniques using common tools and household implements.

Teaching Taiji's New Generation

At the Ji Hong Taiji College, master Luo Hongyuan is unleashing a new generation of taiji elite.

Lawrence Huang, Photos by Lo Hong Yuan

It was 1999 in Virginia. At the annual Taste of China Taiji Tournament, a tiny, 150-pound man was facing an opponent almost twice his size. The audience laughed. It was not a competition! It was a mercy killing.

However, as the game progressed, the spectators were surprised when the smaller man used the force from the bigger competitor to push him off balance again and again. Finally, when the smaller guy won the competition, the audience rose to its feet and gave the winner a standing ovation. This smaller man turned out to be Steve Anderson, a student from Ji Hong Taiji College in Canada. Since master Luo Hongyuan founded the College in 1991, Ji Hong Taiji College has trained a group of elite taiji students who have won numerous international competitions.

From 1995-to-1998, Ji Hong Taiji College students entered 15 North American competitions and took home five Grand Championships and 209 gold medals. In addition, at the 1998 Taiji Legacy International Competition in Dallas, Texas, one student captured four gold medals in push hands competition.

At the 1999 Taiji Legacy Competition, one student won six gold medals in form performance, and another student won a gold medal in push hands competition. Again in 1999 at the Taste of China Taiji competition in Virginia, the school won four of the five push hands gold medals, as well as laying claim to the overall championship in men's restricted step push hands. And last year, the school captured six gold medals in the highest level of taiji competition in Chen's Village.

Finally, in 1997 and 1998, the Ji Hong Taiji School won gold medals in two weight levels of full-contact fighting at the Canadian National San Shou teammember selection competition. This proved once and for all that the school was equally adept in forms, push hands and full-contact fighting.

The magic behind these accomplishments can be found in the ji hong taiji theory system. This new generation of taiji elite has been academically built and practically improved and perfected. Following is a brief introduction to this ji hong theory regarding all the aspects of the structure of this complex system:

1. Five Bow Theory

Master Luo published the article, "Five Bow Theory" when he was teaching in South China

Teachers' University. Traditionally, the spinal column or the backbone forms the main bow, while the hands and legs form the other four bows. Like a fully drawn bow, the spinal column, hands and legs, when stretched, carry potential energy. Then the dan tien (lower belly) directs the internal energy to the five bows.

However, master Luo improved on this concept. In the movements of the limbs, the dan tien takes on the important duty of energizing the limbs, transferring the internal energy (qi) through the spinal column to the hand bows and the leg bows, and finally reaching the tips of the limbs. The result is that the five bows form one unified system, converging all the powers into one single point. Thus, it releases tremendous and explosive power over the opponent.

Master Luo also compares the forming of these five bows into one with an automobile tire. Five bows are like the steel wires in the tire, forming a structure to contain the air pressure. This lays down a solid foundation for a powerful internal force (jin), and further for the generation and exercise of energy (qi).

2. Pressure Theory

Five bow theory sets up a framework for this pressure theory. Like an automobile tire, it cannot hold the air without its steel wires and the rubber frame. Master Luo compares the body to a tire. Bones and flesh are the steel wires and rubber, and dan tien is the air pump, which fills energy into the body like an air-pressured tire. Then the taiji system transforms the body into a strong tire-like air ball. This air ball could work only when it is under pressure. "Qi" (energy) itself does not do any work. It is only when "qi" is under pressure that it transforms itself into power "jing." This is the energy of taiji (qi).

3. Energy Column

After the forming of the air ball, master Luo develops the theory to include the energy in front of the body circumvented by both arms and thighs. This forms an energy column (air column) held by the body. In the pressure theory, this also forms a bigger air ball with our body, arms, and thighs as half the ball, linking the missing half with our mind. This is more commonly called "Hit with qi (energy), hit with yi (mind)."

Master Luo is credited with developing this concept of energy column with rotating axis within the column. Like the earth and moon, all cylindrical objects move around a supposed axis. The central axis is placed along one's spinal column; the external power would reach one's backbones and thereby upset his balance. However, if the central axis is removed outside our system and into the opponent's backbone, one can easily control and upset the opponent's balance.

"The ji hong taiji system is perfect for developing a new legacy that will be used and copied for centuries."

4. Theory of Rootlessness

After finishing the structuring process, Luo moves to rootlessness. In a fighting situation, if we root ourselves and the opponent is powerful, we will be uprooted. The taiji ball goes without roots. Then when the opponent pushes or hits the ball, the ball will turn and transfer his force back on him while ball remains intact.

According to Luo, one needs to remove all the roots to remain stable. As explained in classical taiji theories, you must move like walking on ice or a cat prowling before catching a mouse. Both theories suggest a state of rootlessness.

When we feel external pressure, such pressure will be directed from our body, utilizing the qi column theory, but we should never allow the external pressure to reach to our feet. On the other hand, we will reach our opponent's feet through push hands.

Master Lou further emphasizes the concentration of the energy in dan tien. When we build a heavy and solid dan tien, we will free our legs from rooting to the ground, leaving our opponents no chance of "touching our legs" to uproot us.

5. Principle of Dynamics

Once we adjust ourselves, we can use the pressure created from dan tien to lock our opponent from his legs to the ming men (lower back). Once the opponent is under control, it becomes a matter of dynamics. Simply take the opponent's ming men as the supporting point and his leg as the point receiving the force. Using the opponent's ming men support impacts his legs and allows you to throw him yards away. This is the secret principle that makes taiji so powerful, so invincible.

Master Luo Hongyuan used these five points to develop a complete system for taiji practice and training. He complements this system with practical training methods in forms, push hands, and full-contact fighting. The goal, according to Lu, is to structure a new system that will cultivate a new generation of taiji students.

Many claim the taiji practiced in North America will never reach the standards found every day in China. But master Luo Hongyuan disagrees. He insists the Ji Hong Taiji system is perfect for developing a new legacy that will be used and copied for centuries.

Lawrence Huang is a martial artist and freelance writer.

Hand Techniques 101

Learn the Fundamentals of Striking and How to Avoid Common Errors From Shito-Ryu Expert Fumio Demura

Justin Iverson

You don't do something for 55 years and not get good at it. And that's certainly the case with Fumio Demura. The Southern California-based martial artist has been training in *shito-ryu* karate for more than a half century.

Demura, the director of the Japan Karate Federation and international director of Japan Karate-Do Itosu-Kai, is in huge demand for seminars all the time. He's gone virtually every weekend of every month of every year, teaching techniques to martial artists all over the globe. He knows karate inside and out.

In the following story, the 62-year-old martial artist explains the ins and outs of five hand techniques. He'll cover all the mechanics so you can throw your techniques with authority.

4 ELEMENTS

As you might expect, there are certain elements that constitute a good punch. According to Demura, the items are as follows:
- Good, basic training
- Speed
- Power
- Experience

Of course, the fundamentals are the basis for everything, including the martial arts. And it's the same in other sports, such as golf, baseball and football. If you don't put your hips into the movement, such as a golf swing, the ball isn't going to go as far as it normally would. Similarly, if you don't put your hips into your techniques, your strikes and blocks aren't going to be as effective as they should be.

"Without hip movement, you're not going to be able to hit the ball that far," says Demura. "That is same way with karate punch. You are not just using your arms. Power also comes from your hips."

If you weren't blessed with speed and power, you can work on them. For example, to build your speed, you have to work on speed. This is going to take a lot of repetition and a lot of hard work, says Demura. You might throw 10 techniques in 20 seconds and then bump it up to 12 techniques in 20 seconds. Keep working on it until you've made some progress. Try to beat your time.

To build power, traditionalists pound on the *makiwara*, he says. Hundreds of times. Once or twice per week. Some also do a little weight lifting. Regardless of what you do to build power, make sure you don't get too tight because that inflexibility prevents you from throwing the techniques as fast as you should.

"You have to be loose so you can snap the technique," says Demura. "If you're too tight, that will work against you and make you slow."

Experience also plays a vital role in the whole process.

"Experience tells you several things, including how to hold your hand, what it's like to make contact, and how to move your shoulders and hips," he says.

In this day and age of cross-training, don't hesitate to check out another system. Whatever you do, however, don't neglect your art. More specifically, don't overlook your punches. The more you know, the better you are. The better you are, the more likely you'll win a tournament or escape from a street situation unscathed.

"There are good things and bad things in every style," says Demura. "It doesn't mean one style is better than another. Similarly, don't neglect one aspect of your training, such as punching just to work on your kicking. Everything is important."

TECHNIQUE 1
Jab (kizami-zuki)
When To Use
This can be used to counter or as an offensive technique.

Striking Surface
You should hit your opponent with four joints (the knuckles on your first and second finger).

Tips
- This requires strength and quickness.
- If you're not moving fast enough or strong enough, this technique won't be effective.
- Move your body first.
- To generate power, keep your heels on the ground.
- Follow through on your technique so you're ready to throw another strike.

Common Errors
- Moving your head before you move your body. This increases the likelihood that your opponent will be able to hit you in the nose.
- Lifting your heels to throw a technique.
- Leaning forward, which restricts your power.
- Too much weight on your front leg. This means that your technique will rely almost entirely on arm power.

Fumio Demura (right) and Thanh Nguyen assume the ready position (1). Demura then takes a step and moves his body toward his opponent (2). Note that he does not lead with his head. When he makes contact with the jab, notice how the heel of his back leg is down (3). This ensures that he's packed plenty of power in his technique. Demura also shows the incorrect way to throw a jab (4). Not only is he leading with his head, but his back heel is off the ground so he won't generate much power.

TECHNIQUE 2
Backfist (uraken)
When To Use

This can be used as a counter or as an offensive technique. Typically, this is thrown from side to side, not overhand. Thus, it's an elusive, fast technique that works well in combat because it can't be seen that well.

Striking Surface

The top two knuckles on your first and second finger.

Tips
- Use your opposite hand to block any technique your opponent throws.

- Execute a "deep" step to generate power and to make sure your opponent does not get away.
- When you throw the technique, "snap" your wrist.
- "Snap" back the follow-through so you're ready for the next movement.
- Keep your fist solid. This will generate more power.

Common Errors
- Open hands that are too relaxed.
- Failure to step in. When you reach in, you sacrifice power.

The two fighters square off (1). As he recoils his striking hand and lifts his lead leg, Demura uses his other hand to protect himself (2). When he makes contact, he snaps his hand to create more power (3) and then he follows through (4). Demura also shows the incorrect way to throw a backfist (5), the correct way to make a fist (6) and the incorrect way (7).

TECHNIQUE 3
Reverse Punch (gyaku zuki)

When To Throw

This also can be used as either a counter or an offensive technique. This has more power than a jab.

Striking Surface

Make contact with the four knuckles on the first two fingers of your hand.

Tips
- When you slide in to throw your technique, keep your blocking hand near your face so you can deflect any techniques your opponent throws.
- Go to the outside so your opponent can't hit you with his opposite hand.
- To generate power, move in at the same time your opponent is moving toward you.
- When you throw your punch, turn your hips toward your opponent. This will generate power.
- Snap your technique back so you are prepared for the next movement.
- Hit your opponent "square" or at a 90-degree angle. This generates the most power.

Common Errors
- Stepping too far to the side. This prevents you from throwing the punch with any power or authority.
- Not hitting the opponent at a 90-degree angle. If you don't, you lose power and effectiveness.

Demura and Nguyen assume the ready position (1). When Nguyen throws a punch, Demura slides in to block (2) and then delivers a reverse punch (3). Notice how he turns his hips into the movement to build more power. To illustrate a common mistake, Demura steps too far out (4). Therefore, when he punches, he won't have any power (5).

Demura Up Close
Name: Fumio Demura
Years Training: 55
Styles: shito-ryu and shotokan
School: Japan Karate-Do Itosu-Kaiin Santa Ana, California
Phone: (714) 543-5550
Titles: Director of Japan Karate Federation and international director of Japan karate-do Itosu-Kai
Worldwide Members: 25,000 to 30,000

TECHNIQUE 4
Chop (shuto uchi)
When To Throw
This is an offensive move that should be thrown at your opponent's neck, collarbone or head.
Striking Surface
Strike your opponent with the edge of your hand.
Tips
- Sidestep your opponent as he attacks and then throw your chop.
- When you throw this technique, your body is not going to be completely straight. The technique is going to come from the side.
- You do not use your hips when you throw the chop.
- Follow through when you throw the technique.
- Snap your hand back so you are ready to throw the next technique.
- The key is the distance you are from your opponent. If you're too far back, you'll have to lean forward to make contact with him. In that case, you won't have much power. Therefore, make sure you're close enough to do some damage.

Common Errors
- Raising your heels.
- Improper distance. Some people don't get close enough to their opponent. Thus, when they throw their technique, it doesn't have much power.
- Keeping your fingers open when you throw the chop. When your fingers are open, you'll sacrifice power and possibly hurt yourself.

The fighters square off (1). When his opponent strikes, Demura moves his body sideways so he passes the attack and prepares to counter with his own strike (2). He then unleashes the strike to Nguyen's collar bone or neck area (3). To make this strike effective, it's imperative that you're close enough. Note what happens when you're too far away (4). Demura shows the proper (5) and improper (6) way to hold your hand.

TECHNIQUE 5
Elbow Strike (hijiate)
When To Throw

This is an offensive technique that should be used when you are in tight with your opponent, but you are too close to punch. This is an ideal technique to use when someone has grabbed you.

Striking Surface

The elbow

Tips
- If you slide in to throw an elbow at your adversary, move to the outside of his attacking arm. This enables you to block one strike and keep a safe distance from his other arm.
- For maximum effectiveness, make sure the fist of the arm you are throwing the technique with is close to your chest.
- It's also important to keep your elbow "narrow" or tight to your body. This will also enhance the effectiveness of the strike.
- Throw your hip into the technique.
- Nail your opponent with the tip of your elbow.

Common Errors
- Not getting close enough to the opponent.
- Holding your striking elbow too far away from your opponent.
- Leaning forward when striking. You will not generate power this way.

The fighters square off (1). When his opponent strikes, Demura slides in (2) and blocks the technique (3). Then he launches an elbow strike (4).

Keys to Throwing Hand Techniques Properly

- **Stances**
  You need to be comfortable in your stance so you can be strong and quick.
- **Ki**
  Translated, ki means "life force." When you throw your technique, you must do so with feeling. One punch, one kill is the concept in karate. To do that, you need to have some feeling when you execute the technique.
- **Eyes**
  You also need eye contact, which will give you concentration and focus so you can hit the right target. It's like a golfer. To hit the ball a long way, he has to keep his eyes on it when he's preparing to hit it.
- **Development Power**
  Your mechanics must be right to deliver a technique with full power.

The Secret Is Out

With the release of Iron Monkey, Donnie Yen is no longer a well-kept action secret.

Stephan Berwick, Photos courtesy of Donnie Yen

The underground buzz you've been hearing all these years about Donnie Yen is finally beginning to surface. Once one of the best-kept secrets outside Hong Kong, Yen's fan base is growing so rapidly, many experts predict he's well on his way toward reaching a popularity reserved for such action luminaries as Lee, Chan and Li.

Fans of the Hong Kong action genre were on to Yuen Wo Ping, John Woo, and Chow Yun Fat well before Hollywood. And they knew long ago what the Western world is only now discovering: Donnie Yen is on the cusp of mainstream stardom. With the Miramax release of Yen's 1993 classic, *Iron Monkey,* and his cameo and action work in Wesley Snipes' upcoming *Blade 2,* Donnie Yen is fast becoming Hollywood's latest hot Hong Kong property.

Actors with Yen's versatility are hard to come by. As Yuen Wo Ping's (*The Matrix* and *Crouching Tiger, Hidden Dragon*) true last protege—earned from their collaboration on Hong Kong action classics such as *Drunken Tai Chi, Tiger Cage, Once Upon a Time in China II,* and *Iron Monkey*—Yen has built a reputation as an actor, director and choreographer who can deliver all the big-screen martial arts action an audience can handle.

Currently signed to Miramax and in negotiation with a variety of Hollywood producers, the most-often asked question among movie rank-and-file is, "Where has he been all these years?" Yen recently put his talents to use overseas, where his cult status rivals his burgeoning underground audience in America. In Japan, he action/directed a contemporary sword film based on the Japanese "Manga" comic character known as Shurayuki Hime or Blood Snow Princess. Before working on *Blade 2,* he was in Berlin, as the first Chinese filmmaker in creative control of a major German television production as co-director and action director for one of Germany's highest rated shows, "Codename: Puma."

"Movements are just movements; it's the rhythm, the intensity, the soul that we must try to put behind every piece of action."

(Above): Donnie (holding camera) oversees an action scene from the German television show, "Codename: Puma." (Below left): Getting suited up for his appearance with Wesley Snipes in Blade 2. (Right): Donnie Yen was both co-director and action director for "Puma," which was shot in Berlin.

MARTIAL ARTS

"I need to be the best or at least unique and innovative, otherwise, where is the thrill?"

Donnie Yen's screen presence, martial arts ability, and urban style evoke Bruce Lee's cool in a new era. Like Yen, Lee's films did not rely on gimmicky stunts. Lee's creation of beautifully raw fight sequences lasts to this day. His martial arts credentials, film experience, and cosmopolitan attitude fueled Lee's superstardom. Upon arriving in Hollywood, Yen appeared in *GQ* magazine's 2000 issue on Hollywood's leading men, posing with Bruce Lee's daughter, Shannon Lee—a fitting nod to an action hero whose fans are confident will bring a new image to martial arts films. Here's what he had to say about his current success.

INSIDE KUNG-FU: Much has happened to you since you arrived in Hollywood last year. Can you tell us what's been going on?
DONNIE YEN: I've been busy traveling a lot, working both in front and behind the camera. I was first in Berlin working as a co-director and action director on an RTL primetime action series. During the same time, I signed on with Miramax for a three-picture deal as both an actor and action director. *Highlander: The Endgame* was the first film. After that, I went on to do *Blade 2* as the martial art choreographer with a featured cameo role. And after *Blade 2*, I went to Tokyo to action-direct a Japanese Manga classic that was to be released this Christmas in Japan. Now, I've been busy promoting the release of *Iron Monkey* with Miramax.

IKF: How was it working with Wesley Snipes in *Blade 2*?

DY: Well, first off, I'd like to say that Wesley Snipes is probably one of the most intelligent, well-rounded actors I have ever worked with. What surprised me was the fact that he really is a talented, genuine martial artist who works extremely hard. He really impressed me with how quickly he picked things up and how diligently he would tackle something until he got it perfect. I remember the first fight scene I choreographed for him. The movements in these scenes are highly complex and I actually wasn't sure whether or not he could bring out the flavor that some of these movements required. But Wesley did it, and he performed every movement with perfection.

IKF: How would you compare Hollywood to Hong Kong filmmaking?

DY: Hollywood's way of filmmaking is great because it protects the product and talent with enormous financial and packaging resources. But with my experiences so far in Hollywood, the big-budget and well-planned productions seem, at times, to limit spontaneity on the set. When an artist is under pressure with a limited budget—as is typical in Hong Kong—he is forced to be more creative, because he is under pressure to really perform. Instead of relying on things we couldn't afford, we had to create high-level physical feats. It's cost-efficient, yet translated well to viewers internationally. This was the secret of Bruce Lee, and today of Jackie Chan and Jet Li. But if an actor is to succeed globally, obviously Hollywood is the place to be.

IKF: How do you assess the current and future success of stars like Jackie Chan and Jet Li?

DY: I'm very proud of their success. The U.S. film industry is large enough to welcome more talent, especially after *The Matrix* and *Crouching Tiger*. It wasn't long ago when you saw Asian actors limited to largely minor, stereotypical roles. It shows the world is getting smaller and the American audience's taste for quality action films is more sophisticated. After all, we're in the 21st century—our pace is faster and our desire for greater levels of thrills have been supplied by Hong Kong action films, the undisputed provider of modern film excitement. So I'm excited to see this trend is here to stay. On the other hand, because Hong Kong action style is in such great demand, I also see how poor imitations of these films are taking audiences for a bad ride. Hong Kong-style martial art films are everywhere—in TV commercials, MTV, and even children's programs. I'm not against marketing the Hong Kong cinematic style. If this trend grows, millions will follow. But overflooding the market will eventually rob it of its originality, especially if professionally weak action performers/directors just simply dance along with no quality techniques, or worse, with no soul.

The point I'm trying to make is that it's very important to be true to your art, like martial art, to sustain your craft and make progress.

Similarly, I strive to maintain the essence of what makes a martial art film great so that is stands the test of time, regardless of trends.

IKF: Your long-time film mentor, Yuen Wo Ping, has enjoyed enormous crossover success with *The Matrix* and *Crouching Tiger, Hidden Dragon*. Can you comment on his amazing rise in Hollywood?

DY: During the many years I apprenticed under him, he was always ahead of his time. I'm honored to have been hand-picked as his last protege after he turned Jackie Chan into a star. With the

U.S. release of *Iron Monkey*, the mainstream American audience will finally see our collaboration at its best. *Iron Monkey* is the best film we worked on together and captures the spirit of Chinese martial arts in a way similar to what Yuen accomplished in *Crouching Tiger*.

IKF: Your martial arts performances are famous for exhibiting an extremely high degree of complex skills. How do you approach your action performances?

DY: What really separates a good martial arts film from a great one is not wirework or special effects, but the actor himself. That's why Bruce Lee's fight scenes are still relevant after all these years. For me, movements are just movements; it's the rhythm, the intensity, the soul that we must try to put behind every piece of action.

IKF: Your fans expect you to become a fixture in Hollywood. What's coming up for you?

DY: There are many projects which are in development right now, again, thanks to some of the recent successful Hong Kong-style films. I may star in a TV series by John Woo, and will probably direct a Japanese version of *Charlie's Angels* in Japan. I've dedicated myself more behind the camera for the past few years. But I'll be returning to my acting roots more this coming year. One reason for that is what I see as too many disappointing martial art films that were made recently. The overall standard of martial art choreography and directing has actually dropped, despite exceptions like *Crouching Tiger*. So regardless of what projects I'll take on—in front or behind the camera—I'll take it very personally. I need to be the best or at least unique and innovative, otherwise, where is the thrill?

Showing off the wushu training he received from his mother, Bow Sim Mark, and Beijing's best.

Stephan Berwick is a Washington, D.C.,- based martial artist who was mentored by Bow Sim Mark and studied under Zhao Changjun and Bai Wenxiang in China. He is also a disciple of Chen taiji master Ren Guang Yi.

Jade Leung

Black Cat Rising

Ric Meyers

There are a legion of legends about how the film world can "burn" starlets, but in the case of the brave and daring Jade Leung Chang, it actually happened ... literally and figuratively. The year was 1995 and the beauty contestant, model, and award-winning actress had already suffered success and setbacks.

"But 1995 was a particularly bad year for me," the young beauty remembers. Like Michelle Yeoh, Leung is even more beautiful in person than she is on film, but now her face takes on an wistful expression that comes from accepting pain with prosperity.

"I was starring in *Satin Steel*. It was my big comeback movie. I remember the day perfectly. Sept. 5. I had to run toward the camera and behind me a bomb would go off. It was a very easy shot, which went perfectly the first time. But the director, Tony Leung Siu Hung, didn't think it looked good enough. He asked me, 'Would you mind doing it again?' I said, 'Why not? It's a very easy shot.'"

Those were nearly Jade's famous last words. "So they set up the explosives and the director said 'action,'" she continued. "And I ran. I felt like I was running for two minutes. But this time the explosion was much more powerful. I saw red in front of me ... red color going before my eyes. I remember thinking 'oh my god, I'm going to die.' I'm so scared that my body is on fire and my face is burned. In just seconds I think so many things ..."

As with Jackie Chan's nearly fatal accident in *Armor of God* (U.S.: *Operation Condor II)*, Jade's was captured on film, but what wasn't seen was the frightening aftermath.

"Everybody runs over to me," she remembers. "We're out on location, so

MARTIAL ARTS

somebody had to get transportation to the hospital. I said, 'Please, could you bring me a mirror?' I was so scared, but I didn't cry. My heart was pounding, but I didn't cry. I looked in the mirror. My lips were swollen and my hair was burnt, but it was okay. I was just a little hurt in the face. But then I realized I couldn't really feel my hands. I looked down and saw that they were all wet and red. My skin was burned. Then the pain started. All I said to the director was, "Please don't tell my parents."

Jade Leung still carries the mark of the flames on her right hand and arm. At first glance it looks like a milk-coffee-colored glove or tattoo, but within nano-seconds, you can see that it is a charring discoloration of soft new skin which will never return to its original hue. Leung does not carry it proudly, but she doesn't hide it, either. It is a mark of distinction, in a way—a virtual sign of yin/yang that constantly reminds her what is on the other side of genetic beauty and career luck.

"Finally, after they got me to the hospital and repaired everything and everybody came to my room, only then did I start crying," Jade admits. "I cried and cried and cried. I called my father to tell him, 'I'm in hospital, but please don't tell mom.' But then the newspapers reported my accident the next day, so my uncle and aunt called the house and talked to my mother.

"They said, 'Don't you know your own daughter?' When she came to the hospital, she was crying so hard that I couldn't, or else she'd feel even worse. But I felt very ashamed and guilty in my heart because I hurt her again."

The first hurt came five years before, when Jade Leung decided to leave the safety of her uncle's home in Switzerland to accompany a friend to the Miss Asia beauty pageant tryouts. It wasn't her folks' worst fear, but it was in the running. They had sent her to Switzerland in the first place to protect her from the wilder elements of Asia—much as Bruce Lee's parents had sent him to America. Only Jade was in no danger from picking fights. It was her beauty which attracted the wrong element.

It was that beauty that saw her being picked to compete in the Miss Asia pageant while her friend didn't make the cut.

"I didn't go to the finals, but it was a good experience for me," she maintains. "Thankfully they gave contestants a lot of money to live on, so I gave myself two years to succeed or else I'd go back to my uncle's. I started doing modeling work, but then one film company, D&B, was looking for a new action actress."

Essentially they were looking for the "new Michelle Khan." That was Michelle Yeoh's screen name in the years prior to her marrying Dickson Poon, one of the bosses of D&B. But, as Angela Mao before her, once Michelle married, she retired from the screen. Her immediate replacement in the *Yes, Madam* series was a Taiwanese actress renamed Cynthia Khan (borrowing *Yes, Madam* co-star Cynthia Rothrock's first name). But then *La Femme Nikita* premiered internationally, and D&B knew a great Hong Kong film could be created from it.

They called the "new" script *Black Cat* and went looking for just the right gorgeous girl who could combine fear with defiance. Jade Leung was that girl. "There was an acting and fighting audition," Leung says. "There were many actresses vying for the role, but

"I looked down and saw that my hands were all wet and red. My skin was burned. Then the pain started. All I said to the director was, 'Please don't tell my parents.'"

when they looked at my face they said it gave them a 'Black Cat' feeling. So they chose me and my career began."

Producer/director Stephen Shin soon knew he had made the right choice, and plans for a sequel went into immediate production even before Jade won the "Best New Performance" award at the Hong Kong equivalent of the Oscars. But what many of the voters might not have guessed was that Jade's look of defiance mixed with fear wasn't all acting.

"Before then I knew nothing," Leung admits. "I didn't know martial arts. I didn't know how to act. It was such hard work and I was so scared. I worked with Kong Tao Hoi, who was the action director. He taught me what I needed for the film, but not really martial arts. That's what really hurt—they only gave me about two weeks of lessons, then it was off to Vancouver to make the movie."

Still she survived, and even flourished.

"At this point I can look back on it with a little objectivity. It was hard work but a good memory because it's very difficult for one girl to do anything in Hong Kong. Many girls never get to play anything close to a lead in an Asian action picture, so I feel very lucky, but also I remember I was very confused. I was so young and it was happening so fast. I would ask myself over and over again 'Why?' But I never had an answer."

Black Cat 2: The Assassination of President Yeltsin went into immediate production, but since the original *La Femme Nikita* didn't have a sequel the crew could borrow from, this effort floundered. Even so, it allowed Leung to regain some of her balance and experience things she never would have otherwise.

"For *Black Cat 2*, we got to film in Russia, which was very interesting to me. We went many places to film, and I saw how everyone around was so very poor. I could put my own confusion in perspective. And, by then, I knew my character so I felt better about my acting. I could control the emotions better."

This is not to say, however, that everything was great on the set.

"We worked 15-to-18 hours a day, every day. I was so tired that whenever the director said 'action,' I would almost panic. But I knew that this was my opportunity, and I was so lucky to have been chosen, so I tried very hard. One crew guy said, 'I don't know how you do this.' It turns out

that the crew was always hoping that I might get ill or hurt, so they could take a rest!"

Little did anyone know that they would get plenty of rest because D&B decided to stop making films altogether. "I had many companies asking me to star in their movies over the next few years, but I was contracted to D&B and they always objected," Jade explained. "So everybody is calling me a 'superstar,' but I couldn't work anymore, so I was very upset and confused. I was very young, so I didn't know what to do."

What she wound up doing was waiting until her contract expired. It expired in 1995. She threw herself into every film she could, appearing in five that year. But came Sept. 5. And the flames. But even that didn't stop her. By the end of the year she was already working again. And if she wondered why she should be punished with the scarring on her arm, that was put into tragic perspective on a fateful holiday.

"It was Christmas Day. I was doing a film in Shanghai. I knew a young stuntman from China on that set. He worked very hard. At lunch I would often teach him Cantonese. He was doing a stunt with another girl and got killed right before my eyes. I couldn't understand it. How could he die and I didn't? I felt so … I don't know. I looked at my hand and realized my burning was just a little thing in comparison. I grieved for him and his family, but I never felt bad about my accident again."

Jade accepted her luck, both good and bad, and worked diligently at her craft. Her fans might have been confused by her subsequent choices—appearing in everything from dramas like Alfred Cheung's *Green Hat* (1996) to Category III (R-rated) thrillers like *Peeping Tom* (1997)—but finally, Leung knew exactly what she was doing.

"No actress wants to play only one kind of character in her career," she explains. "After *Black Cat* and *Satin Steel*, I worked very hard to do different things. Having just gotten more comfortable with my acting, I wanted to stretch and test my talent. I wanted to play every different kind of character in all kinds of movies. In Hong Kong these days it's very difficult to get into the movies, and once you do, it is very difficult to escape typecasting. But this is my dream, so I want people to think of me as more than an action actress. For me it's very fun to do different characters, no matter what kind of movie it is."

So Jade starred in the well-received thriller *Leopard Hunting* as well as the condemned *Raging Angels*. She didn't turn her nose up at television work either. She appeared in a series about firefighters (Lie Huo Xiong Xing), as well as a costumed historical martial arts serial (Nan Long Bei Feng). She returned to her most famous role in 2000, with *Black Cat in Jail*, as well as portraying a goddess in *Phantom of Snake* and a spoiled mistress in *Money Laundry*. But no matter what she appeared in, her fans agreed: she was always better than the material.

Today she finds her chances even better. She now appears alongside one of the kung-fu film greats, Sammo Hung, in a Mongolian martial arts epic which was titled *Flying Dragon, Leaping Tiger* before *Crouching Tiger, Hidden Dragon* made those two animals cinematically famous. The coincidentally named epic calls for Jade to utilize everything she's learned in her decade of trials and triumphs.

"When I was very young I'd always see Sammo Hung's films," she says. "He's such a great action actor. So I was very happy and honored to make a film with him. We also had fun filming in

Mongolia. In the scene where I have to cry over his body, he was always making funny faces just out of camera range. I told him, 'Please, how can I cry if you keep doing that?" He is a very kind and funny guy. He was also very considerate. He didn't help me with the kung-fu in that film on the set, because he understands that the action director must be in control. He had some suggestions for me, but never on location."

Now entering her second decade of acting, Jade Leung looks forward with renewed optimism. After meetings in New York and Los Angeles, she's returning to Hong Kong, where she has to make a choice between two films which are vying for her services.

"But both are action films," she assures me with a smile, wanting to let her fans know how much she appreciates their support over the years.

Finally, when I asked what was the one thing she had learned in this business which often burns its young, her reply was quintessential Jade Leung. "I learned how much my parents love me. You know, even when I became *Black Cat* they never asked me for anything. They only wanted to know if I was all right. They never intruded. Whenever they met someone who knew me, they'd only ask them to tell me that they send their love and that they were there if I needed them. That's why I didn't want them to know how badly I was hurt. I didn't want them to feel bad because they only wanted their daughter to be safe."

Philosophic and beautiful, Jade Leung always leaves an impression.

Ric Meyers is a former Inside Kung-Fu *"Writer of the Year."*

MARTIAL ARTS

Wang Hui-Juin's 7 Principles of Tai Chi

Dr. Peter Uhlmann

Tai chi players are confronted by a multitude of styles and traditional concepts. Often, these are conflicting and contradictory. There is some reality in the joke that each tai chi player's teacher changes the light bulb differently. My teacher, master Wang Hui-Juin (Henry Wang) studied with many martial arts masters and eventually developed seven basic principles that can be applied to any tai chi style, and indeed any martial art. Though we practice the Cheng Man-Ching short Yang form, the seven principles would also apply to Chen, Wu, and other styles.

The seven principles are fundamental to master Wang's teaching and integrated and interrelated. For correct tai chi practice, all the principles must be observed. The principles are relaxation, concentration, circle, center, coordination, proportion and balance. Here is how each principle applies to the tai chi form.

- Relaxation
- Concentration
- Circle
- Center
- Coordination
- Proportion
- Balance

Relaxation

This aspect is emphasized in all tai chi schools. Relaxation is not the same as being flacid or loose as if lying on the beach. One must consciously focus the mind to relax the muscles, and sink the body's "chi" energy to the ground. When someone attacks us we instinctively react with tension. We must learn to overcome this and be soft instead. This is difficult and takes years of practice. It is almost like going back to infancy when we would fall and not get hurt. Relaxation is also seen in bamboo bending in

While there is some reality to the joke that all tai chi players change a light bulb differently, everyone can agree on the seven principles of tai chi.

Master Wang Hui-Juin shows the seven principles of tai chi in action while assuming the "Fair Lady at Shuttles" (1); "Bend the Bow to Shoot the Tiger" (2); and "Golden Pheasant Stands on One Leg" (3).

the wind, while the tree which resists is uprooted. We carry a lot of tension in our bodies and need to think about relaxing muscles all the time. When relaxed our limbs feel very heavy and over time there are healthy changes to our skin, bones and muscles.

Concentration

This begins with learning the many postures of the tai chi form. If the mind wanders the player forgets positions and sequences. The mind is important in high-level martial arts. By one's focus and intention, the tai chi player can mobilize and utilize chi energy for healing or combat. It is impor-

According to master Wang Hui-Juin, the seven principles of tai chi can be used with any form. Here he shows how they work with "Grasp the Sparrow's Tail" (1); "Press" (2); "Single Whip" (3); and "Turning the Body to Sweep the Lotus" (4).

tant to practice in peaceful surroundings, preferably early in the morning so the mind is clear and concentration is easier. Like meditation, concentration requires the mind to avoid interrupting thoughts and focus on tai chi only. With practice the impossible becomes possible.

Circle

This is fundamental to tai chi practice and theory. The famous yin/yang symbol is a circle. Master Wang talks about creating a "globe shape" with our body with the dan tien as the center. Inside our body are many circles and spirals similar to a large beach ball. Just like the ball we should be able to absorb incoming forces into our center and then release them.

If we cannot create circles and spirals, we won't absorb and root, nor can we deflect or repel incoming energy. Tai chi movements should avoid any straight-line action. Arms and legs should be supple and the joints open. When I push against master Wang, he spirals my force down into his root. Yet he feels soft, not rigid as he is also relaxed. There is a lot of energy in a circle (think of an inflated car tire) and the tighter the spirals, the more energy is available.

"Movements must flow at an even rate of speed and blend into each other in a seamless fashion."

"By one's focus and intention, the tai chi player can mobilize and utilize chi energy for healing or combat."

Center

This is the path from our head, down our spine and dan tien, through our feet and to the ground. Our center connects us to the sky and ground energy. All movements should arise from the center and then extend to the limbs. First the trunk turns, followed by the arms and legs. When a fish swims it uses its center—not its head or tail—to initiate movement. I like to imagine a brace and bit used for drilling into a piece of wood.

The top of the brace is similar to my head, the handle is my waist, and the bit is analogous to my feet. The tool must be centered while the handle turns for the bit to bite into the wood. If the brace is tilted off center, it will not screw straight. In a similar fashion, the ability to center oneself will develop the ability to "root" into the ground.

Center implies concepts differing from traditional tai chi teaching. Many teachers demand a 70-percent-to-30-percent weight distribution. Master Wang says this is "double weighting" as the arm and leg on one side bear the load at the same time. It also means that one shifts the body's weight and then turns. Master Wang teaches distributing the weight 100 percent-to-0 percent or 50-50. This means the body never leans away from the centerline.

He also turns his center first and then shifts his weight. This is a major difference and is difficult for many teachers to accept. However, when they try to turn and then shift they will immediately feel their foot "screw" into the ground. I know of no other sport that requires a 70-30 posture. Imagine riding a bike or walking with such an unnatural weight distribution. Yin and yang should be in equal balance.

Center also implies that the head is connected to the trunk and does not turn independently. If you are walking and someone calls you, you automatically turn your trunk and then your head follows. You would never turn your head around and then the body.

Coordination

This is commonly experienced in casual walking. We balance our left foot with our right arm and vice-versa. Also they move at the same time. It is important to coordinate arms and legs and upper and lower body while performing the tai chi form. Movements must flow at an even rate of speed and blend into each other in a seamless fashion. Coordination is closely related to proportion.

Proportion

Simply stated, one's left hand is related to one's right foot. The left elbow is related to the right knee. The left shoulder is related to the right hip and vice-versa. If the left knee is bent, the right elbow should be bent proportionally. When weight is applied to one foot the opposite hand should feel connected through an energy path. Proportion also implies up and down and back and forth as well as right and left. Proportion assists in providing the globe shape described above. When an incoming force is applied to the right arm, for example, it should be felt in the left leg.

Balance

Balance permits fluid movement from one position to the next in a relaxed manner. With the 100-0 percent or 50-50 percent concept, balance and center are integrated. In the 70-30 percent concept there can be balance but no center. In tai chi most position changes require a movement of 45 degrees or multiples thereof. At these angles balance is most easily achieved.

No one principle is more important than the others. They must all be applied for proper form and they are interdependent. These principles also apply to life in general and not just tai chi. For tai chi to be more than just an exercise we need to apply balance and proportion in our lives. We need to maintain our center and stay focussed and relaxed. We need to learn to let go.

Master Wang emphasizes that tai chi must have a proper theory, form, and practical function. The theory originates in Daoist philosophy. Four ounces should move a thousand pounds. The form should follow the seven principles. Finally, the practical function should be consistent with the philosophy and form. Many tai chi students learn a form and are told to be soft and relaxed. Then they practice push hands and use a lot of force and technique unrelated to their tai chi form. Push hands often resembles wrestling rather than tai chi.

Master Wang teaches "search center" instead of traditional push hands. Search center avoids pushing and use of force or technique, and instead relies on chi energy, softness, and the seven principles. Search center requires a separate article to properly explain. Search center and the seven principles can lead to exceptional skills in tai chi and other martial arts while emphasizing softness and internal energy.

Chance Action Fighting

Wing Chun's Method To Manipulate, Weaken and Destabilize Your Opponent

Gregory E. LeBlanc, M.S., L.Ac., Story and Photos

Wing chun kung-fu is best known for its powerful, relentless, linear attacks. Practitioners seek the path of least resistance and then repeatedly strike to specific targets on the opponent's centerline. The goal is to end a conflict as decisively as possible, taking the most direct route available.

While many people know that, many are unaware that wing chun consists of several systems of training, and striking techniques only play one part of the whole picture. Pushing and pulling—which also play an integral role in the art—are used to manipulate, weaken and destabilize the opponent and are usually used to supplement the primary attacking techniques.

Pushing and pulling are part of a class of fighting movements called "chance actions," because they are only used when an opportunity or chance presents itself. When you combine all of these elements together, you've got the unified wing chun open-hand system as Sigung Wong Shun Leung taught to Gary Lam (Lam Man Hoc).

SKILL DEVELOPMENT

After learning the basics, students next delve into the second level of training. This focuses on chance action techniques and emphasizes a different approach to skill development, especially a different way of doing *chi sao* (sticky hands).

In the beginning stages of training, chi sao is all about hitting the opponent and trying to not get hit. In the second level, the student starts to develop abilities to control the opponent's fighting structure and also begins to develop "feeling" or a "natural reaction to fighting." Translated, if you can control the opponent and react based on instinct, you can do what you want, when you want and how you want.

Training to control the opponent is significantly different than trying to hit only. This means you must discipline yourself to not always hit and you can't be afraid of being hit. It also means beginning to train chance techniques such as pushing and pulling. You should also be getting a feel for what the opponent is doing and how he is doing it.

Chi sao training of this nature is often referred to as "playing," which is learning to control your opponent instead of always trying to beat him. It is definitely not free fighting. All-out fighting would not allow you the opportunity to develop these skills. If you're going to advance to a higher

When his opponent strikes (1), Gary Lam counters with a bon sao deflection (2) and then utilizes a jam sao (line deflection) to counter (3) his opponent's tan sao (defensive move designed to change the direction of an opponent's attack).

level, you cannot be obsessed with hitting. This is easy to understand but very difficult to do. You must be able to have the discipline, self-control and character to not always strike.

As Lam says, "You must train with a open and big heart."

In essence, you must turn off your muscle power and strive to develop subtle technique, keen sensitivity and learn how to harness your body's innate structural power.

DEVELOP THESE SKILLS

Chi sao offers a training environment to develop these higher-level chance action skills, such as pushing and pulling. To really progress, you must often slow down your techniques so that correct footwork and body structure are not lost to speed and an uncontrolled desire for making the hit.

Lam can often be heard saying, "If you want to go faster, slow down. If you want to be stronger, train softer."

Pulling training begins with learning the basic drills. These cover an outside and inside arm pull, as well as an outside arm bar pull. These techniques serve as first and second actions on the opponent's leading or follow-up attacking strikes and serve to throw the attacker into environmental obstructions, to the ground or into another opponent. Pulling also serves to disturb, destabilize and disrupt an opponent's correct body structure, balance, direction and main attack.

Pulling and pushing are often combined together, changing direction and throwing off the opponent's natural reaction to recover his balance. Chance actions are typically followed by footwork techniques such as a leg break or a throw and hand strikes such as lap sao and pak sao.

TWO CATEGORIES OF PUSHING

Pushing training is separated into two categories: one-handed and two-handed techniques. When you execute one-handed pushing *(toi sao)* techniques, you use the lead hand to push on your opponent's centerline. Usually, you apply pressure just below the shoulder at the humeral joint. You use your other hand to misdirect the opponent's position and to bring him slightly off balance. Lam calls this "making the opponent wrong."

The idea of two or more movements for every one fighting action, such as initially making the opponent wrong just prior to performing the push, is a subtle but prevalent concept used in wing chun.

Two-handed pushing (*po pai* or butterfly hands) is a more complex technique and features eight different lead in hands. Furthermore, instead of ejecting the opponent away from you with the arms held straight such as in toi sao (one-handed pushing), po pai pushing follows the opponent at a close range for the entire push. This is done to maximize the power of the push and to also protect the wing chun practitioner from being hit by a counter strike.

In addition to pushing with po pai, you can also strike. Using internal power, a *yin* style iron palm strike is delivered to the opponent's internal organs along with the push. Po pai is an action that must be executed with impeccable timing to be effective and relies heavily on the practitioner's development and use of structural power.

Po pai can be used to project the opponent outside the fighting distance, and like the toi sao, can be used to strike the opponent against objects in the environment, including other opponents.

IMPROVE YOUR ODDS

Pulling and pushing, as well as all other chance or secondary actions, must be used with caution and never be thought of as primary attacks. The main reason for this is what's called "chasing hands." This is one of Sigung Wong Shun Leung's most important edicts. His conviction was that your principle goal should always be to attack directly to the enemy's centerline and therefore the most important targets. Any divergence from this philosophy was nothing short of opening your own defensive gaps and becoming a target yourself.

To break with this commandment entails following the movements of the opponent's actions rather than perusing the primary centerline targets that are the head and neck. This is an easy sin to make when trying to learn chance action fighting; it takes a correct combination of actions and events to execute a chance technique properly and safely.

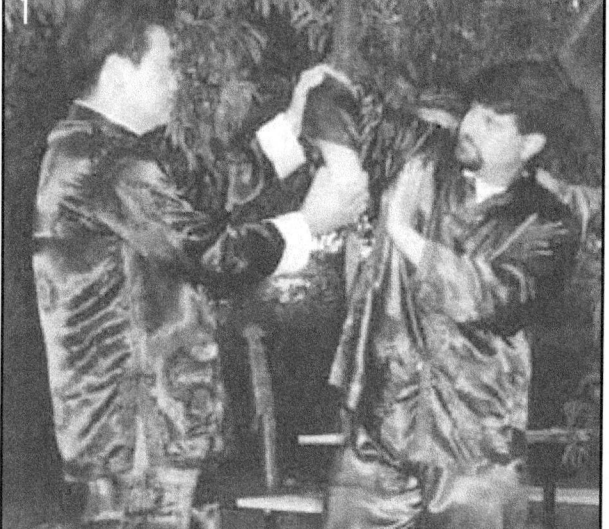

Gary Lam (left) uses a chokyu (breaking the bridge) to break his opponent's arm bridge (1). His opponent then counters with a punch, which Lam deflects with a spear hand deflection (2).

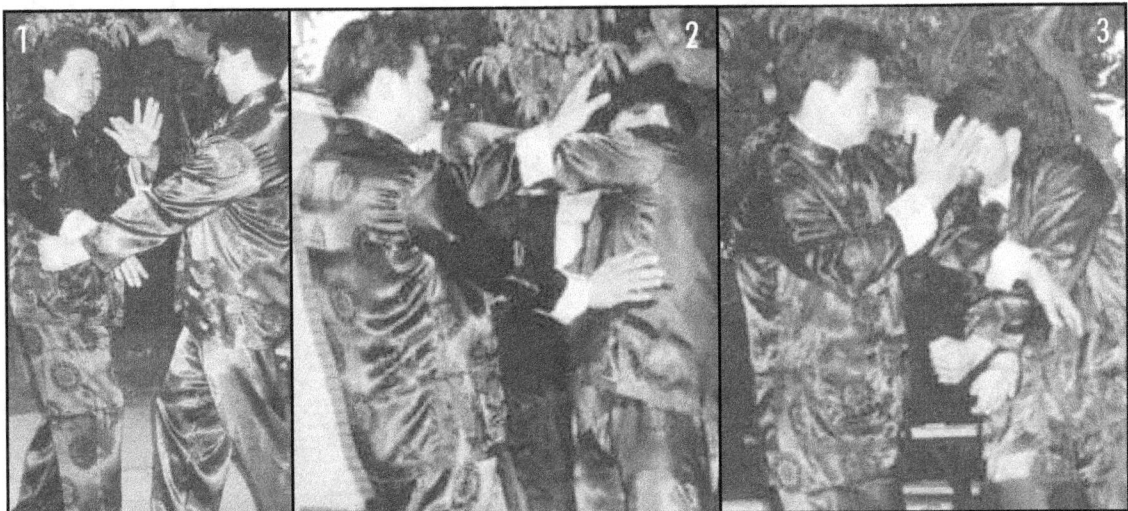

Gary Lam blocks his opponent's strike with a lower downward action to protect the lower body (1) and then uses a po pai (two-handed push) to move his opponent (2). Lam concludes with a downward defensive cutting action (3).

Turning a chance action into a primary technique will spell disaster against a seasoned opponent. It will provide a waiting bridge for the enemy to cross or will open a gap in one's defenses that may be impossible to close once violated. Sigung Wong Shun Leung said that training anything else other than how to attack and stop the enemy is training to be a target. Thus, in our tradition, chance actions serve to provide a deeper experience and a more developed background to a person's training, broadening their options and honing the primary attacking techniques.

Fighting is gambling. In wing chun, that's why you learn how to put the odds in your favor as much as possible. Wing chun accomplishes this goal by being as direct in action, simple in solution and as economical in movement as possible.

About the author: Gregory LeBlanc makes his home in Los Angeles California, where he manages a Chinese medicine practice and studies wing chun kung fu under Gary Lam. For more information, check www.garylamwingchun.com.

MARTIAL ARTS

Stick Attack

Grandmaster Cacoy Canete reveals the details of escrima takedowns and other self-defense moves

Doug Jeffrey

Following is an interview with Cacoy Canete, an 82-year-old *escrima* grandmaster from the Philippines. In this story, the legendary martial artist hits on a variety of topics, including the history of doce pares escrima, takedowns with sticks and other self-defense concepts.
—Editor

Martial Art: First, tell us a little about doce pares escrima.
Cacoy Canete: To do that, we'll need to go back a few years. Ferdinand Magellan's sword-wielding conquistadors fell to Maharaja Lapulapu, who used escrima to defeat the Spanish at the battle of Mactan.

Now, we'll jump ahead a few years. In the late 1920s, escrima attained a high level of popularity in Cebu City, the second largest city in the Philippines (Cebu island is located in the center of the Philippine archipelago). In 1932, the most renowned escrima-dors, who were mainly from Cebu, founded doce pares to promote the only original native martial art of the Philippines.

The name doce pares reflects the Spanish influence on the Philippines and signifies "Twelve Pairs," referring to the 12 basic strikes and 12 basic defenses of escrima. It also reflects the 12 original founding masters of doce pares.

MA: How about those the sticks? How long are they, how much do they weigh and what are they made out of?
Canete: They are 29 inches long, they weigh 150 grams and they are made of rattan. Incidentally, in a street self-defense situation, the length, weight and type of wood does not matter. In that type of situation, anything (or size) that can be held in the hand can be used as a Cacoy doce pares stick.

MA: What about maintenance of the stick? What is the best way to store them when they are not being used? Do they need a special type of coating or anything to preserve them?

Canete: Varnish preserves the sticks. The best way to store them is in a Cacoy doce pares stick bag. However, a Cacoy doce pares training stick is very inexpensive, and it doesn't really need any kind of maintenance.

MA: What are the keys to successfully executing a takedown with sticks?

Canete: You have to destroy or break your opponent's balance and control his limbs with the *olisi* (stick). That will result in a takedown. Speed is obviously very important, too. And of course, it's important to control your opponent's stick hand and body when you're trying to take him down.

MA: You have to get close to your opponent to take him down. What is the best way to ensure your safety before you execute the takedown?

Canete: Control your opponent's weapon and wrist, and break his balance by pulling with your right arm and pushing with your left hand.

MA: Before you actually do that, you have to close the gap.

Canete: The best and safest way to close the gap is with a quick and sudden entry using the stick or your hand to control your opponent's olisi hand. Then you can go for a takedown. You can also execute a surprise movement when your opponent is off guard. Or, you can distract your opponent by moving one way and then reversing your movement to close the gap. That may also be safe.

MA: What are some things you must never do when trying to execute a takedown with sticks?

Canete: You must never be off balance. When you're involuntarily off balance, it is difficult to perform a takedown technique. It also gives your opponent an advantage to counter your technique.

MA: Do you need one or two sticks to take someone down?

Richard Bustillo and Cacoy Canete (right) square off (1). Canete blocks Bustillo's strike with his stick and a hand check (2). Canete then immobilizes Bustillo's weapon hand and strikes his neck (3). Then he traps Bustillo's weapon hand and arm with his stick (4) and sweeps him off balance with a push-and-pull technique (5).

Canete: A takedown is easier with one stick because you've got your other hand to control your opponent's wrist, arm or neck. However, you can also take someone down with two sticks or just your hands.

MA: Once you take your opponent down, what is the best way to finish off the attack?

Canete: Once an opponent is down, make sure you disarm him. Then you can strike the vital areas of the body.

MA: What are the best targets?

Canete: In a contest involving weapons, the primary target is the opponent's weapon hand. You want to be able to disarm him. Most will surrender when they lose their weapon. However, should an opponent continue to fight, strike his hands and legs. This should reduce the likelihood of being countered.

MA: What are the advantages of using sticks for self-defense?

Canete: You gain an understanding of self-defense with or without the use of the sticks. Of

> **Canete Up Close**
> - Last surviving founding member of the 1932 Doce Pares Escrima Club
> - Amateur boxer, Cebu City
> - U.S. Armed Forces guerilla
> - Retired lieutenant, Philippine Army Military Police
> - Wrestler, Philippine National Wrestling Association
> - Black belts in shorin-ryu karate, kodokan, aikido
> - Retired captain, Reserve Armed Forces of the Philippines
> - Presidential champion trophy, 1st National Arnis Masters Open
> - Cebu Sports Hall of Fame, Philippines
> - Sports Commissioner of Escrima, Cebu City
> - Filipino Martial Arts Hall of Fame, El Paso, Texas

course, using the stick is a big advantage because of its length and the speed in which you can use it, provided you've had the proper training. We study lines of attack, angles of defense and unique counters.

MA: What are the disadvantages?

Canete: There are none. On the other hand, if your fundamentals are weak and you have no speed, you will be in trouble.

MA: In a self-defense situation, would you rely entirely on the sticks or would you use kicks and/or punches if necessary?

Canete: Initially, I would rely on the advantage of using a stick. When the opportunity presented itself, I would kick, punch or grapple.

MA: Does that mean you'd drop the stick to finish him off?

Canete: The stick is a big advantage in self-defense and should not be released. You should

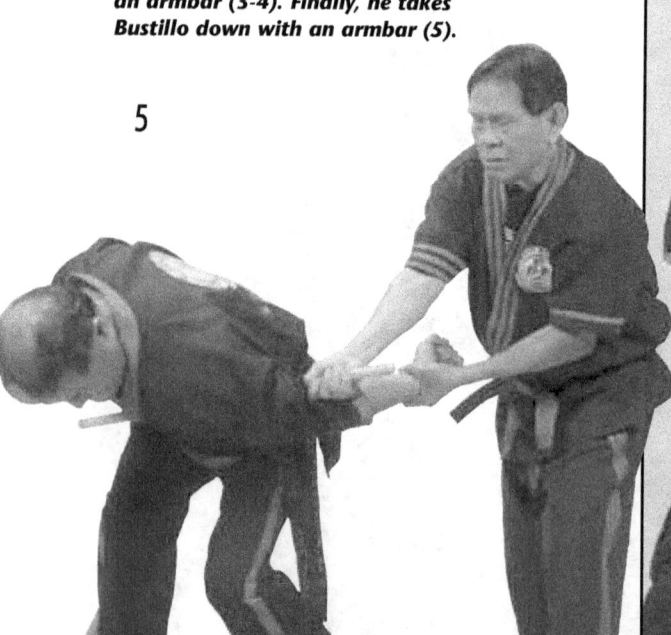

Bustillo assumes a mid-thrust stance (1). When he strikes, Canete blocks the thrust (2) and sets up an armbar (3-4). Finally, he takes Bustillo down with an armbar (5).

MARTIAL ARTS

> You gain an understanding of self-defense with or without the use of the sticks. Of course, using the stick is a big advantage because of its length and the speed in which you can use it, provided you've had the proper training.

only throw kicks or punches at an open area of an opponent's defense so you can incapacitate him.

MA: What if you lose your stick during an altercation? What is the best way to proceed?

Canete: If your opponent has a weapon, move in as quickly as possible and try to disarm him. If your opponent does not have a weapon, your empty hand skills can be applied as if you had sticks in your hands. Remember, the olisi is an extension of the hands ... with proper training.

MA: What are the principles or concepts behind the sticks? For example, angles, physics, etc.

Canete: The stick can be delivered accurately at any angle. More importantly, understanding the principles of strikes gives you the ability to angle for position in defense. Understanding the concepts of gripping and striking a stick increases your ability to use any striking, blunt or bladed weapon.

MA: Are things like speed and strength important with the use of sticks or can you rely entirely on the stick itself to accomplish your techniques?

Canete: Speed and strength are certainly an important factor in the use of our sticks or in any other martial arts techniques.

MA: Is there a special way to hold the sticks?

Canete: We em-ploy a full grip three inches above the butt end. That is special. There are, however, many other ways to hold the sticks. It depends on each individual's style. Our full grip is special because of the variety of striking capabilities, takedown techniques and disarming techniques that can be applied.

MA: Has escrima evolved throughout the years?

Canete: Through research and actual combat, I have progressively improved the traditional doce pares escrima. I cannot speak for the other escrima styles. Throughout my combat experiences, I have researched ways to develop power and speed with the many twirling, striking, thrusting and curve striking training exercises. I have found ways to train my olisi against various resistance materials for accuracy, endurance and strength.

MA: Is training with sticks realistic? Some might argue that you don't carry a stick with you so why would you train with one?

Canete: It is quite realistic. Sure, without the stick, both arms and hands can do the job. However, whether armed with the stick or unarmed, our stick training enhances your speed and coordination in both hands for empty-hand self-defense techniques. Training with sticks also teaches you how to strike or grapple with empty hands.

Doce Pares Headquarters

Doce Pares maintains its headquarters in Cebu City, Cebu, in the Philippines. This is just a few miles from the site where Lapulapu used escrima to defeat the Spanish conquistadors of Magellan in 1521.

The headquarters is the site of a training gym and is a frequent meeting point for escrimadores and martial artists throughout the world. All martial artists are warmly invited to visit the Doce Pares headquarters either while on tour of the Philippines as a vacationer, student or observer.

MARTIAL ARTS

Make Your Defense OFFENSIVE
The Science Behind Wing Chun's Blocks

Eric Oram

Looking back to my early karate days, I clearly remember the frustration I experienced during sparring. No matter how I tried to apply the multitude of techniques I thought I knew, somehow I always felt like a dog chasing his own tail at the end of the day. In spite of all the trophies, encouragement and praise, the truth of the matter was all of my "skill" disappeared when the situation became random.

Why?

I realize now that my reflexes had not been properly trained. My subconscious mind had not been given a clear and effective road map to follow when engaging a live opponent. All of my understanding was just that: understanding an intellectual and conceptual exercise, not a visceral understanding with the conscious mind free of thought, allowing the "moment" to take over.

My reflexes were never free to roam. They were consistently held captive while I tried to understand the situation, then I would react to it. And it was always too late ... pow! Got hit again ... pow! That side kick ...

If you don't know where you're going, you don't know when you're there. Even if the destination is known, you must still have an accurate map to show the way. And not just any route ... as the crow flies.

SCIENCE LESSON

In the October issue of *Martial Arts & Combat Sports*, I discussed the science behind the blocking system of traditional wing chun kung fu, as taught by Grandmaster William (Churk Hing) Cheung. Without recounting the entire conversation, following is a list of the principles that were discussed:
- Guard your centerline. The shortest distance between two points is a straight line. Guard the quick path; force your opponent to take a longer (circular) path.
- Watch the nearest elbow or knee point. This point will tele-

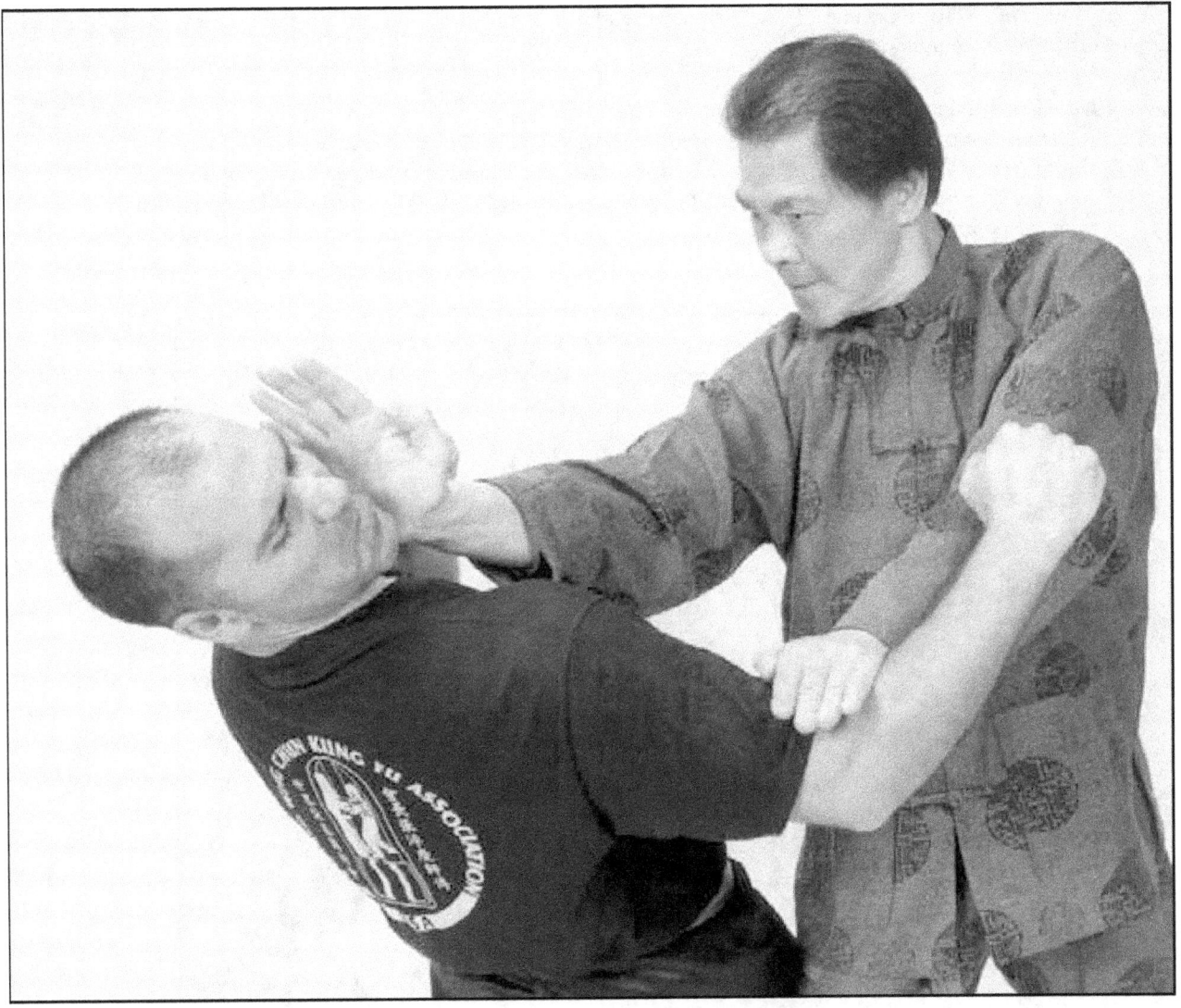

graph to you which attack is coming. The elbow is slower than the fist and more accurate to read than the body or the eyes.
- Assess the angle of the strike. Is it linear or circular? Assess the gate of attack. Is it attacking the upper, middle or lower gate?
- Intercept the line of attack. Two objects can't occupy the same space at the same time. Your object must occupy the path.
- Don't fight force with force. Redirect and release the opponent's force only. Don't stop it cold because this allows the opponent to initiate a new strike. Instead, allow the force to continue and exploit the opening at the peak of the strike's commitment.

The focus of these principles is to guide the practitioner from the pre-contact stage to contact—establishing the map to assessing an attack and preparing the proper defense against it. Now that we are there—at contact—having successfully deflected the attack … what is the next step? What is the absolute priority at this next instant?

In The William Cheung (TWC) system, the idea is to put the opponent on the defensive. In other words, counterattack.

ALL ABOUT CHI SAO

There is an entire training system within the wing chun system that is called *chi sao*, which is also known as "sticky hands." It is dedicated to developing sensitivity and reflexes at the point of contact. With relaxed, fluid movement, the William Cheung (TWC) practitioner should launch from the point of touch like a loaded spring.

Grandmaster William Cheung (left) and Eric Oram square off (1). Notice Master Cheung is guarding the centerline, occupying the most direct path in, and his even weight distribution. Cheung also watches the leading elbow to determine the path of the strike. Because the straight path is covered, Oram launches a right hook (2). Cheung follows the elbow and identifies it as circular and then intercepts and deflects the strike with a left lop sao block. Cheung then releases the remaining force in the hook punch (3) and follows through with another strike to the head (4).

Cheung and Oram square off (1). Note how Cheung guards the centerline. Oram jams the line with a jab, and Cheung identifies the angle as linear. Thus, he uses a pak sao to deflect the strike to the side (2). Cheung prepares to counter, but Oram immediately attacks again, trying to keep Cheung on the defensive (3). Cheung identifies the new angle and interrupts his counter to flow into a right lop sao block. Cheung releases the force, and positions to the outside (4), and then he follows through with another strike to the head (5).

The Lop Sao

The lop sao is a semi-circular block that can intercept from underneath, to the side, or on top of the strike, depending on the angle of attack.

The Pak Sao

The pak sao is a small circular block and can be used from underneath, on top, and to the side of the attack.

The Bil Sao

The bil sao is another small, circular movement that is primarily used at a slightly longer range, due to the block's extension. It mainly approaches the attack from underneath and from the side.

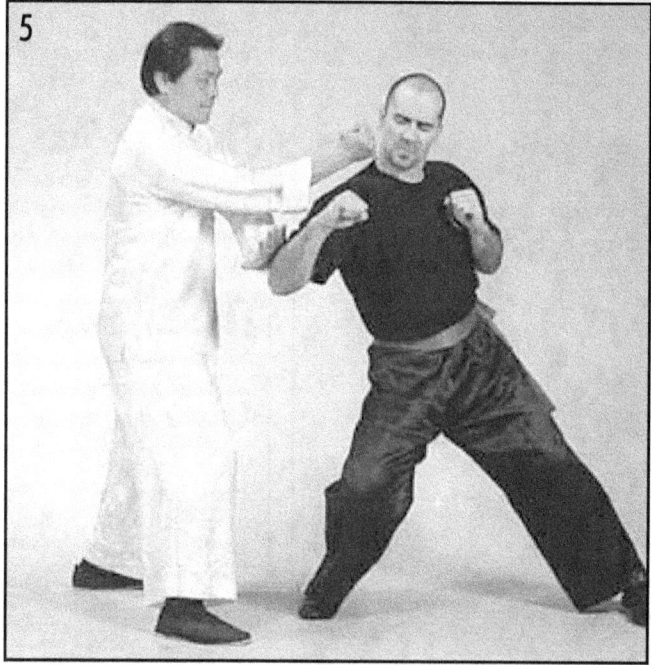

Cheung and Oram square off (1). Oram attacks with a hook to the head (2), and Cheung intercepts the circular strike with a bil sao block. Before Cheung can launch the counterattack, he feels the excessive force from the hook driving in. Cheung releases the pressure by slipping to the outside (3) and then has the angle to set up the simultaneous block and counter, due to the excessive commitment of the Oram's force (4). Cheung then follows through with another strike to the head (5).

This forward energy is then loaded into the blocks and the strikes of the system. It's important to allow the reflexes to flow easily and instantaneously from the moment of contact into the counterattack, using the opponent's own force to determine the opening. The objective is to shorten the response time of the reaction and the speed and economy of the movement.

But speed is only the rate of motion. The reflexes are still in need of a guide from the point of contact. Through the chi sao, the practitioner's energy is properly prepared for the map we are about to follow.

CAN'T WIN ON THE DEFENSIVE

Throughout the years of training with grandmaster Cheung, I've heard him say a thousand times, "You can't win on the defensive!"

How true it is. If you block two, they get you with No. 3. If you block 10, they get you with 11. That is why we must put the energy back into the direction of the opponent as quickly as possible—get him off of the agenda of attack and over to blocking and defense. This will change the dynamics of the encounter entirely.

While the blocking arm reads the opponent's force, the other arm immediately counterattacks. Therefore, it is also imperative we have command over both arms at the same time—not just one after another.

Thus, the most important ingredient, which also makes the TWC blocking system complete, is the overall position of the block. This should position you for your counterattack.

There are two lines, or leverage systems, that are set up to operate simultaneously. The line of the block and the line of the counterattack. Therefore, each single position should provide leverage, the proper angle and the correct distance for each line.

To achieve only one or the other leaves the situation incomplete. If you engage the opponent—at the moment of contact—strictly on defense, then what's to prevent the opponent from striking you again? You have blocked the strike, but the next moment is free to either your next attack or theirs. We need to eliminate the "or theirs" from that equation. If we do not, we can only pray that we are faster and more powerful than the opponent (a contest of force, not timing and strategy).

What, then, is the key to the positioning?

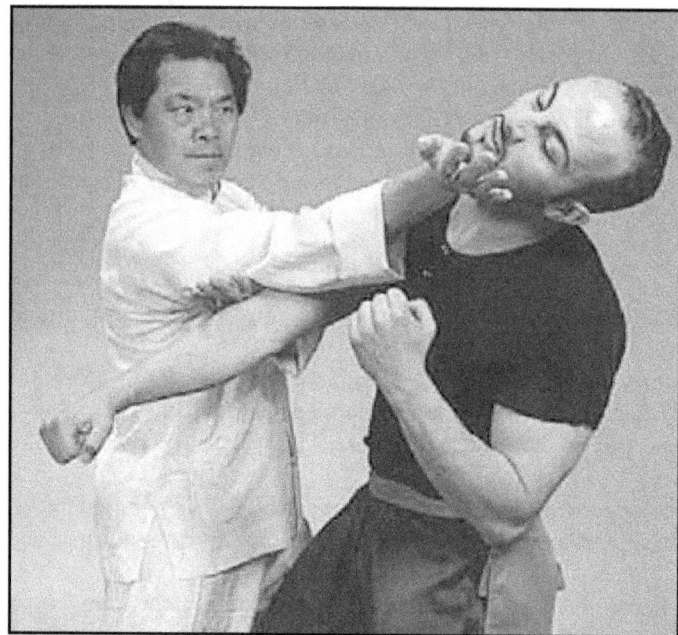

That nasty old nuisance: footwork.

BACK TO BASICS

The two key ingredients for the footwork in the TWC system are balance and mobility. We need a stable base to support our blocks, launch our attacks and absorb the opponent's force to a degree. And we want a free, neutral base to move the block and striking team to any location at any time. This mobility requires a balanced, 50/50 stance. The balance cannot afford to linger on one side or the other or it will loose the opportunity to follow any sudden changes in the distance and/or angle we are after.

It is rather like a tennis player waiting for the serve—neutral and free to follow the ball according to the direction and angle of the ball's commitment. (This is not to say that wing chun is strictly defensive in nature, having to wait for the opponent to attack first before responding. There are certainly measures for bridging the gap offensively, but our context here is the defensive scenario.)

At the same time, we must maintain a centered, balanced stance to provide the leverage and the correct distance for the block and counter. If we can't reach the target, we have no follow through and therefore no power. If we are too close, we will be too cramped to extend through the push of our attack. Understanding the footwork, therefore, is a crucial ingredient in executing the block and counter system as intended in the TWC system.

THE ROOTS

The Chinese have a saying, "Before there was the flower, there was the root."

So, the keys to setting up the correct position are:
- **The Defensive System** discussed in the aforementioned interview.
- **The Target**—What angle do you need? Can you reach it? And not just to impact but also with the follow-through. Our step must put us in position to push well beyond the surface of the target—like an arrow or a bullet—striking all the way through. This is where the power lies.
- **The Next Threat**—What is it? What angle does it need? How can my positioning set up my counterattack to also cut off the line of the next weapon?

Putting all of the elements together now, the final map looks like this:

1) Pre-Contact
- Protect our centerline.
- Use the eyes to determine which block is needed (watching the elbow).
- What is the angle?
- What is the gate?
- Maintain a neutral and balanced stance, so that you are ready to spring anywhere at any time.

You need to be able to place yourself in position to block and immediately counterattack.
- Intercept the line of attack.

2) At Contact
- Don't fight force with force.
- The touch sensitivity interprets the contact and senses the opening.
- Have the forward energy ready to respond instantaneously to what you see and what you feel.
- The footwork must support the offense and defense (two arms) at the same time so you can put the opponent on the defensive.

ULTIMATE OBJECTIVE

In the end, we essentially engage our entire bodies in this reflex/response process, which is, again, the ultimate objective. Engrain this map deeply into the subconscious mind through thousands of hours of repetition and follow a precise map with simple, effective, scientific movement.

If your movement follows this guide and address each of its elements, you will make it virtually impossible for the opponent to stay on the offensive. To do so, would be putting themselves at great risk of getting hit.

My objective here is to share what works for me and why, in hopes that it may spare the reader the same frustrations I experienced early on in my martial arts practice. Understanding the principles involved is a relatively simple task, once they are laid out. Like Occum's Razor tells us, the simplest solution is usually the best.

Getting it into the reflexes, however, is another matter. That is the exclusive job of the practitioner and it requires repetition. For this, the only thing left to do is simply get back to practice.

Warrior Training with Baguazhang

The secret to creating real power is linking the muscles with the mind.

Dr. John P. Painter

"To practice Chinese boxing without developing strength and skills would leave one with nothing in the end."

—Old martial proverb

This Chinese proverb is an often-quoted maxim from the internal schools of baguazhang. Shifu Johnny Kwong Ming Lee, a highly respected baguazhang combat instructor said, "Unfortunately today much of the baguazhang taught to Americans does not have the true power. This power was developed by long and correct practice of the principles imparted to the masters of old. We must learn to discuss the production of baguazhang's internal and external power from the standpoint of modern science in the hope that the art of baguazhang will once again achieve the proper place of power and respect it deserves."

The idea that a small, skinny person trained in form and meditation can generate more speed and strength than a large, muscular person with the same training is in a word, fantasy. It is true that through correct training the small, slight person can with no apparent measurable increase in muscular strength seem to develop greater power and speed than a strong, clumsy person. Internal training,

Classical baguazhang training for modern sport competition is quite different from baguazhang warrior training as practiced by palace guards and soldiers. Today, emphasis is on grace, balance and aesthetic appearance.

1. Formal training begins with quiet sitting to prepare the mind.

2. Daoyin yoga helps to limber the joints and increase circulation.

3. Zhan zhuang/quiet standing® opens joints and stimulates qi flow.

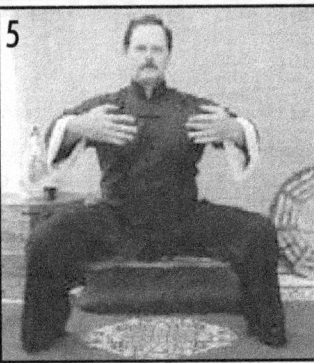

4. Zhan zhuang/power standing® for 15 minutes begins serious internal work.

5. Ten minutes of deep horse stance while holding the ball will warm up the legs.

6. Circle walking with stone spheres is used as a neigong skill to understand maximum and minimum power points and to strengthen the deltoid muscles. We slowly walk the circle raising and lowering the spheres and testing correct angles.

such as form practice, coupled with standing meditation (zhan zhuang) often produces this effect.

In truth, what has occurred is an increase in body efficiency. The individual is not physically any stronger in terms of general strength; he has just learned to use the body in a new way that focuses the general strength into a more functional strength. Such power still does not guarantee that our trainee is now a martial warrior.

Science dictates that the individual who increases muscle mass and general strength and is trained in correct martial disciplines will be physiologically able to generate much more speed and power than someone of a lesser muscular development no matter what methods the less-powerful individual employs.

External muscular strength is known as mingjin or conspicuous strength. Mingjin is the force from using the external muscles. It can be clumsy or with correct training becomes coordinated strength. This ability to use strength is the essence of functional strength—strength you can use in martial arts. That is the subject of this article.

Baguazhang Warrior Way
Few modern baguazhang schools stress the warrior way of baguazhang. Part of the reason lies in the lack of clear information on this type of training. The other reason is that these methods are

MARTIAL ARTS

Circle walking used as a waigong using iron wrist rings and a 30-pound weighted vest to develop strength.

Cables can be used to develop whole-body power from the ground to the palm. It is important to link all parts and not isolate movements.

extremely arduous and demanding in time and energy.

Baguazhang warrior training means the development of an individual who is in top mental and physical condition and who can survive in a hand-to-hand encounter with multiple opponents under any conditions and on any terrain. The closest modern analogy would be that of a U.S. Navy SEAL or Army Ranger. This level is time intensive and is mostly undertaken only by professional bodyguards, law enforcement and specialized military-like warriors.

Jiulong Baguazhang Warrior Training

The Li family of Sichuan province developed its specialized methods for baguazhang warrior training around 1916 while working for military warlords as mercenary-type bodyguards. In 1928 Li, Zhang-Lai and his son Li, Longdao were employed to train soldiers for General Jiang Jieshi (Chiang Kai-shek) as he worked to reunite inner China.

After moving to America in the early 1940s Li, Longdao began training this author, then a sickly young Texas boy, in these methods to improve his health. Li was a severe taskmaster steeped in tradition yet unafraid to learn and change. He encouraged me to, "Constantly look for new way of science to improve training for health and combat. When you find some method that is better than older way embrace this and improve the system." I have never forgotten these words and today I continually seek to improve my knowledge and skill with modern sport science while preserving and blending it with the best of the ancient ways.

Real Combat Training

Some people claim that internal martial art masters only trained their qi and neigong (inner skills). This is not entirely true. Waigong (outer skill) training was popular with not only baguazhang masters but taijiquan and xingyiquan masters as well. My shifu said to me, "You need internal power, speed and muscular strength to fight. The muscle must be supple, never stiff, and able to relax but if the muscle is not strong then qi does not have a solid house in which to reside. This is hard training, you have to learn to suffer much and eat bitter!"

Written accounts of baguazhang masters like Cheng, Ting-Hua report that he and others used to train with equipment for power development. Master Cheng was said to wear a leather vest filled with iron while training his footwork. He would often lift two buckets of water suspended by a rope handle and walk the circle with them suspended from his outstretched palms, lowering the weight up and down as he walked. In his courtyard hung a bag suspended by a rope from a tree. This bag filled with sand is said to have weighed 300 pounds. Cheng would push and strike the bag with his palm every day. It is said that he could make the bag swing high in the air with a single slap of his palm.

In jiulong combat baguazhang we say there are three levels of training. First is the mind, then the body, and finally the warrior spirit. Each level has numerous subcategories. For this article we will focus almost entirely on the second level of the body and physical training.

Running the nine palace course. This training involved weaving through a series of nine posts set into the ground. One can dodge or strike to the poles to develop footwork and test power applications while on the move.

The steel pole hangs from a chain so it can swing freely. It is pushed or struck with the palms. This one is filled with concrete and weighs 200 pounds.

What is Martial Power?

Martial power involves reacting instantly with total mind and body energy to a violent encounter. Those who posses this total body power seem to strike with almost superhuman strength. Striking with what appears to be almost superhuman power is not a feat of magic, although it may appear to be to those who do not understand the physics principles involved. If we wish to strike with maximum power/force we need to understand that the faster one moves and the heavier the mass moving, the more powerful the force of a strike will be.

This is the secret of the one-inch punch or the amazing pulsing force of fajin (pulsing force) derived from yiquan standing methods. It is also why the so-called "internal" martial arts use what is known as zhengjin or "whole-body" power. The concept is to get the entire amount of mass (body weight) behind the strike moving at maximum speed in minimum time and distance. This means that not only the arm must move fast, but the entire body must also move fast. No matter how you slice it moving fast requires muscle, coordinated muscles that can generate explosive force.

I am not advocating the development of the Mr. America-type physique. Huge, overly developed musculature produced through slow repetition-type progressive resistance exercises in the Daoist concept is yang taken to the extreme and has nothing to do with the subject of this article.

What I am advocating is the intelligent development and maintenance of useful muscle capable of generating explosive power through balanced strength development. This type of training will produce some muscle hypertrophy (size increase) in the overall physique as a byproduct of progressive resistance training.

Speed and Mass Create Power

The key elements in creating usable power for combat martial arts are speed and explosive power. Strength is nothing more than the ability to do work; power is the ability to apply strength very

MARTIAL ARTS

Internal power is not magic. It is a combination of the mind learning a method of releasing the full potential of our muscles. Here, the author breaks a pair of regulation Smith & Wesson model #100 handcuffs. Chain links are welded and tested to withstand well over 500 pounds of pressure. Photo taken before witnesses at the Rangers Training Center, Dallas, Texas, 1998.

Painter assumes wandering dragon posture as Leach begins his attack with a Bowie knife (1). Deflecting the thrust with wedge principle Painter moves in to Leach's space (2). Continuing to slide forward Painter strikes Leach on the neck with his forearm, momentarily stunning him (3). Wrapping his left arm under Leach's leg, Painter lifts and simultaneously presses down on the man's neck (4). Leach is catapulted into the air as Painter strikes with a palm heel to the chin. He is unconscious before he strikes the ground (5-6).

quickly. Research indicates that power is improved only when muscle is trained at a speed equal to or greater than the performance. This is why athletes using traditional slow-repetition weight-training techniques are not improving muscle function in ways that will develop speed and explosive power necessary for successful martial applications.

The most effective modern method of training for explosive power is with plyometric exercise. Plyometrics is the display of explosive energy after quick, intensive loading of the muscles. This loading pre-tenses the muscle with greater force than can be volitionally generated and then uses it in the main action.

We use a formula to show power, which is a term that can be used in place of explosiveness. In other words, the greater your explosiveness, the greater your power and vice versa. In the accompanying formula we see that power (P) is equal to force (f) times distance (d) per unit of time (t): **P = f x d/t**

This means the more strength you can generate, the greater your explosive power. Thus, if you increase strength, power will also go up. Conversely, if you keep increasing strength but execute the movement slowly as many internal artists tend to do, the muscles begin to "learn" slowness and there will actually be a decrease in the amount of power/explosiveness you can generate. For maximum results you must develop increased strength, together with increased speed during the exercise.

For explosive power or plyometric training, start with the sphere at the waist and as you step forward literally throw it upward. Allow the ball to fall with your arm becoming limp and return to the starting point and immediately lift it up explosively again. In the accompanying photos I used rubber cables, a medicine ball and stone spheres to strengthen the shoulders and arms. During circle walking you should not hold the spheres or medicine balls in a fixed position as some older manuals indicate. This will develop static strength only in that particular shoulder position.

Plyometric exercises require that a rapid loading (eccentric or yielding phase) of the muscles be accomplished just prior to the contraction phase of these muscles. In this case the lifting phase is throwing the ball upward. You can also do this with the rubber cables or any heavy object. Be very careful with this method, because it is deceptively taxing on your strength. I recommend you do no more than two days a week of this type of exercise with at least 72 hours between each session.

Higher Levels of Power

We have all seen martial artists who have discovered this whole-body force. They may not be impressive in a weightlifting environment, but he can crush you with his ability to apply all the strength he possesses in sparring or combat. To develop the tremendous power of external and inner strength one has to first develop the physical connections that link each segment of the body and then use the mind to develop functional strength.

In Chinese this functional strength is known as anjin or hidden strength. Anjin strength involves coordinating the muscles with the mental intent, yi, and then making it work as one unit so that one begins to use zhengjin instead of separately using parts of the body to move and strike. When the yigong or intention skill is added to the equation we reach even more subtle strength levels. Fueled by stronger, more reactive muscles, the mind can produce the true internal power of legend.

Dr. John P. Painter holds a Ph.D. in Naturopathic Chinese medicine and is a captain in the American Rangers Law Enforcement Training Institute. A member of the Inside Kung-Fu *Hall of Fame, he has 32 years' experience teaching the Chinese internal martial arts of taijiquan, xingyiquan and baguazhang. Contact Dr. Painter at P.O. Box 1777, Arlington TX, 76004; or thegompa@aol.com. The jiulong web site is www.ninedragonbaguazhang.com*

BEST OF CFW — VOL. 1
MARTIAL ARTS

The Perfect Warrior

Hwa Rang Do's Circle Principle Will Bolster Your Defensive and Offensive Skills

Doug Jeffrey

You slide onto your slippery seat just as the clock clunks over to 2:10. Your bespectacled teacher, chalk in hand, is waiting for the tardy bell to stop before he starts another loonnnggg, boring session of formulas, graphs, numbers, gobbledygook and whatever else he talks about while you're daydreaming.

You think, "Does this guy have to start right on time every single day? Come on!"

To make matters worse, the 102-degree summer heat has turned your bungalow into a kiln and you can't even escape the torture of your trigonometry class with a few quick glances at that cute girl in back because she's out today.

What are you going to do?

In case you didn't know, formulas, theories, numbers and all that good stuff doesn't have to be a huge drag. If you don't believe me, just get yourself into Gil Kim's Hwa Rang Do Academy in Huntington Beach, California.

OK, he's not really teaching any advanced math classes and you won't be computing any formulas with X, Y or Z. However, you will quickly find out that you can have a blast with concepts, theories and terms like the circle principle, momentum and centrifugal force.

Best of all, you'll probably develop a greater appreciation for this Korean art, and you might discover that there are some concepts that may just come in a little handy for you in training, competition or on the street.

THE CIRCLE PRINCIPLE

The first thing we need to do is start with a definition. The circle principle—which can be used in blocking, kicking, grappling and striking—involves circular—as opposed to linear—movements.

Just how important is this circular principle?

"It's a must, of course, for the martial arts," says Kim. "If you don't include it in your training, you're missing out quite a bit."

To prove his point, Kim notes that the same concept is used in other sports. Take a look at how a baseball pitcher winds up for added velocity before he throws a pitch. Of course, everyone has seen figure skaters turn into a blur—much like that coyote in that old cartoon—while they spin like an out-of-control top.

Gil Kim Up Close

- Born: Seoul, Korea
- Age: 50
- Former self-defense instructor for the United States Marine Corp. at Camp Pendleton in San Diego, California
- Founder and director of United Hwa Rang Do Federation
- Vice-president of World Martial Arts Association
- Chief master instructor of *ki mood do, ki gum do* (ancient Korean sword art)
- Owner: Hwa Rang Do Academy in Huntington Beach, California since 1977
- Instruction includes self-defense, weapons and meditation
- Phone: (714) 846-8008

BEST OF CFW — VOL.1
MARTIAL ARTS

> **Training Tips**
>
> Keep the following points in mind when executing circular palm or fisted blocks:
> - Stand relaxed with your knees slightly bent. Most of your weight should be on the balls of your feet.
> - Keep your upper body straight and relaxed. Keep your blocking hands and arms loose.
> - Depending on the type of attack, utilize full extension from the shoulder joint or half extension from the elbow joint.
> - Open your hands for redirecting and trapping.
> - Use fisted hands for powerful counter strikes.
> - All of the turns and pivots have to come from the center of your hips.

"Spinning [the circular principle] is a natural thing," he says. "Take it and embrace it because it is a gift."

Ash Merritt, who has been training with Gil Kim since 1979, says he has trained in other styles, and the circular principle makes a difference ... a big difference.

"This increases your speed, no doubt," he says. "It creates unbelievable power."

Justin Betance, a 22-year-old student of Kim, agrees there is a huge difference between linear and circular moves.

"The difference between the two movements is like night and day," says the recent UCLA grad. "Instead of meeting force with force (as you would with a linear defense), you alter the direction of their technique and only expend a minimal amount of energy (with a circular defense)."

Of course, saving energy is vital, especially if you're facing multiple attackers.

Betance, who has been training with Kim for more than three years, knows this stuff works because he had to use it once in the street.

"Utilizing the circular principle, I was able to restrain the other party and take him to the ground," he says. "I would have to stay that it prevented a fight."

If you want to find out other reasons why Kim advocates circular movements, keep reading.

WHY IT'S GOOD

According to Kim, there are several reasons why you should incorporate this circular motion into your repertoire. They are as follows:

ADVANTAGE NO. 1

When you execute circular techniques, it enables you to maintain your balance better, says Kim.

"You deflect your opponent's technique, you turn, spin around and come back where you started," he says. "This enables you to counterattack with less effort. This movement puts you in position to follow up easily."

ADVANTAGE NO. 2

Spinning creates speed, and speed creates power. Whether you're executing a block or throwing a technique, you're going to generate both of these vital characteristics, he says.

"Think of how much power and speed you can produce when you attach a stone to a rope and twirl it above your head," says the former forms and fighting competitor. "That circular motion, which is centrifugal force, can also benefit your [martial arts] techniques."

ADVANTAGE NO. 3

Quickness is another benefit, but you're not going to be quick unless you're relaxed.

"When you're relaxed, you will definitely react quicker," he says. "When you become like water, you are like a wave, flowing over the ocean. On the other hand, when you're tense, you slow down, like a rock. In this case, you don't glide like you're on oil or some other liquid."

Of course, you're not going to be relaxed unless your mind is focused.

"Physically and mentally, you have to be as sharp as a needle," he points out.

Merritt, who operates his own hwa rang do school in Ft. Mojave, Arizona, agrees that relaxation is paramount if you want to execute the techniques with power, speed and effectiveness.

"If you're not relaxed, it's like driving with your parking brake on," says the 48-year-old hwa rang do stylist. "The tension causes you to slow down. It's friction."

On the other hand, when you're loose, you'll see a huge difference, he adds.

"It's like a wave," he says. "When it finally breaks or crashes on the shore, what power."

THE THEORY BEHIND EACH

Let's now turn our attention to the specifics of blocking, striking and weapons, just a few of the areas in which the circle principle produces some desirable benefits.

The fighters square off (1). Justin Betance throws a right, which Kim redirects with a left, inside circular palm block (2) and immediately counters with a right vertical fist (3). Kim then secures his opponent's right arm in preparation for an outside, bent-arm armbar throw (4). Kim executes a 180-degree counter clockwise body turn and competes the technique (5). He then secures his opponent with a knee to the neck and a wristlock (6).

BLOCKING

Let's say you're preparing to block a monster right from that big guy in class who—because of his extra large frame—you've been trying to avoid since the first day he stormed into class. Sure, you could execute a simple traditional outside block (moving your arm across your body at a 90-degree angle). Or, as Kim recommends, you could move your arm in a circular motion to block the strike.

Blocking a strike in a circular manner—as opposed to a straight block—enables you to cover a "broader" area, he says. This, he notes, increases the likelihood that the block will be successful,

Ashley Merritt approaches Gil Kim with a knife (1). When Merritt attacks with a straight stab, Kim simultaneously blocks and cuts his opponent's weapon hand with a downward circular move (2). Next, Kim is able to steal the weapon and point it at his opponent (3). As an option, Kim could also execute a quick circular move over his opponent's shoulder and strike to the neck (4). Kim concludes the sequence with an outside leg sweep takedown (5 and 6).

regardless of how quick or strong your opponent is.

"This technique will enable you to deflect the strike or disrupt his balance," says Kim.

Once you do that, you can go in for the counterattack. You can follow up with combinations, strikes, joint locks, a takedown or a throw.

Some might argue that the traditional block has more power than the circular motion. In fact, they might even point out that the shortest distance between two points is a straight line and all that good jazz. And, because of this—anything, including a block—will have more power if it goes from Point A to Point B.

Nice try, but you're going to get an argument from Kim, who says that a circular block will have just as much power as the old-fashioned straight block.

The circular move also is beneficial because you don't have to stop and start again before you perform the next technique. As that old saying goes, "An object in motion tends to stay in motion."

While you're in motion, you can finish one movement and carry on with another, he says.

"You don't have to stop and start," he notes. "You can carry on with the momentum from the block to execute a counterattack. It's very fluid. You can react faster."

> ## Hwa Rang Do History
> - Hwa rang do was conceived 1,800 years ago by the Buddhist priest, Won Kwang Bopsa.
> - Translated, hwa rang do means "Flower, man, way" or "The way of the flowering of manhood."
> - King Chinghung, of Silla, called upon Bopsa to instruct young members of the royal family in a variety of activities, including the martial arts. They became known as the hwarang warriors.
> - The art has a code of ethics, including loyalty to country, loyalty to parents and courage in the face of an enemy.
> - The art can be subdivided into four major paths of study: internal power, external power, weapon power and mental power.
>
> *Source: "The Original Martial Arts Encyclopedia"*

STRIKING

Now, let's look at a similar example with striking. Instead of punching in a linear fashion straight ahead, twist your upper body, bring your arm back, throw the technique in a circular fashion and … bam. You're got the equivalent of a United States "Smart Bomb."

"If you throw a spinning back hand or some other type of technique that has a whipping, circular motion, that will generate extra centrifugal force," he says. "And that means more power."

WEAPONS

The same principles apply here, he says.

"The circle principle will give you more speed and create more chances of making combinations because of that speed and movement," says Kim.

BE AWARE

While Kim has taught and used the circular principle in his training and teaching from Day No. 1, you do need to be aware that there is one limitation. In order for this to work, you can't be in a different area code than your opponent. You have to be up close and personal.

"If you're not close to him, you have to close the gap to make it work," he says. "These are close-quarters tactics."

Of course, depending on the circumstances, you may or may not want to get in tight. Circumstances will dictate what to do.

"You may just want to stay put and see what your opponent does," says Kim.

If you do move in, apply some of these concepts with the circular principle. And if you throw a strike, add a little something extra for that old trig teacher you used to have.

MARTIAL ARTS

The Best of Both Worlds

Jihua "Jenny" Tang is combining the best of yesterday with the promise of tomorrow.

Dave Cater

Jihua "Jenny" Tang doesn't see herself a trailblazer. But she is. She doesn't see herself as the standard bearer for a new breed of Chinese practitioner.

But she is.

And she certainly doesn't see herself as an honest-to-goodness connection between the old and new; tradition and innovation.

But she is.

Jihua (pronounced jee-wah) "Jenny" Tang is a combination of everything that is good and right with today's Chinese martial artist. She was raised to respect the ways of her ancestors, to learn as they did. At the same time, she realized there had to be more to life than spending hours upon hours trying to perfect a Chen-style kick or a Yang-style empty stance. Those things would come in time, she believed. But life had to go on.

The Learning Curve

Maybe it wasn't so much what she learned, but rather how she was taught that made the biggest impact. Although Tang began her training at seven—an age when many Chinese youngsters are pushed from the comforts of their home for the more austere confines of a martial arts "school/camp"—she joined because she wanted to and stayed because she liked it.

Of course, it didn't hurt that her aunt was her instructor. Or that the instructor was the famed Wei Qi He, the sister of Tang's mother. Or that He performed at the White House in front of President Richard M. Nixon in 1974.

"During the summer holidays my aunt was teaching at the Shanghai Sports Palace," Tang fondly remembers. "She started a new group of students my age and invited me to come to practice. I went and I liked it. That's how I joined."

MARTIAL ARTS

Jenny Tang learned her tai chi skills from her aunt, renowned internal stylist Wei Qi He.

No being ripped from mother's arms. No being dragged down the street into a waiting car. No being told she'd see her parents on the next holiday.

It was fun. Pure and simple enjoyment.

Quick Study

The three hours of kung-fu went quickly for the only child of middle-class Chinese parents. Stretching, training in the fundamentals, the rudiments of a group form honed to a razor's edge.

"It was both fun and work," remembers Tang, who also studied ballet. "At first I was just going there for fun, but then I decided I really like it and I wanted to be able to perform there with the other kids."

Wei Qi He, now one of the most-respected internal voices in the West, treated her niece like another daughter. (Jenny notes, however, she always called her aunt "coach.")

Young Jihua fell in love with the movement, the style, and the grace of tai chi. And when it came time to pick a specialty, she disdained the flips and spins of competition wushu for the more-demanding Chen.

"I think Chen is more interesting for kids because there are more kicks and jumps," noted Tang, born in Shanghai. "I enjoyed the movements."

On With The Show

But deep inside, what she really enjoyed was performing—as part of a group, in front of a group. Which just happened to occur weekly at the Shanghai Children's Palace, where Wei Qi He's students conducted martial arts demonstrations before visiting dignitaries and other foreign officials.

The work was hard, Tang now admits, but the rewards far outweighed the sacrifices.

"I would go to school until 3 and then practice from 3:30-6:30 p.m.," relates Tang, whose parents never studied martial arts. "We even trained on the weekends. My aunt treated me just like any other student. At times it was hard but when I found out we could perform, I really wanted to do it."

Jihua "Jenny" Tang

Born — Feb. 5, 1974
Birthplace: Shanghai, China
Parents: Father was a science engineer and later a high school geography teacher; mother was a sales representative
Martial Arts: Wushu and Chen and Yang style tai chi
Started studying: Age 7
Instructor: Wei Qi He
Place of study: Shanghai Sports Palace
First Style: Wushu
Later studied: Chen and Yang style with an emphasis on the 24 form
Specialty: Horse tail tai chi sword
Facts: As a child performed at Shanghai Children's Palace. Later appeared at the International Wrestling Festival in Tokyo and the Nagasaki Holland Village
Professional Experience: Performed as a martial artist, singer and dancer at the Tiger Balm Garden in Singapore from 1993-96
Arrived in the United States: 1998
Education: Received bachelor's degree in computer science from Philander Smith College in Littlerock, Ark.
Languages: Speaks fluent Mandarin, Cantonese, Shanghaiese and English
Achievements: Recently crowned Miss Asian Arkansas; started a college martial arts class; later taught at a fitness center
Contact: www.geocities.com/jjt88

The beautiful, but rarely seen horse tail or mane whisk tai chi sword features a tassel at the end.

While everyone else was doing wushu, Tang stayed with Chen, a style that typically asks more from the female practitioner than the practitioner is willing or able to give. The strong kicks, deep stances and concentrated power demanded of the Chen style performer usually thin the ranks long before most discover its benefits. But Tang, the only student in her group choosing tai chi as a specialty, found something to like in a style that seldom likes back.

"It was something different, plus my aunt thinks it's good for kids to try tai chi," she notes. "I was the only one doing it and for me, Chen wasn't boring. The 24 simplified Yang form was only three or four minutes while the Chen form was really long."

Back To Basics

Tang maintains the secret to mastering Chen may lie in a fundamentally sound wushu background.

"If you don't have a wushu background it may be hard for you," she adds. "But if you have a wushu background, it's easy."

(At this point, the 5-foot-2, 110-pound martial artist with hair down to her waist rises to demonstrate in a three-foot-by-three-foot space.)

"You have the basics of Chen in one movement—a crescent kick to a drop stance where only your feet and not your knees touch the floor. Add to that a fajing punch and you're there. Wushu definitely makes it easier."

Tang used those talents to delight fans in Tokyo at the International Wrestling Festival. Three years later, she joined forces with the Shanghai Opera Team and Shanghai Acrobatic Team to perform at the Holland Vacation Village in Nagasaki.

When Wei Qi He left China for the United States in 1989, a 15-year-old Tang assumed assistant coaching duties at the Shanghai Sports Palace. She continued to instruct young students on the virtues of martial arts until she graduated from high school in 1992 and took a position as an entertainer at the Tiger Balm Garden in Singapore.

"I worked there as a performing artist—mainly martial arts—but also acting, singing and dancing," she recalls. "They interviewed many people but just took two acrobats and me."

Universal Language

Tang was attractive to Tiger Balm Garden officials not only because she knew her way around a stage, but also because she was the only Chinese who could speak fluent English.

"I not only took English classes in school, but I also took lessons at night," notes Tang, who also speaks Mandarin, Cantonese and a local dialect called Shanghaiese.

At the same time the contract offer came from Tiger Balm Garden, she also received overtures from the Richmond, Va., city manager's office. Her aunt had started a martial arts program and they needed an assistant coach. As much a Jenny wanted to come to America, the timing wasn't right. For the next three years she performed at Singapore's popular theme park, while also teaching martial arts and tai chi on the side.

Tang returned to China in 1996 and served as translator for two America teams visiting Shanghai—one led by her aunt and another led by kuoshu great Joe Dunphy in Maryland. The decision was made and in 1998 Tang was accepted at tiny Philander Smith College in Littlerock, Ark.

There was a bit of a culture shock, to say the least. Philander Smith, designated a Historical Black College University, had an enrollment of 1,000, 95 percent of which was Black. International students comprised the remaining five percent. Although she knew no one, Tang created a martial arts class at the school during her first year and later taught tai chi at a local fitness center where she had as many as 20 students. She will graduate this year with a bachelor's in computer science, carrying a 3.8 average.

Along the way, Jenny made the move from Chen to Yang style because she was attracted by its free-flowing movements. Comparing the form to a musical score, she notes that Yang is like a graceful opera that slides from one note to the next in a natural progression, while Chen features both very high and very low notes interspersed with drastic transitions.

Tang has made a splash on the tournament circuit by demonstrating the rarely seen horse tail or mane whisk tai chi sword. She learned the weapon from Junhai Lu, son of the great Zheng Duo Lu, who taught the weapon to Wei Qi He.

Jenny Tang, the reigning Miss Asian Arkansas, meets with Arkansas Governor Mike Huckbee.

Photo courtesy of Jenny Tang

"All the control is in your wrist, just like a sword," she says.

Tang also made a splash recently when she was crowned Miss Asian Arkansas. The 28-year-old beauty beat out nine other contestants vying for a trophy, a $500 travel voucher and a chance at competing for Miss Asian America.

"I was going to sing the music from *Crouching Tiger, Hidden Dragon* but they didn't have the music," explains Tang, who sings in the school choir. "So I did my form. I was really confident and everything went very smoothly. It was fun."

Tang, who hopes to find a job in the computer field while also teaching martial arts, would like to create a tai chi program that benefits seniors, specifically those confined to hospitals. She also wants to make the instruction simple enough so martial artists and non-martial artists alike learn to appreciate its benefits.

"The basics are everything," she insists. "Once you understand the basics you can very easily learn a form in a day."

The long road to a new day began 21 years ago for Jihua "Jenny" Tang. Through it all, she has experienced the very best martial arts has to offer—at her own pace and in her own way. No one forced her to train. No one made her learn. There was never a compelling reason to push forward or draw back. Just a sincere desire to appreciate the real value of martial arts training.

Jenny Tang didn't set out to be a great martial artist. She didn't plan on becoming a leader. And she didn't make it her life's work to become the best example of yesterday weaved gently, yet so eloquently with the promise of tomorrow.

But she is.

The Mechanics of Spiral Throws

The spiral throw may look easy, but there are enough twists and turns to confuse even the seasoned practitioner.

Tim Cartmell, Photos by Matt Huang

All throws can be grouped into three basic categories. Traditionally, throws are labeled according to the type of technique to which it applies (i.e., hip throws, sacrifice throws, joint techniques, flips, sweeps, etc.). In other words, how the thrower makes the other fall.

In contrast, we will organize throws in relation to the movement the person being thrown makes through space before hitting the ground. This means throws will be categorized from the point of view of the person being thrown and not the partner doing the throwing. From this point of view, all throws may be placed into one of three broad categories, namely, circles, arcs and spirals.

Simply put, circular throws are those which cause the opponent to rotate either forward or backward around a central axis (his hips) with the feet moving approximately 360 degrees. Examples of circle throws are the fireman's carry of Western wrestling and the tomoe nage (foot in stomach) throw of judo. Arcing throws cause the opponent's head to move in an arcing plane to the front or rear of the baseline (the line drawn between the ankles with one or both of the opponent's feet remaining stationary). Examples of arcing throws are "clothesline" takedowns, the o-soto-gari (major reaping throw) of judo or the shiho nage (four directions throw) of aikido.

Spiral throws cause the opponent's upper body to twist either forward or backward as it moves downward with the opponent's feet either leaving the ground (as in a circular throw) or remaining relatively stationary (as in arcing throws). Examples of spiral throws are the head-twisting throws of baguazhang, the Japanese whizzer of Western wrestling or the salto of Greco-Roman wrestling.

In this article, we are going to cover the mechanics and application of spiral throws. First, it is important to shift our point of view from "doing" specific techniques to an opponent and "causing" him to fall through a particular pattern in space. The latter orientation will allow for much greater flexibility and spontaneity in applying technique that is essential when actually trying to throw an uncooperative opponent. Once you understand the principles and have internalized the basic mechanics of the types of throws, you can change and modify your techniques as needed.

Certain principles must be employed to throw an opponent efficiently and without undue effort. These principles hold true for all types of throws. Some of the more important and basic principles are:

Non-Opposition of Force

This is perhaps the most basic rule to follow. The ideal is to never directly oppose the force of

The opponents clinch in a common over-and-under position (1). Tim (in blue shirt) steps toward his opponent's rear corner with his left foot and presses his right palm on the back of the opponent's leg (2). By leaning to his left, Tim breaks his opponent's posture and sets him up for a rear spiral. The push behind the leg acts as a fulcrum for the throw. Tim needs only to twist his body to the left, which causes a transfer of momentum through the opponent's shoulder (3). This forces him to fall in a spiral to his rear.

our opponent with our own force. In a direct confrontation of power against power, the contender with the greatest strength will invariably win. The practical worth of any technique should be considered in light of its potential universal applicability or lack thereof (can you make it work on a much larger and stronger opponent).

The most difficult part of any throw is usually the entry and set-up. Using force against force we will not only preclude any chance of setting up a throw against a stronger opponent, it will also cause a weaker opponent to reflexively pull back and go on the defensive, making the application of any technique more difficult. Understanding the functions and structural weaknesses of the opponent's body and the methods of maximizing the use of gravity, we can engineer entries and techniques that allow us to circumvent our opponent's power and throw larger and stronger fighters.

Connect and Join Centers

The next step in throwing an opponent without struggle is to connect with him physically and join centers. The purpose of joining centers is to become "one body" so the opponent must move as an extension of yourself. Yours will be the dominant center and the opponent will have no choice but to follow your movement. As long as you and

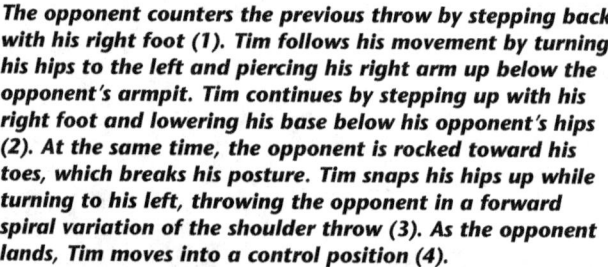

The opponent counters the previous throw by stepping back with his right foot (1). Tim follows his movement by turning his hips to the left and piercing his right arm up below the opponent's armpit. Tim continues by stepping up with his right foot and lowering his base below his opponent's hips (2). At the same time, the opponent is rocked toward his toes, which breaks his posture. Tim snaps his hips up while turning to his left, throwing the opponent in a forward spiral variation of the shoulder throw (3). As the opponent lands, Tim moves into a control position (4).

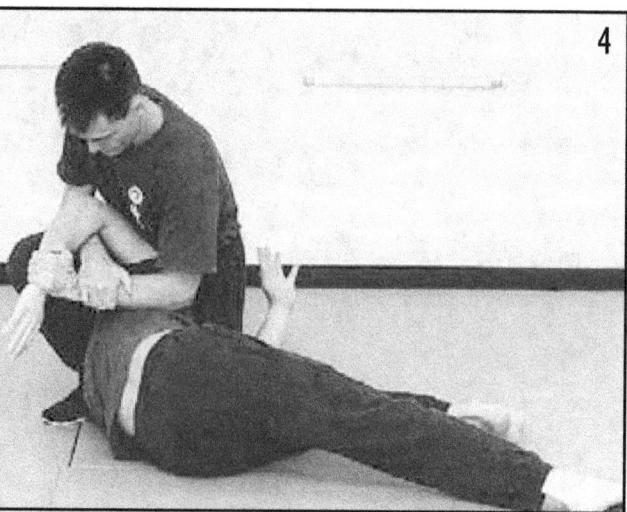

the opponent move as two separate entities (have two separate centers) there will inevitably be opposition and struggle. Until we join centers from a dominant position, we must follow our opponent's movement and look to establish a connection without fighting his force directly.

Apply Force Where The Opponent Cannot Resist

Once you have joined centers with a dominant physical connection, the next step is to lead the opponent without giving him an opportunity to effectively resist. This prevents the opponent from counterattacking or stopping your momentum. It is important to keep all the slack out of the connection with our opponent's center so he has no freedom to escape. Now we can transfer our momentum through our hold and into the opponent without resistance. The key is knowledge of the body's structure and weak angles.

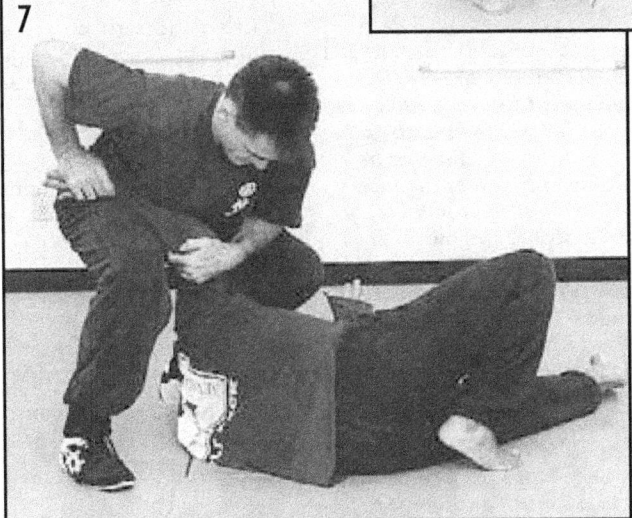

The opponents square off in a guard-up position (1). Tim advances with a right backhand strike. The opponent blocks up with his right hand (2). Tim reaches up from below and grabs inside the opponent's right wrist with his left as he simultaneously frees his right hand to strike again at the face (3). The opponent blocks the strike with his free hand. Tim grabs the opponent's left hand with his right and pushes it up under the opponent's right armpit as he goes in and strikes with his right shoulder (4). Tim swings his left foot back and lowers his base as he hooks over the opponent's arms with his right arm. He traps the opponent's arms so he is unable to defend the throw (5). Tim snaps his legs straight and bows forward while twisting to his left for a front spiral throw (6). The throw ends in a control position (7).

MARTIAL ARTS

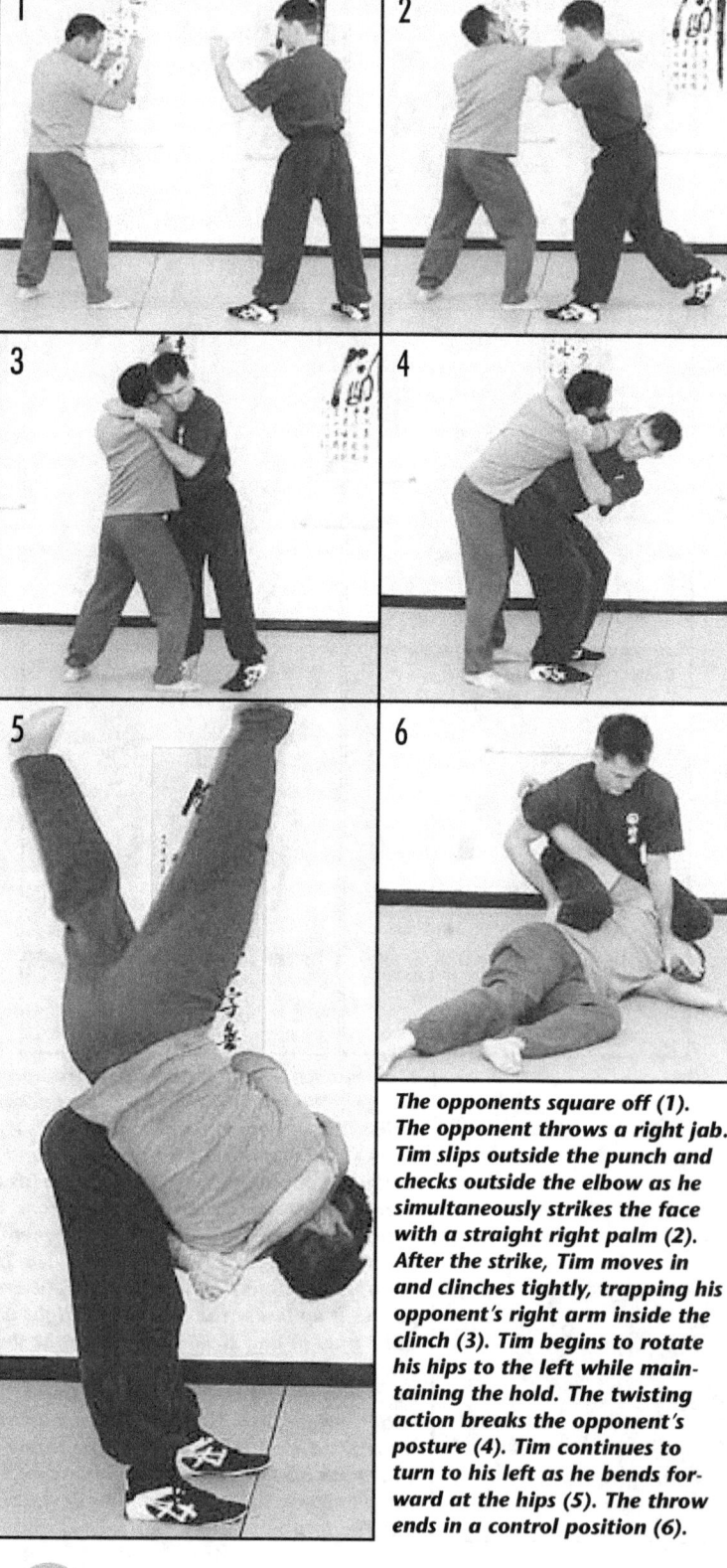

The opponents square off (1). The opponent throws a right jab. Tim slips outside the punch and checks outside the elbow as he simultaneously strikes the face with a straight right palm (2). After the strike, Tim moves in and clinches tightly, trapping his opponent's right arm inside the clinch (3). Tim begins to rotate his hips to the left while maintaining the hold. The twisting action breaks the opponent's posture (4). Tim continues to turn to his left as he bends forward at the hips (5). The throw ends in a control position (6).

Transfer the Momentum Through the Hold

Besides applying our force where the opponent cannot resist, we must also be aware of why certain forces are applied. The goal more or less dictates the type, intensity and duration of whichever forces are appropriate to any given situation. Since our immediate goal is to break the opponent's posture and throw him to the ground, the manner in which we apply our force will be different than if our goal were to strike the opponent and cause local tissue damage.

Applying a ballistic force as we move to throw will most often be counterproductive, since too much force knocks your opponent away, disjoins your centers and ruins the throw. Once you have joined centers with the opponent and established a hold, transfer the momentum of your mass through the hold into the opponent's center to create a reciprocal reaction in his body. The key to a smooth transference of momentum from your body to his is to continue moving into him at a natural rate of acceleration (as determined by your position and direction relative to gravity). Smooth acceleration that transfers your momentum through your opponent will cause him to move where you desire without giving him a chance to escape (transference of momentum too slow) or without knocking him away (transference of momentum too fast).

Misalign the Opponent's Posture

Once connected to the opponent and dominating his center and movement, you need to break his posture before attempting the actual throw. Breaking the posture may or may not actually cause the opponent to physically lose his balance. For example, your skeletal structure can be misaligned without you falling to the ground unless additional pressure is applied. Breaking the balance automatically results in the attempt to regain balance or a fall will occur.

To break the posture, you must seek to misalign the opponent's skeletal structure through natural ranges of motion so that subsequent moderate pressure will bring him to the ground. One advantage of misaligning the skeletal structure over breaking the balance is that by forcing him off balance, he will instinctively struggle to regain balance and often a contest of strength ensues. Breaking the alignment of the frame does not alarm the opponent or automatically engage the righting reflex. Since applying force is based upon the system of bony levers of our frame, misaligning the structure effectively weakens the opponent's ability to use force, no matter how strong the muscles might be.

Cause the Opponent to Fall

Now we come to the actual part of the technique recognized as the "throw" itself. If you have properly set up the opponent, causing him to fall should be the easiest part of the process. Although there are a limited number of ways to set up a throw and break the postural alignment, there should be a virtually limitless number of ways to cause the fall. It is important to realize the methods of causing an opponent to fall are not separate from the methods used to break his posture and thus should be viewed as a continuation of that process.

An ideal throw has set-up, entry, joining centers, transference of momentum, a breaking of the alignment, and takedown as one smooth flow of movement. It remains important at this stage of the technique not to use brute force. Even as the opponent falls, if you attempt to accelerate him by using force you will more likely than not give him pressure to resist against. This will help him to partially reduce the speed at which he hits the ground. Cause the opponent to fall without giving him anything to hang onto and the throw will have maximum effect.

The principles described above are universally applicable to all types of throws. Below are examples of spiral throws, which are special in that they may be used to effect the same types of landings as circles and arcs, and are the most difficult types of throws to counter. In addition, in a combat format, spiral throws very often cause the most damage because of the unusual positions at which the opponent hits the ground (they make break falling difficult).

Spiral throws are divided into two categories: those which cause the opponent to spiral and fall to his front, and those which cause the opponent to spiral and fall to his rear. The technical examples that follow show the applications of several variations of the over the hips, front spiral throw.

Tim Cartmell's books are available through cfwenterprises.com

MARTIAL ARTS

The Secret Behind Baji Basics

Without a clear understanding of internal power, you will never advance past physical mastery.

Neil Thomas, with Jason Tsou

Feeling the burn welling up in my thighs, I am instructed to execute another "double planting fists" technique from the baji quan (the eight extreme style's) basic training. But this time, I am told to keep low. "Don't bob up and down as your transition from one posture to the next."

Buckets of sweat are pouring down our faces as our legs scream for a timeout. Jason Tsou, my teacher, is drilling us, or should I say torturing us, with the basic, single-movement drills of the baji/piqua systems. Mustering all my strength, I try it again. With arms extended shoulder high, I slowly bring them both into the center, like two inward blocks, rise onto my toes as high as possible, then with a snappy downward punching movement, I stomp both feet simultaneously as hard as I can.

"Slower! Not so fast!" he reminds us. "Okay, let's do it again by the numbers ... Yi ... Er ..." Pause ... Jason has stopped to correct somebody's posture while we hold our positions. My legs are shaking so badly I'm almost having an out-of-body-experience, or more of a déjà vu really. Thoughts of paying my dues years ago "standing in horse" creep past my mind. Shouldn't my long, hard hours of basic training be behind me by now? I mean, I'm in good shape, right?

Suddenly, I'm shaken back to reality by Jason's voice. "San ..." Pause. My legs are begging him to say the next number! Suddenly I hear, "Tuck your butt in!" Tuck my butt in? Doesn't he realize I'm lucky to be standing! "and Ssi!" We execute the downward double punch. "Okay, take a break."

Thank God! That was close. I thought I was on the verge of passing out, but instead my legs exploded. I'm now on all fours, unable to stand. I'd be embarrassed if I had any energy left. Finally, I decide I've been down here too long and had better stand. And so, imitating "The Evolution of Man," I force myself upright. Step ... and step ... and step. As if coming down from some sort of anaesthetic, I make my way to the nearest wall.

"Training by the numbers forces you into the proper position and stance. It gives you enough

Baji kick.

Baji chi szi post standing stance.

Shoen yao rocking weight shifting basic #1.

Shoen huan weight shifting basic #2.

time to pay attention to the details," Tsou explains, adding, "like how and when to shift your weight, and what muscles you are using to execute a particular movement. You can put it all together later."

Combat-Ready Techniques

Never have I experienced basic training so demanding, techniques that involve so many muscles and require so much exertion as the ones in the baji/piqua system taught by sifu Tsou in Monterey Park, Calif. But he assures us that these basics are the foundation of good kung-fu, and we believe him wholeheartedly. After all, we have all seen him demonstrate, or been an unlucky participant in a demonstration of power issuing. There is no illusion as to whether or not these basics work. It's more a question of, do we have the wisdom and drive to continue?

"In the beginning," Tsou tells us, "there were no fancy forms with which to demonstrate, just combat-tested training techniques, which would ready a student for battle."

Tsou pauses, then, as if letting us in on a valuable secret says, "If all you practiced were these basic lines (single-movement training), you would be better prepared for combat than collecting all the flashy forms we see today. These lines are the key for the building and storing of qi and training the body to move correctly," he adds.

"Practicing baji basics is like depositing money qi into your bank (the tan tien). Practicing piqua basics is like going to the ATM to make a withdrawal. They use the qi you've stored while practicing baji. It's balanced. If you haven't practiced baji first, you have nothing to use when doing piqua."

Standing on legs of Jell-O, with a shirt that looks as if I just took a shower in it, I am content in the knowledge that I survived another lesson…

Back to Basics with Baji

The old masters that developed our styles and forms were really quite clever. They understood perfectly the essential elements one needs for good kung-fu. Blocking and countering are merely the

Shoen jou bear walk shifting basic #3.

"Baji/piqua create such a formidable martial art foundation even demons are afraid of those who master them."

first level of training. Hidden within most techniques are the keys to developing high levels of internal power and nothing is more important than a clear understanding of those training goals. This may sound overly simplistic, but without this level of understanding, you will never advance past physical mastery.

The style that opened my eyes to the importance of basic training was baji quan. So, for those who've become dissatisfied with your progress after years of study, or who'd like a deeper understanding of your practice, I'd like to share some baji basic techniques and concepts that I've picked up, which may change the focus of your workout.

Baji is a simple, yet rich, system containing only a small number of forms. Each form requires a tremendous amount of basic training to set the foundation. The most important techniques one must master first are found within the system's first form and training level known as xiao baji (the small eight extremes).

Xiao baji's form, bajijia is made up of 24 powerful techniques, a third of which are practiced as single-movement training techniques. This is when you take each posture and practice it repeatedly on alternating sides. Tsou refers to this as a "line" and each of these eight "lines" is practiced with three different training emphasis or focuses. The first is learning the eight main postures, with a focus on position and proper body alignment. The second level involves stomping techniques with a

Beginning posture.

focus on rooting, and at the third level a chi gong technique is added with an emphasis on breathing. But, we're getting ahead of ourselves. Before you should even attempt learning the lines, you need to prepare your body with basic training exercises.

As in most systems, baji's first training level begins with attention to proper posture, form and footwork. This process trains the eight essentials of body alignment: feet, knees, hips (or kua), tailbone, shoulders, elbows, hands, and head, while you develop leg and lower back strength. When thinking about kung-fu stances, most of us envision low, deep stances. However, baji differs in that the depth of the stance depends on the body structure of each individual student. Rule No. 1: Never sacrifice alignment for depth; alignment is a key to producing internal power later. Keep this in mind as you practice.

The Basic Baji Stance

Many veteran martial artists have spent time standing in static postures to develop the strength needed for advanced training. But this first baji stance separates the men from the boys. If practiced regularly, a kind of "qi ball" develops in front of your stomach and abdomen. According to Tsou, this posture not only builds your lower back muscles, it drives qi up your spine to help remove blockages.

With feet together, slowly bend your knees as if you were going to sit. Keep your back straight and your chin and tailbone tucked in a little. At the same time, extend both your arms in front of your chest as if you were driving a car. Your shoulders should be relaxed with your scapulae slightly rounded. Your fists should not be clinched but hollow, like a garden rake. (Note: baji was originally called batzuquan, meaning rake fist after this fist posture, but it was considered too crass and changed to baji). Remember to keep your knees together, round your scapulae to hollow your chest area and relax. Your legs are your qi pumps and within a few breaths, begin sending qi up the spine to the head. If practiced correctly, you won't be able to hold this posture for very long. Start by placing your back against a wall and hold this posture for about one minute. Gradually you will be able to hold it for two, then three minutes. At this point, it's time to lose the wall and hold the posture in the open. Don't get discouraged. None of the martial artists I know could hold this posture for long in the beginning.

Bear Walking

Another good basic is shoen bu or the bear walking technique. This technique is broken down into three categories: shoen yao (weight-shifting drills); shoen huan (lunging drills); and shoen jou (diagonal shuffling drills). All categories are usually practiced at two levels: concentrating on posture and footwork, and concentrating on sinking your qi. This is accomplished by practicing each walk with a forceful stomping technique designed to condition the feet, stimulate acupuncture points in the feet, and open your qi channels or pathways to the head.

Bending kick.

Kick.

Shoen yao, the first weight-shifting drill, is performed by placing your feet over a shoulder-width apart and flexing your knees. Your arms extend downward and are rounded to your sides like a bear on its hind legs. Now slowly inhale, shift all your weight to one leg, exhale, and lower your stance a little. Inhale again, slowly shift your weight to the other leg as you lower your stance, and exhale. Within eight breaths, four on either side, you should reach a deep horse stance. Now slowly reverse the process until you are back standing. Remember to keep your shoulders relaxed and your palms facing the ground. As you shift your weight, try to be soft and sensitive with your feet and palms. Visualize and feel the energy from the ground.

When adding a stomp to your bear step, your feet are together with all your weight on your right leg. Your arms are at your sides, totally relaxed, with your left toe barely touching the ground for balance. As you begin to shift your weight to the other side, lift your qi by physically lifting your left shoulder, mentally lifting your center of gravity, and directing your intent. Now, with a driving force, drop your weight onto your left side with a stomp and lift your right foot until just your toes are touching. I know this sounds awkward, but I can't think of any practice that will teach you how to sink your qi to your feet any faster.

Shoen huan, the first lunging drill, is performed like kneeling. Place your left foot in front of your right, about one stride, and sink your weight until your right knee is almost touching the ground. Your arms extend downward and are rounded to your sides, again like a bear. Inhale, step forward with your right foot and drag your left foot up behind until you are in the same position, but on the opposite side, and exhale. Remember to keep your back straight and keep your arms and palms rounded. Feel the energy around you.

Shoen jou, the first diagonal shuffling drill, is performed by stepping diagonally with your left foot into a 60/40 stance. Again, your arms extend downward and are rounded to your sides, like a bear, with your back straight. Now inhale, shuffle diagonally to your right into the same stance, but on the opposite side, as you exhale. Remember to keep your back straight and keep your arms and

Shan tsai double-planting fist.

palms rounded, feeling the energy around you. Remember, this should also be practiced as a stomping technique.

Single Punching Drill

This basic utilizes the shifting from one bow and arrow stance into another to produce punching power. Stand in a right bow and arrow stance facing right, with your left punch extended to the front. Slowly bring your punch back into your body as you begin to pivot. This transition takes you through a low horse stance, facing front with the arms creating a push-and-pull motion in front of your abdomen. Then snap to the left side in a bow and arrow stance as you extend your right punch forward.

Sounds easy, right? Well, it is, if you don't put any effort into it. As you pivot, remember to grind the soles of your feet into the earth. Power begins in the feet; in a punch it's generated with the rear foot driving it. As for your hands, 50 percent of your power is in the punching hand and the other 50 percent is in your elbow strike. That's right. Both arms are connected at the spine and should move in unison, executing a punch in front and an elbow to the rear. Repeat 99 more times, slowly and with power, and tell me if you've broken a sweat.

Single Kicking Drill

I hate even thinking about this one. You begin by stepping forward as in shoen huan posture, but instead of relaxed with rounded bear arms, place them in the "holding-a-steering-wheel" position, as in first stance practice. Now, without rising in your stance, snap a front heel kick out horizontal to the ground and hold it for a couple of breaths. Slowly lower your kick to the ground in the same lunging posture, opposite side, and snap your other kick out and hold. Remember to keep your shoulders and arms relaxed. Repeat on either side.

The Lines of Xiao Baji

Now that you're warmed up, it's time for single-movement training or as we affectionately refer to them "the lines." As I've already explained, the eight postures come from the form, xiao bajijia. Each is practiced repeatedly alternating on either side, while concentrating on proper alignment, stance transition and good footwork.

Once you feel strong and competent, you can advance to the next level. This is where you learn how to shift your weight and apply various stomping techniques like the one you've learned doing the bear walk. Stomping forces your body to sink its qi into the ground and root your stance. The resultant reaction force travels back up the legs, to the spine, and out the arms. This is the beginning of learning how to issue real internal power. In fact, the lines of xiao baji teach you how to control and issue four types internal power:

This level scares many students away from baji practice, because the punishment on their bodies is simply too hard. My first day, I broke most of the capillaries in my inner thighs practicing stomping. But the injury healed as I got stronger. For the small group that trains seriously, however, these lines should be considered the heart of baji quan.

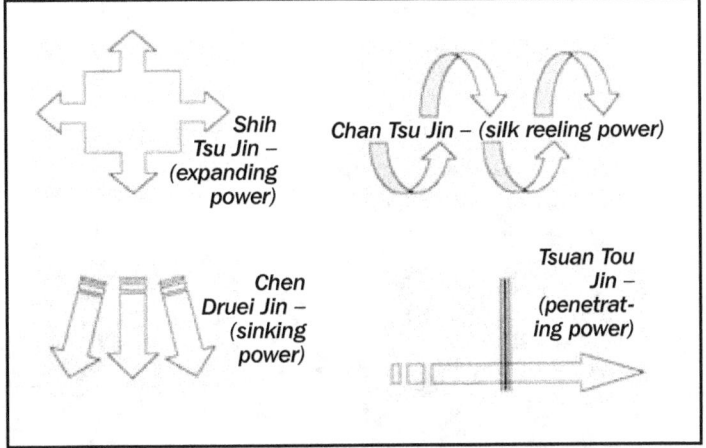

Bridging your internal training with the external will be found at the third level. At this stage of chi gong training you will quit stomping and begin holding each posture for eight focused breaths. This level must be mastered before higher levels of the art are explored. While holding each posture and breathing, you focus on sinking your qi to your tan tien. It's a method of xujin or storing energy. At this level your major muscles become fatigued and let go. This allows your minor muscle groups to take over and opens your qi channels for better qi storage, as well as issuing power.

Piqua Zhang Basic Training

From the first moment I began practicing basic piqua drills, I knew they would be my daily medicine. Never have I experienced basic training so demanding, techniques that involve so many muscles and require so much exertion, as these taught by sifu Jason Tsou of Monterey Park, Calif. But Tsou assures me that these basics are the foundation of good kung-fu, and I believe him wholeheartedly. After all, I have seen him demonstrate, or been an unlucky participant in a demonstration of power issuing. There is no illusion as to whether or not these basics work.

It's more a question of, "Do I have the wisdom and drive to practice?" Since I have already discussed baji basics in the first installment of this article (March 2002), I'd like to share some piqua basic techniques and concepts I've picked up, which may change the focus of your workout.

Piqua zhang is an old kung-fu style believed to date back to the Ming dynasty (A.D. 1368-1644). "Pi" translates as chopping, "qua" means to suspend, and "zhang" indicates the use of the palm. Together, this name reflects two main characteristics of the style. To deliver these strikes with power, a skilled practitioner needs to condition his upper spine and shoulder muscles, as well as coordinate quick, lively footwork. Sounds simple, right? Nothing could be further from the truth.

Back to More Basics

The first, seemingly gentle training drill emphasizes total relaxation with a focus on building flexibility in the back and shoulders. It is referred to as "pi" or chopping technique and trains your slapping strike. Begin with the feet a shoulder-width apart and your left arm behind your lower back. Extend your right arm directly over your head and swing it down to your left hip as if slapping the air. Return it overhead and swing it down to your right side in a backhand slap. Repeat this drill at least eight times then switch sides. All these drills are performed on three levels—high, medium and low.

Pi's second level is performed starting in a tall horse stance. As you execute the slapping strikes, you sink low into your stance. Then, you can relax your stance as you raise your arm to strike again. This sinking motion brings your legs into play as pumps. The up-and-down motion not only strengthens your legs, but also pump your blood and your qi throughout your entire body.

Pi's third level is performed in a low horse stance without the up-and-down motion. Your focus should be on compressing and relaxing your spine. The spine acts like a bow, drawing and releasing power into each strike. (*Photos 1-4*).

The next drill focuses on building flexibility in the back, shoulders and waist. This drill is called "bao" or embracing technique. You begin with your feet a shoulder-width apart. Your right arm is stretched straight up, while your left is stretched down at your side. Bring your right arm down across your body in a relaxed chopping motion to your left hip. At the same time, swing your left arm up to your right shoulder. Let both hands gently slap your body, then return them to your original position and repeat. This resembles a soft whipping motion of the arms and will loosen the joints, while simultaneously conditioning the skin to being hit. Remember to always practice on both sides.

The second level to the bao drill is performed in a moderate horse stance with both arms stretched out to your sides. Using your waist to begin the movement and your spine to generate the momentum, turn slightly to your left and swing both arms across your body and gently slap. At the same time, you should incorporate your legs by lowering your stance. Relax the torque by opening your arms and executing the movement on the opposite side. Remember to begin the movement with a torque of the waist; then the arms swing as you sink. Again, this will bring your legs into play as pumps. The level-three drill again focuses on your spine to produce power.

This is accomplished by staying in a horse stance and using your spine, not your legs, to generate the torque. The effect resembles those Chinese toy drums on a stick. By spinning the handle back and forth between your hands, you generate torque that drives the little balls to strike the drum. *(Photos 5-8)*.

Drill No. 3 is referred to as "qin," meaning to press or push with the hand. You begin by placing your feet a shoulder-width apart with your arms stretched outward. Now, bring your right arm directly in front of your right shoulder as in an inward block, and bring your left arm, palm up, under your right elbow. Continue the arm circles by lifting your right elbow and dropping your right hand until the arm is horizontal. As your right hand circles down and out to the side, your left hand circles up over your head as if you were brushing your hair. Keep this coiling motion going by extending both arms outward at the same time with palm strikes. Sound simple? Well, it's not. It took me several weeks of constant practice before this one clicked. *(Photos 9-12)*.

You'll have fun with qin's second-level drill. Stand as if you were going to do the first level, but this time you're going to shift your weight and pivot to your left. As you turn your waist, swing your right arm down and out in front of you, palm down. Your left arm swings down and out behind you at the same time. As your arms reach the zenith of their swing, come up on your rear toes. Now allow both arms to drop as you shift to the right side, pivot and swing your arms up and out in front and back, only this time your arms are reversed. This action resembles a bird flapping its wings.

After swinging to either side, allow your arms to relax and lower your body into a crouching posture, bringing your arms in close as if you were clutching a football, or right palm up and left palm down. Your stance is low, with your weight mainly on the right leg. This is a coiling or winding-up action. To release this strike, you must pivot around sharply to a left bow stance as you thrust a right palm strike straight in front and your left to the rear. As you fire the strike, you must fully extend balancing your power issuing to 50/50 in both arms. This drill teaches you how to use your back and rear leg to produce power.

The last drill I'll give you is the third-level called "kao," meaning to lean. It should be performed, you guessed it, in a low horse stance with both arms extended. Slowly begin to shift your weight to your left leg as you swing your right arm down in front of you and back up over your head like a sword. As your right arm circles down to chop, start circling your left arm up over your head. Now pivot into a right bow stance as you bring your left strike down and circle the right up behind. Continue circling your right arm back up overhead as your left swings down through the target. And sharply pivot back into a horse stance as you drop the last right palm strike.

These strikes should be linked to form one fluid movement. This drill is designed to build flexibility and teach you how to use your waist to generate maximum power. *(Photos 13-18)*.

Tsou refers to the next phase of piqua training as "the four lines." Each incorporates a single movement from the above drills with unique footwork. These drills teach you how to generate power with a sharp "whippy" quality, while maintaining focus on proper body alignment.

But, before you even attempt learning these lines, you need to prepare your body with the basic training exercises above.

Why Blend Baji and Piqua?

The old master Li Shuwen, who blended these two styles, was really quite clever. He understood perfectly the essential elements one must possess for good kung-fu. Both systems are very simple, containing only a small number of forms. However, each form requires a tremendous amount of basic training to set the foundation.

First, you must master xiao baji with its basic drills. Along with physical strength, they teach your body how to cultivate vast amounts of qi and store it deep within the structure of the body for later use. Many people today mistakenly think that training the external is counterproductive to internal development. However, the division between external and internal is an illusion. For it is only through exhausting the major muscle groups that the minor ones can take over. This process brings with it endurance and rooting ability. It also allows you to relax in your postures. The body must be able to relax for qi to flow smoothly. Heavy qi sinks to your root and vital qi moves to your head creating equilibrium and balance.

Basic training in piqua will develop total-body awareness. By practicing waist-turning drills, your body becomes more flexible along its middle axis. This allows you to use centrifugal force to generate large amounts of torque.

Additionally, focusing on the spine develops the ability to compress and release energy like a spring. It's much like drawing and releasing a bow. Developing these two skills will help you take the qi you've stored practicing baji and effectively distribute it throughout the body.

It is important to have a clear understanding of these training goals. Without it, and I can't stress this enough, you will never reach the high levels of the art. This may sound overly simplistic, but through this level of understanding are the keys to developing the high levels of internal power. Let me explain. Many contemporary martial artists believe the keys to mastery are in the advanced forms. If they can just find an instructor willing to teach them the details of advanced forms, their skills will automatically be transformed or elevated to the master level.

Unfortunately for most, once they chalk up another form in their repertoire, they still find their skills lacking. Some become disillusioned, claiming that either their teacher doesn't know the secrets, can't do them himself or is unwilling to teach them. The simple truth is that the student's focus is on the wrong training. For those who measure your progress by the number of forms you've acquired, these basics may seem a little extreme. Form practice certainly has its place, because it teaches us lively footwork, coherent smooth transitions and fluidity in our movements. They show us how to change tempo, build stamina and convey the unique characteristics of a particular style.

But for those who've hit a plateau in their training and become dissatisfied, or would just like a little deeper understanding of what your training is all about, the answer is simple. Go back to your basics and take another look.

Break down each exercise and ask yourself some important questions: Is my body well-balanced? Am I rooted, with a low stable center of gravity? Are my joints aligned and relaxed, properly relieving the stress on the tendons and ligaments? Is my back straight? Do I sacrifice form for speed? Do I bob up and down in my footwork? Is my breathing coming from the abdomen, slow and relaxed, or is it high in my chest? Your basic training should effectively set the stage for your internal training. Without this foundation firmly in place, you will never experience and enjoy the power, beauty and benefits your art's higher levels can offer.

Conclusion

We've covered a lot of ground, but this is by no means the entire regimen of baji basics. There are still wall training, post training, sandbag training, two-person drills, and applications. Quite a foundation. It can take up to two-to-three years just to complete the first level of baji basic training. When mastered, baji/piqua create such a formidable martial art foundation, even demons are afraid of those who master them.

Neil Thomas is a 30-year veteran of the martial arts and studies under sifu Jason Tsou in Monterey Park, California. Sifu Tsou was a long-time disciple of the late grandmaster Liu Yunchao, founder of the Wu Tang Federation in Taiwan.

Martial Science

The Art of Kenpo, Which Is Linear and Circular, Is Designed to Let You Move Smoothly from Striking to Grappling and Vice Versa

Doug Jeffrey

"OK. Got it. Go ahead with the next move," the photographer says to Larry Tatum, a *kenpo* stylist from Pasadena, California who has a worldwide organization. Her unheeded words drift aimlessly off into the dark photo studio. Tatum—suddenly oblivious to the shoot, time and the importance of the impeccability of his form—stands motionless because an old, familiar song from the 1960s has drifted across the radio.

"That's the Dave Clark Five," says Tatum, a broad grin developing over his movie star face.

"Are you sure?" another interjects. "It might be Herman's Hermits."

"I don't think so."

Now everyone stops to listen.

"Actually, I'm not so sure," says the confident Tatum, suddenly not sounding so confident.

"They're showing their age," whispers Jill, Tatum's wife.

The musicians chuckle at their inability to positively ID the artist, and Tatum—silver feather earring dangling from his ear, long sandy-blonde hair reaching for his shoulders—turns back to his partner to continue the shoot. They run through the next movement and then Tatum pauses again.

"The concepts and principles [of kenpo] are integrated into the self-defense techniques for each belt level," he says. "As the student goes through the curriculum, he is exposed to all the concepts and principles of fighting. That does not mean that the student utilizes all the principles and concepts, but he picks and chooses and works within his parameters. It doesn't matter if it's grappling mode or strictly kicks or hands. He is exposed to it.

"As he learns about the concepts and principles, he learns that the technique was only an idea. What is more important is how he can rearrange the pattern of technique to fit the situation. Beyond that, it is then important that he works within the underlying principles of kenpo. So you can see that kenpo is more of a martial science than martial art or martial style."

Up Close
- Name: Larry Tatum
- Age: 53
- Began training: 1965
- Trained with Ed Parker from 1965 to 1988
- Name of school: Larry Tatum's Kenpo Karate Studio
- Name of organization: Larry Tatum's Kenpo Karate Association Schools all over the world, including South America, Europe and the United States.
- Headquarters: 111 W. Green St., Pasadena, CA 91105
- Website: www.ltatum.com

FIRST IMPRESSIONS

First impressions are interesting, especially when you're looking at someone who exudes style. Someone such as Larry Tatum. When you first see him—especially with his attractive wife at his side—you'd probably guess that he is your typical rock star or movie star, which is actually not too far from the truth. The 53-year-old kenpo stylist is also a musician and actor.

As soon as you hear the Vietnam vet discusses the concepts of kenpo, you'd swear that he was a college professor. If there were only enough hours in the day ...

Then, when you see Tatum in his karate *gi* (uniform) doing the art that he's done so expertly throughout the years, he looks very much the part of the martial arts master, which he is.

You can see, in essence, that every impression you may have of Tatum is correct. However, in this particular story, we'll narrow the focus to his role as martial arts master.

MARTIAL ARTS

When his opponent winds up to throw a big right (1), Larry Tatum responds with an inward block (2). Tatum then delivers an outward hand sword that Cliff Seminerio parries with his lift hand (3). This deflection sends Tatum's strike over his opponent's arm, just above his elbow (4). Tatum takes advantage of this angle of opportunity and grabs his opponent's elbow (5). Tatum then steps back and dislocates his adversary's shoulder (6).

KENPO'S STRONG POINTS

Tatum, who has been practicing the art for more than 37 years, says kenpo—unlike other styles—is a balanced system that features 100 percent hands and 100 percent legs. In addition to that, it is also linear and circular. Add these elements up, and you've got a well-rounded, versatile system.

"Kenpo blends with encounters as they happen," he notes. "Kenpo rides the middle."

For example, let's say an attacker uses linear moves on a kenpo stylist. The kenpo stylist may respond with linear-to-linear moves or he may show a few circular moves.

"If the opponent comes with a linear attack, we can blend with the assault with intermittent speed and power with both linear or circular or moves supported by checks that govern our opponent's ability to counter past his first strike," he says. "Our emotions are also brought into balance so our emotional levels of response are brought into balance."

Of course, the kenpo stylist can also "shift gears from striking to grappling [contact manipulation] and vice versa," notes Tatum.

"He'll go with the move that fits the situation."

The situation dictates when those gears should switch, and experience is the key to making that determination, he says. However, you can also throw a little logic into the equation, too.

"Let's say I got into a confrontation with an opponent," he says. "[During the course of the clash], I may find that it's better to apply a contact manipulation [grappling] move than it is to strike. That doesn't mean that I couldn't strike, but the circumstances just may send me to a target that is quicker. It's all about awareness and experience."

There's an obvious benefit to this versatility.

"This makes you a [more] balanced martial artist," he says. "It's like a college educated man who goes into the work force. The degree enables him to adapt and blend in. It is the same with kenpo. It's like having a college degree in martial science. When you go into another environment, you can instantly blend in because you've been exposed to it."

WHEN THINGS GO WRONG

In the best-case scenario, everything flows smoothly. You make the transition from one method of fighting to the other and you walk away unscathed. Of course, there's this little thing called "Murphy's Law." You know, anything that can go wrong, will go wrong. So, what happens if you make the wrong decision? What if it's better to strike than to grapple or vice versa?

"Definitely, someone could make the wrong decision," he says. "The art is a funny thing. If you try to push it past your limitations or use it when you are wrong, it works against you. I have seen guys who force the issue. Subsequently, they are convinced the art is sloppy. However, when you are in a righteous position and know how to defend yourself, the art works best."

Larry Tatum (right) and Cliff Seminerio square off (1). When his opponent pushes him (2), Tatum steps back (following the angle of least resistance) and snaps his arm (3). Tatum then hooks Seminerio's arm (4) and finishes by raking down on his arm into a left, outward hand sword (5).

MARTIAL ARTS

Larry Tatum and Cliff Seminerio square off. As Seminerio starts to push (1), Tatum delivers a snapping arm break (2). As Seminerio pulls back to throw a roundhouse punch, Tatum grabs his left arm (3) and cranks his wrist counter clockwise (4. When his opponent goes down with pain, Tatum hammers down on his forearm (5), thrusts a finger to his eye (6) and drills him in the chin (7.

From the beginning of their journey along the martial path, kenpo students are versed on linear and circular moves on every technique, as well as the contact manipulation moves.

"Of course, students are also versed in grappling as well as striking, but we never overemphasize one or the other," he says. "We blend or integrate these together so the student knows what to use in a street situation and when he has to make a split-second decision."

A PRAGMATIC STYLE

The art also allows a person "to develop individually."

"Rather than force a student to adapt to a system, it works the other way around," he says. "The system adapts to the student."

In some styles, if you can't execute the basics as they are designed, you fall along the wayside, he says. That won't happen in kenpo.

In kenpo, Tatum explains, the motion is natural and built upon everyday movement. Furthermore, the range of motion is the natural range of the human body. That, he says, is the key as to why people come back to the art.

"It's a pragmatic style," he says.

As an example, Tatum says imagine how your arm moves when you raise it to brush your hair back.

"Your elbow comes up, and that is an upward elbow," he says.

For that move to have an effect in a fight, all you have to do is add some "definition and purpose." Thus, you can see the natural motion that extends beyond the natural movement.

Next, take your right hand and point at something across the room. Then, add a little definition and purpose and you've got a finger strike or punch.

Example No. 3. Put your right hand on your hip and make a fist. Move your right arm across your body toward your left shoulder. You've got an inward, horizontal elbow strike.

Four, scratch your right shoulder with your right hand. That movement could be an upward elbow strike.

"All of these are simply built-in a logical extensions of natural movements, and this makes them more instinctive," he says. "You just move within your own natural motion and your God-given motion. These are designed around the way the human body was built and that is where logic took over. All you have to do is add speed, power and definition to any movement and it becomes a dangerous weapon."

These natural movements are important for another reason, too. If and when you get into a confrontation, your reactions will be programmed, the muscle memory will be right on the money and you'll be instinctive.

"The mind is like a computer," he says. "When you are in a confrontation, especially on the street, the conscious mind does not react fast enough to comprehend what's going on because everything is accelerated. Reality takes on some distortion. Your heart races, your hearing goes because of a surge of blood, your breathing is unregulated and you become euphoric. It's almost like looking at everything underwater."

An experienced fighter doesn't have to worry about those things.

"He learns how to control those things," says Tatum. "He slows his heart, he keeps his breathing regulated and his senses become heightened rather than dulled. He may not win the fight because the other guy may be stronger or faster, but at least he has a chance."

And that's the importance of locking that information and moves into your mind—survival.

"Your subconscious mind comes into play when this happens," he says. "It feeds the defense techniques that are logical. Your subconscious mind locks in things that are logical in a fighting situation."

Of course, good, old-fashioned speed doesn't hurt either.

"You don't just throw one technique and move," he says. "In kenpo, you rely on multiple strikes and targets in a short time. Within two seconds, you can apply five strikes ... easily."

THE OLD PANASONIC

"We need one more technique to wrap up the shoot," says the photographer. "Give us one that captures the essence of the art. You know ... something fast, effective and practical."

In the blink of an eye, Tatum runs through multiple techniques with flawless control, turns to the photographer and says, "How's that?"

"Good. Let's go with the last one."

Almost on cue, the second he's done, "Respect" blares out of the old black Panasonic. A wide grin forms on Tatum's face as he starts to peel off his uniform top.

"Aretha Franklin," he says with the confidence and certainty of a college professor answering a freshmen's question. "She's cool."

Respect, confidence, cool, effective, practical.

Words that apply to Larry Tatum ... and kenpo karate.

MARTIAL ARTS

Choy Lay Fut's Renaissance Man

Shane Lacey is changing the way the world sees and practices choy lay fut.

David Tadman

Shane Lacey may be the best martial artist no one knows about outside Northern California. A four-time International Four-Star Grand Champion, Lacey is a master of hand-to-hand combat and weapons. While buk sing choy lay fut is his core style, Lacey also has extensive training in wushu, wing chun, chow gar, fut gar, and muay Thai. Lacey is among a new breed of martial artists who embraces traditional values with revolutionary techniques. Here is his story.

INSIDE KUNG-FU: What is your martial arts background?
SHANE LACEY: I studied the basic shaolin, which is sil lum, and then moved into the northern styles of shaolin, which is influenced a lot more with jumping and kicking. This was good for me as a young kid because I liked to move around a lot. As I grew older and filled out my frame, I then was taught buk sing choy lay fut. I also do close-range fighting like wing chun. I am also very proficient with muay Thai, and have an extensive background in wushu and submission fighting.

IKF: Your base martial art is buk sing choy lay fut. Tell us more about this style.

SL: Buk sing choy lay fut is a dynamic style that incorporates a lot of long-range techniques. The kicks vary from low-to-high and are pretty standard with the northern style influence. The hand techniques are very rapid and fluid and they range from low-to-high as well.

IKF: You teach the physical as well as the philosophical elements. Can you tell us what kind of philosophy you express to your students?

SL: I stress two different types of philosophy with my students. For the children I try to emphasize more of the discipline and respect for one another. With my adult students, I stress health with the conditioning of the body and the mind. It is very important that each individual who comes to

me for teaching must enjoy what he is learning. This gives a sense of peace, which allows you to lift the burden off your mind. This allows you to understand the martial art better.

IKF: You teach lion dancing. Can you tell us about that and what it means to your style of kung-fu?

SL: I teach a very traditional form of lion dancing that most other kung-fu schools teach as well.

MARTIAL ARTS

Shane Lacey shapes up in a traditional buk sing choy lay fut leopard fist stance (1). The attacker throws a right jab, which Shane blocks (2) with a right chuen san (forearm block). The attacker follows with a left cross (3). Lacey shifts back into a bow stance and uses a left poon kiu (circling hand) to redirect the punch downward (4). He leaps in with a right fei charp (flying leopard fist) to the throat.

Profile

Name: Shane Lacey
Birthplace: Perth, Western Australia
Birthdate: April 28, 1969
Height: 5-11
Weight: 165 pounds
Heritage: Considered Eurasian; Half-Chinese, a quarter Irish and a quarter Portugese.
Martial Arts Experience: Buk sing choy lay fut; jow ga, northern style shaolin, wushu, muay Thai.
Earned black belt: All black sashes.
Outside Loves: Fine dining, movies, dancing.
Facts: Won The Four Star Grand Championship four times at Tat Mau Wong's tournament.
Contact: You can contact Shane at (510) 792-5259 or www.buksing.com

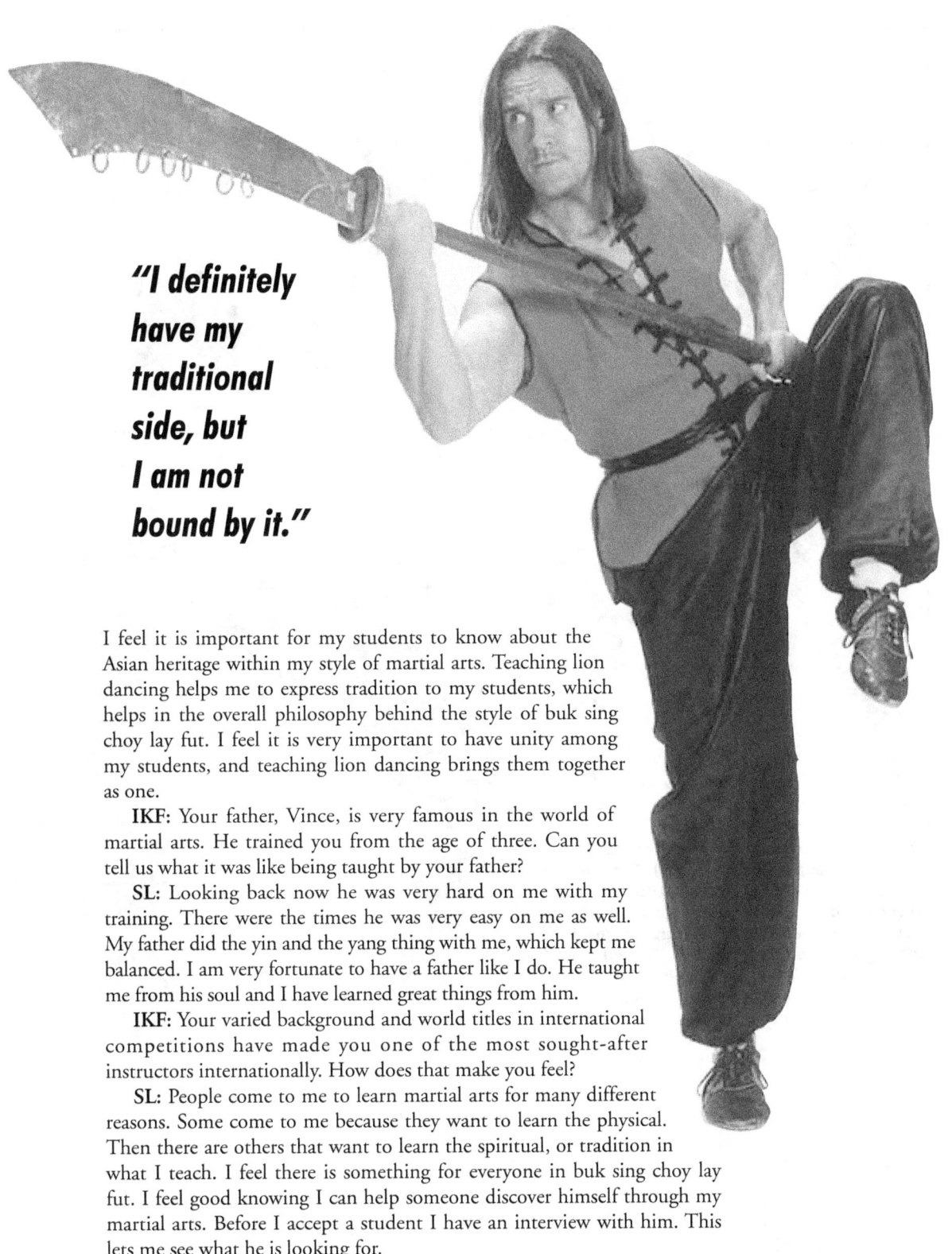

"I definitely have my traditional side, but I am not bound by it."

I feel it is important for my students to know about the Asian heritage within my style of martial arts. Teaching lion dancing helps me to express tradition to my students, which helps in the overall philosophy behind the style of buk sing choy lay fut. I feel it is very important to have unity among my students, and teaching lion dancing brings them together as one.

IKF: Your father, Vince, is very famous in the world of martial arts. He trained you from the age of three. Can you tell us what it was like being taught by your father?

SL: Looking back now he was very hard on me with my training. There were the times he was very easy on me as well. My father did the yin and the yang thing with me, which kept me balanced. I am very fortunate to have a father like I do. He taught me from his soul and I have learned great things from him.

IKF: Your varied background and world titles in international competitions have made you one of the most sought-after instructors internationally. How does that make you feel?

SL: People come to me to learn martial arts for many different reasons. Some come to me because they want to learn the physical. Then there are others that want to learn the spiritual, or tradition in what I teach. I feel there is something for everyone in buk sing choy lay fut. I feel good knowing I can help someone discover himself through my martial arts. Before I accept a student I have an interview with him. This lets me see what he is looking for.

Shane Lacey shapes up in a traditional buk sing choy lay fut leopard fist stance (1). The attacker throws a left jab to the face (2). Lacey blocks it with a left chuen sau (forearm block). He then turns the left chuen sau into a larp sau (grab) and begins to raise his right leg and hand (3). Shane uses a right so tui (sweeping kick) low to the attacker's calf (4) and simultaneously chops with his right arm to the throat.

IKF: You were the Four-Star International Kung-Fu Grand Champion from 1988-to-1993. Tell us about it.

SL: The Four Star competition was best-suited to all my abilities as a martial artist. The competition was a mix of forms and fighting. I am fortunate to have always been trained in both. The competition featured martial artists from all over the world. I stayed focused and self-assured and I came out on top. I gave it my all.

MARTIAL ARTS

IKF: You are also a broadsword champion?

SL: I learned the northern broad-sword forms first. I felt I was lacking more explosiveness and dynamics. This is when I went to the wushu style of broadsword. I feel both styles of broadsword helped in my becoming a champion.

IKF: You teach alongside your father at the Academy of Champions in Fremont, Calif. Is your approach to teaching different than your father's?

SL: My father has more of a rigid and traditional way of teaching. I grew up in Australia and also lived in Hong Kong and here in the United States. I feel this has given me a broader view on how people learn martial arts. Through my years of training in the martial arts, I have come to realize that there are many ways to teach the same technique by doing it differently. I definitely have my traditional side, but I am not bound by it.

Shane Lacey shapes up (1) with charp chui (leopard fist horse stance). The attacker fires a low right side kick (2). Shane retreats with tau ma (retreating unicorn stance) and blocks the sidekick with his right gwa chui (backfist). Shane twists out of the unicorn stance, lifts his left knee and prepares his left arm to block and grab (3). Spinning around, Lacey uses his left arm to grab the attacker's right jab (4). He then flies in with a right fei san chui (flying roundhouse punch).

"Kung-fu is something that you can't learn overnight. You must take it home with you and work on it, then bring it back and keep practicing."

IKF: I know that buk sing choy lay fut has set patterns of instruction. What are your feelings on cross-training?

SL: I cross-train quite a bit. My workouts consist of cross-training with aerobic and weights. I cross-train in many styles of martial arts. What I do try to emphasize when I am cross-training in martial arts is not to intermix the styles. I would not go from a choy lay fut movement to a wing chun movement. I would more or less practice in one style, stop, and clear my mind, then move into a different style, and transform into that style.

IKF: Some say you are slowly changing the way choy lay fut is taught. Is that true?

SL: I am not really changing it; I am rearranging it. In this I mean the structure of teaching. I feel that each student is an individual and depending on his needs, I as an instructor must attend to them all as individuals. I am not as structured in my teaching with set patterns. I will teach what needs to be taught depending on each individual's make-up.

IKF: What is the most important thing you try to get across to your students?

SL: I try to get across that kung-fu is something that you can't learn over-night. You must take it home with you and work on it, then bring it back and keep practicing until you can master it. I also try to get across to my students that each time you work on perfecting a movement you find out more about yourself. It's important that my students know the techniques taught to them will help them discover more about themselves as a whole. This comes with perseverance and hard work.

IKF: You are making a name for yourself in action cinema. Give us a brief resume.

SL: I started doing many different types of commercials that needed some type of action or martial art character. After doing commercials for a while, I got into television in Australia and Hong Kong, doing many action, martial arts-types of roles. As of now, I am going over a few scripts that interest me.

IKF: Hong Kong martial arts action cinema has become very big here in the United States. You have been doing Hong Kong-style action for many years now. As one who has seen both sides, what is your feeling on the difference between Hong Kong action cinema and the action cinema here in the States?

SL: Hong Kong action cinema takes that extra leap. You are looking at two different cultures that express themselves differently on film. In Hong Kong, you will find more risk in action cinema. But now we're seeing more of a change in the United States. Movies like *Matrix* are showing the influence of Hong Kong cinema.

IKF: What would be your perfect role?

SL: Something with meaning, something with heart. I would love to do a character that has Charles Bronson, Bruce Lee and Mel Gibson meshed into one.

IKF: As a martial artist, what do you hope to express most in your films?

SL: I want to show the beauty of my martial arts. I want people to see the fluidity in what I do. Most of all, I want people to walk away from a film I do and feel good about the experience they just had.

IKF: Is buk sing choy lay fut on the right path?

SL: Buk sing choy lay fut is a complete martial art because there is something—the fighting, the philosophical and the spiritual—for everyone in this style.

MARTIAL ARTS

Extreme Hwa Rang Do

This Korean Art's Aerial Kicks Push the Human Body to Find the Maximum Range of Physical Expression.

Hyung-Min Jung

In the past few years, the *hwa rang do* system has stayed out of the spotlight. But that dormancy has come to pass, and hwa rang do is coming out of its cave like a hungry tiger with an appetite for conquest. At the forefront of that charge is Taejoon "Henry" Lee, the elder son of hwa rang do's founder, Dr. Joo Bang Lee.

Taejoon Lee is one of the most colorful figures of Korean martial arts, and his insights into the system founded by his father are no less exciting than the man himself.

"Hwa rang do is a compilation of my father's martial expertise that came on the scene in the 1960s in Korea," explains Lee. "Many people look at some of the techniques that Korean martial arts are known for, and they credit them to styles like *taekwondo* and *hapkido,* but the reality is that many of those techniques showed up in other systems after my father started teaching publicly in Seoul. From Seoul, the instructors that trained under my father spread out to influence other systems and schools."

KOREAN FOOT-FEST

One such branch of techniques is the amazing aerial kicking that the Korean martial arts are well known for, and hwa rang do kicking in particular may be indeed at the vanguard of that Korean foot-fest.

"If people just talk to anyone who trained with my father back in the 1950s and 1960s, they'll know that hwa rang do practitioners were doing some of the 540 and 720 spin and combination kicks that some tournament forms competitors started doing only in recent years," says Lee.

"When I was a little kid back in Korea, there used to be footprints on the ceiling of my father's *dojang* (martial arts school) from the jumping *dora chagi* (spinning kicks) that his students used to practice."

Hwa rang do's radical flying foot attacks fall

MARTIAL ARTS

Lee Up Close

Chief Master **Taejoon Lee** is the elder son of Hwa Rang Do's founder, Dr. Joo Bang Lee and oversees the West Coast Hwa Rang Do Headquarters. You can visit him on the net at **www.hwarangdo.net** and see him in action with his latest film project at **www.k-towncowboys.com.**

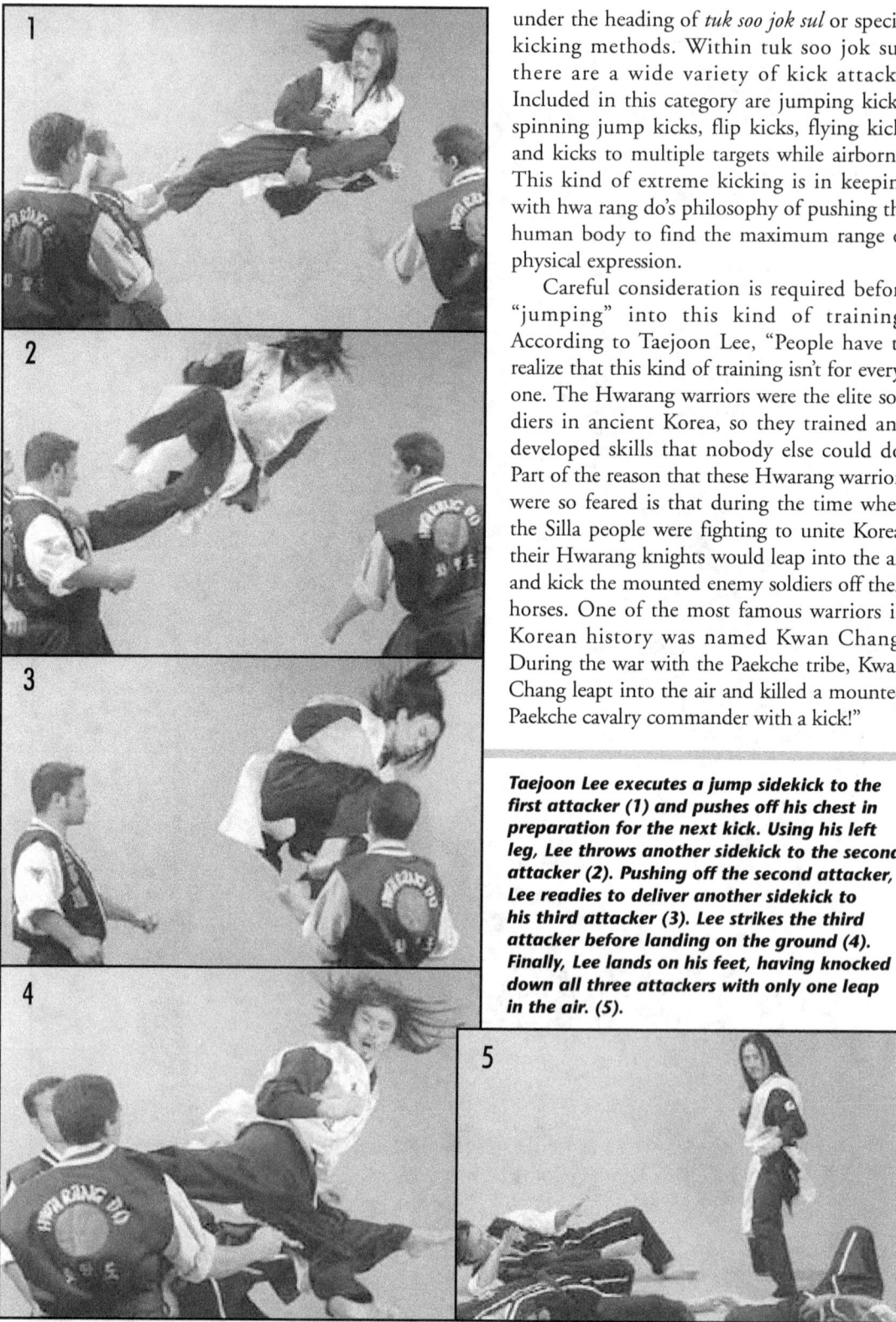

under the heading of *tuk soo jok sul* or special kicking methods. Within tuk soo jok sul, there are a wide variety of kick attacks. Included in this category are jumping kicks, spinning jump kicks, flip kicks, flying kicks and kicks to multiple targets while airborne. This kind of extreme kicking is in keeping with hwa rang do's philosophy of pushing the human body to find the maximum range of physical expression.

Careful consideration is required before "jumping" into this kind of training. According to Taejoon Lee, "People have to realize that this kind of training isn't for everyone. The Hwarang warriors were the elite soldiers in ancient Korea, so they trained and developed skills that nobody else could do. Part of the reason that these Hwarang warriors were so feared is that during the time when the Silla people were fighting to unite Korea, their Hwarang knights would leap into the air and kick the mounted enemy soldiers off their horses. One of the most famous warriors in Korean history was named Kwan Chang. During the war with the Paekche tribe, Kwan Chang leapt into the air and killed a mounted Paekche cavalry commander with a kick!"

Taejoon Lee executes a jump sidekick to the first attacker (1) and pushes off his chest in preparation for the next kick. Using his left leg, Lee throws another sidekick to the second attacker (2). Pushing off the second attacker, Lee readies to deliver another sidekick to his third attacker (3). Lee strikes the third attacker before landing on the ground (4). Finally, Lee lands on his feet, having knocked down all three attackers with only one leap in the air. (5).

MARTIAL ARTS

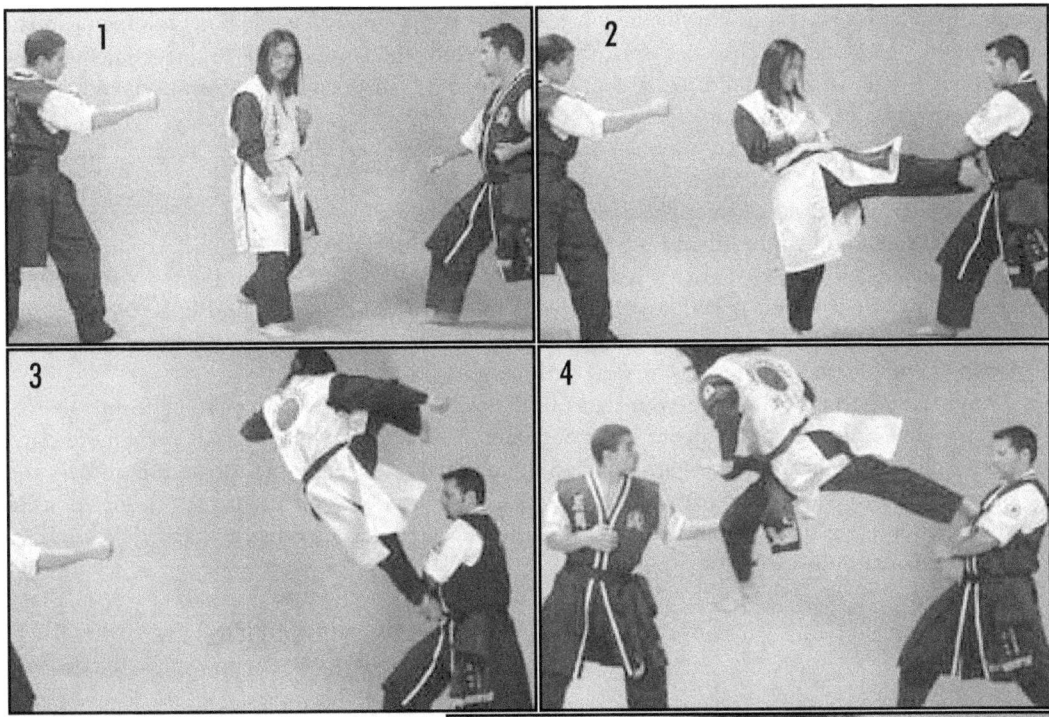

SERIOUS INJURIES

But as a result of attaining such height, there is also a long drop back to the ground. This is where a great deal of injuries can occur with martial artists. There are countless incidents where aspiring martial art students are sidelined by serious knee or ankle injuries sustained while practicing jumping kicks. Yet Lee has a quick answer for this situation.

"Injuries are a mark of something missing in the training, whether it be an issue of technical explanation, proper demonstration or safety precautions," he says. "In many cases, it's a situation in which the student isn't taught the proper method for jumping and landing. Anyone can jump up high with a little practice, but are they prepared for the landing?"

RIGOROUS TRAINING

To prepare his students, Lee has a rigorous training regimen that builds

Taejoon "Henry" Lee faces off with two attackers (1). Lee throws a front kick at one opponent, who blocks it and grabs his leg (2). Lee then pushes off with his other leg and leaps into the air, swinging his right leg over the opponent (3). Lee kicks the first opponent and searches for his second attacker (4). Lee spots him and punches him on his way down (5).

muscular strength to attain height for the jump and power for the kick, while also building ligament and tendon strength to be able to absorb the impact from the landing. He begins from the most simple duck-walk drills to build leg strength and progresses to practicing the components of the most complicated of hwa rang do's kicks.

Following are some tips that are really important to remember when you're jumping and landing, explains Lee.

- You have to land "like a cat, not like a sack of bricks," he says.
- Your feet should touch the ground toe first, then follow with the heel.
- Some people land heel first after a jumping kick, and the shock of the landing goes straight up their legs to their knees. If you land with your forefoot first, the ankle and knee together will absorb a lot more shock and give your body more time to decelerate. That prevents the kind of jarring injuries sustained most of the time with jumping kicks.
- Also, it is important to tighten your dan jun or lower abdomen when you're performing these jump kicks. When you tighten your lower abdomen, it's like you're making your body more compact, lighter, so that when you jump and spin, your center of mass isn't spread out all over the place. When your center of mass is smaller, it's easier for you to maintain your proper posture and positioning in the air, much like it is when you see a professional figure skater do a jumping spin and land on the ice.

JUMPING, FLYING KICKS

Once the basic jumping and landing skills have been mastered, the next step for a hwa rang do student is to progress through a series of jumping and flying kicks, starting from the simple standing jump kicks, to flying single kicks (usually for breaking), and then aerial combination kicks. Lee was one of the first martial artists in the United States to popularize the flying side kick breaking techniques, taking a running leap over several people to shatter a stack of boards. The aerial combination kicks progress in difficulty from double jumping front kicks (where both legs kick out at two separate targets simultaneously), to combination kicks in which the kicker strikes an opponent three times after leaving the ground.

Another type of tuk soo jok sul is the *wol jang jok sul* or kicking techniques after stepping or pushing off an object with the foot.

"You know the kicks you see a lot of action stars doing in films?" asks Lee. "In hwa rang do, we do many of those same kicks that you see on the screen, but without the wires to hold us up."

To emphasize his point, Lee stands up

and positions two of his students with kicking targets, one at chest height and the other at head height. He sprints toward the wall, leaping up and pushing off the wall with one foot, changing his direction towards the first target and kicking it solidly with his other foot. With the same foot, he spins in midair and nails the second target—some six feet away from the first target—with a spinning round kick before alighting on the mat again.

"That's the essence of wol jang jok sul," says Lee. "We use this kind of foot technique to attack multiple targets and change direction in midair. At the beginning levels, students learn to take a few steps off a wall and then push off the wall to kick a target that's a few feet away from it. Later on, at higher levels, we can use an aerial kick as a means to change direction and strike the next target. Just now you saw me jump up the wall and hit the first target using the wall as a means to push off and change direction, but I used the force from the first kick to propel me backward so I could kick the second target."

Such flying technique may seem almost unbelievable to the untrained observer, but this kind of technique is simple physics, based on inertia—the propensity of an object in motion to remain in motion and an object at rest to remain at rest. Each time the foot touches a stationary object, there is resistance to motion. For instance, when Lee begins to sprint toward the wall, his body is accelerated into motion. When it hits the first target, the target provides resistance against which his kick pushes to propel him backward and upwards into the next target. However, don't let the simplistic explanation fool you. There is a great deal of physical coordination required for such maneuvers.

ASKING FOR TROUBLE?

This kind of kicking may seem as if it would offer ample opportunity for an opponent to grab an outstretched leg, but Lee merely grins at the suggestion.

"If someone were lucky enough to grab a leg, part of wol jang jok sul training is to use the free leg to kick the opponent with a telling blow, and free your leg," says Lee. "In addition, we set up our aerial spinning kicks, like the 540's with both legs, using one leg when you first leave the ground to gage the distance or create a diversion, and the second kick has the finishing power from the spin."

"Agility is defined as the ability to change directions rapidly," he continues. "Wol jang jok sul requires a great deal of agility—twisting the upper body, balancing in mid-air, and torque from the waist—to create the proper angle and motion for that kind of aerial combination kicking. We are basing our movements on the harmonized motion of proper breathing, leg strength, waist twisting and torso alignment to create powerful movement in different directions while airborne. It's physics combined with ki power to make the body lighter in such a way as to facilitate the jump and the following kick. That's the wirework you see in movies, but done in real life, with real kicks and real people. This is part of hwa rang do's basic philosophy of maximizing human potential. It's not just about training the simplest techniques for combat, but more to challenge yourself to achieve options that are unthinkable for the average person."

PART OF THE PICTURE

Hwa rang do is well-known for its spectacular joint locks and throws, and its students regularly demonstrate their competence in the "standing-grappling" range. According to Lee, however, this is just part of the picture.

"Some martial arts instructors have made the grave mistake to say that they are well-versed in grappling when, [in reality], they are only familiar with the part of grappling that is comprised of standing joint-locks and throws," says Lee. "They're seeing only half of the picture."

For a person to really understand empty-hand grappling, he has to know what to do if the fight goes to the ground, he says.

"Fortunately, hwa rang do is a complete martial art and offers us a way to grapple confidently in any range: stand-up distance, stand-up in-close and on the ground," he adds.

In all of hwa rang do's techniques, the goal is to move in close, execute a takedown, and finish the opponent in the quickest, effective means possible, he says.

"However, going to the ground together with the opponent and wrestling is not the goal, but merely an option," he adds.

In traditional Korean culture, during an honorable match with an opponent, the person who is knocked down loses and submits of his own accord, accepting the loss. Only in self-defense when you are fighting for your life does the need to go to the ground arise. For this purpose, hwa rang do has extensive techniques to subdue the opponent on the ground.

BASIC CURRICULUM

Hwa rang do's basic curriculum, which can be applied for ground fighting, includes but is not limited to the following defenses:
- Clothing grabs *(hoshin we bok sul)*
- Body grabs *(che gong sul)*
- Wrist grabs *(hoshin wan sul)*
- Offensive throwing techniques *(kongkyuk too gi sul)*
- Throws *(hoshin bang too gi sul)*
- Two-handed grabs *(hoshin yang soo gi sul)*
- Offensive choking *(kongkyuk jo ru gi sul)*
- From seated position *(hoshin jwa gi sul)*
- From prone position *(hoshin wha gi sul)*
- Offensive pressure point techniques *(kongkyuk jwagi jiap sul)*
- Special joint dislocation techniques *(teuk soo gol jel gi sul)*
- And, of course, this does not take into consideration all of the striking techniques with both the hands and the feet found in hwa rang do.

Lee says, "As there are a limited number of ways that the body can be attacked with a grab, the responses fall into similar patterns, regardless of whether standing or on the ground. We all have the same joints that can be attacked, even if we don't all feel pain in the same way."

Thus, you have to think about the limbs and then think of how they can be attacked, he adds. There are three basic sections of the body, and you can divide those further, depending on how accessible the joint is and "how easily you can elicit a pain response."

According to Lee, the basic targets are as follows:
- Arm: fingers, wrist, elbow, shoulder
- Leg: ankle, knee, hip
- Torso: lumbar spine, neck

These are the points of greater vulnerability for grapplers to focus on when working for a submission or joint displacement. On a strategic level, the chief master lays out some very simple points for those who choose to grapple.

"The nature of human beings is that they usually will do the opposite of what you want them to do, so you have to gear your response accordingly to create stronger leverage for yourself," he says. "If you pull them close to you and they push away, you have to be ready to take advantage of that and capitalize on the openings in their positions. Think of it like playing chess. You set up your moves intelligently and then seize the opportunity when it arises. Furthermore, like all things, it is easier to control when it is closer to you than further away."

As it is in stand up fighting, distancing is crucial on the ground as well as spacing, says Lee. You have to limit the space and distance between your opponent and yourself. The greater the spacing, there is a greater chance of execution of a technique. Therefore, to be an effective grappler—you have to learn to lessen the space for defense and apply techniques effectively with limited spacing, he adds.

JOINT LOCKS ON THE GROUND

All of the joint locks that practitioners learn in the standing range can also be applied on the ground. The big difference is that there are new challenges to be aware of because of the different body position, he says.

For example, you don't have the same mobility on the ground that you would have on your feet. At the same time, the ground supports the body for movement in other ways and vectors. The legs, which are used for positioning and balance while standing, are used as extra limbs, "much like an octopus," to control and gain leverage over the opponent, he says.

EFFECTIVE TECHNIQUES

Lee also notes that certain points are universal in executing effective grappling techniques. They are as follows:

- A good triangular base offers maximum stability with mobility.
- Keep your back away from your opponent, just like in stand-up fighting. This keeps your attention geared toward the threat at hand.
- Your elbows should generally stay in toward your ribs. This reduces the likelihood of suffering an arm lock or exposing your midsection, just as in standing range combat.
- Position yourself in such a way that you prevent your opponents from getting a comfortable or advantageous position.
- Lee, who distinguished himself as a high-school wrestling champion by using the grappling moves of hwa rang do, mentions another point that spells the end for many wrestlers and ground fighters.

"Relaxed and well-paced fighting are important for ground work as well," he says. "Oftentimes, people will panic when they get to the ground ... at least for the first few times. They struggle too hard when they need to be relaxing and tensing their muscles intelligently, not just all the time when they're freaking out, hyperventilating. As I said earlier, you have to set up your moves, sparing energy and effort until you're committed to making something happen."

According to Lee, that's a point that you see in all of the best fighters, and the best human beings. They all have three things: physical capability, mental clarity and emotional stability. Besides, it's easy for people to forget that many of the same principles of economy of motion that martial arts people use while standing still apply while on the ground, even while the body positioning might be different.

Hwa Rang Do
An Abbreviated Introduction

Hwa rang do has suffered much historical confusion over the years, a great deal of which was caused by language barriers during the time that the art's grandmaster, Dr. Joo Bang Lee, came to the USA. In short, following are a few highlights.

- According to Dr. Lee, Won-Kwang Bopsa organized a system of hwarang's martial skills based on the *um-yang* (yin-yang) concept of opposite forces working in harmony.
- At King Chinhung's request, Won-Kwang Bopsa took the system already in placed and organized the outline for a thorough system of education for the youth who would become the future Hwarang, involving Buddhist religious study, literature, science, fine arts, medicine, and total understanding of military and combative arts.
- The military training of the Hwarang involved a plethora of weapons, archery, horsemanship, strategic theories and empty-hand combat (with movements that blended hard and soft, linear and circular).
- The only supreme grandmaster of hwa rang do, (known in Korean as "Do Joo Nim" or "the owner of the art") Dr. Joo Bang Lee, began his martial skills studies with his father. Then, together with his brother undertook devoted study with Su-Ahm Dosa (a title for a hermit monk). Su-Ahm Dosa taught the Lee brothers a system called "Um Yang Kwon," which was a particular lineage of the Hwarang training that had been handed down in secrecy for more than 50 generations. The training under Su-Ahm Dosa included total military training, as well as traditional Oriental medical wisdom.
- In 1960, Dr. Lee founded the *hwa rang do* (way of the flowering manhood) system and registered the name with the Korean government.
- In 1972, Dr. Lee relocated to the United States of America and registered the name Hwa Rang Do, attaining an international servicemark.

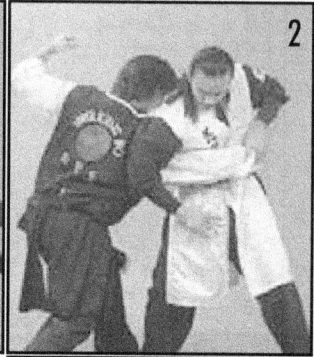

"One must be like a snake and slither into position without alerting the opponent of what is taking place," he says. "Then, when you are prepared to strike, you must act with 100 percent commitment and determination. This is much like a snake as well—it consumes its pray slowly yet methodically, trapping and suffocating its victim, never relinquishing its grip."

This is an art that's designed to be employed effectively with minimal force using leverage, not with the biggest muscles.

- Lastly, you must learn to tolerate pain and not succumb to it, but rather learn to endure it and lessen the pressure by body positioning, leverage and angles. He illustrates his point by attacking his assistant with a figure-4 shoulder lock from the mount. When his assistant extends his arm to push Lee's chest away and lessen the force on the shoulder, Lee whips his body around and cranks on an armbar, strikingly similar to a standard Brazilian jiu-jitsu combination.

COMPARED TO BRAZILIAN JIU-JITSU

When asked about a comparison with Brazilian jiu-

When his opponent locks up with him (1), Taejoon Lee (right) attains control of his opponent's right arm and starts to execute a Figure-Four (2). Lee finishes the lock and steps forward with his left leg while pressing his opponent's shoulder down with his right arm (3). Lee then spins right and kicks out his opponent's right leg, forcing him to the ground (4). To prevent the opponent from spinning out, it's important to maintain pressure on his arm while falling to the ground. Lee steps over his opponent's back and leverages himself on top of his opponent's back (5). Lee secures himself and presses down on his adversary's shoulder blade with his right elbow. Meanwhile, he

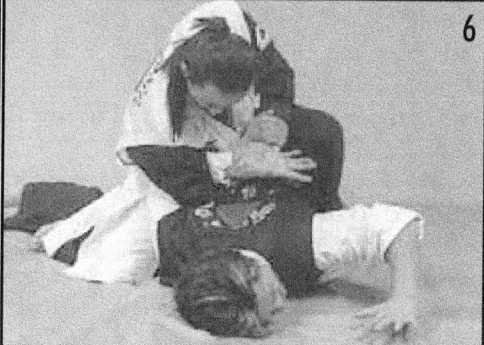

jitsu, Lee offers a refresher course on the history of Brazilian jiu-jitsu's more ancient origins.

"Brazilian jiu-jitsu had its origins in the judo and jiu-jitsu taught to the Gracies by Maeda, a Japanese national," he says. "Considering that Japanese jiu-jitsu could trace its origins back to Shinra Saburo, but you pronounce that same name in Korean as Silla Sam-rang, well, that indicates that he was a Hwarang warrior of the Silla kingdom."

As the modern descendants of the Hwarang warriors, practitioners of hwa rang do actually learn the same fundamental techniques that gave rise to what the Brazilian jiu-jitsu players use, he says. So the guard, the side mount positions, and the mount are really nothing new.

"Yet we also have the pressure point techniques that relate back to our study of traditional Oriental medicine," he notes. "That's something special that we use a little more in our grappling to set up the submissions by releasing the opponent's resisting muscle. But essentially, hwa rang do ground grappling per se is no different from that of the Brazilians or Japanese. The only difference is when you look at our system as a whole—encompassing long range, medium range, close range and ground fighting—that you realize the real uniqueness and completeness of hwa rang do.

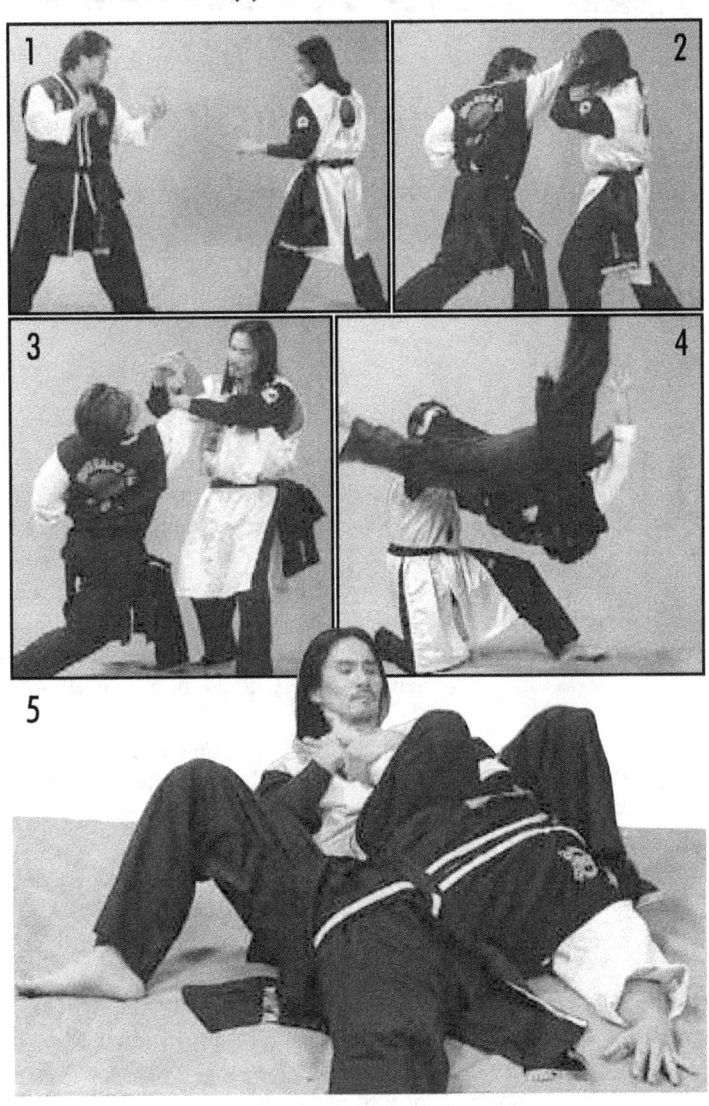

Taejoon Lee (right) faces off with his opponent (1). When his adversary throws a punch, Lee moves to the outside, blocking and trapping his opponent's arm (2). Lee then wraps his left arm over his opponent's arm and grabs his other wrist, trapping the arm in a Figure-Four lock and attaining a C-lock (3). Lee drops to his knee and throws his opponent to the ground, maintaining his Figure-Four (4). Lee steps over his adversary's head with his left leg and leans into an armbar (5).

MARTIAL ARTS

Liangong, the Chinese Way to Better Health

As a general health maintenance and preventative set of exercises, liangong may be among the greatest, yet least-known systems ever devised.

Wen Mei Yu

Useful and easy to learn, liangong is a modern health exercise developed from the ancient medical movement techniques of China's past. Its creator, Dr. Zhuang Yuan Ming, was a doctor in Shanghai in the early 1970s, who was familiar with both Asian and Western healing methods. He also studied tai chi from a well-respected master.

Dr. Zhuang gathered a group of health professionals to help him refine liangong early in its development. I lived in Shanghai then and joined this group as an established taiji and qigong instructor. My role was to teach the exercise, report my observations, and solicit student opinions. Liangong was formally presented to the Chinese public in 1974. It became very popular and I continued to teach it.

I moved to Southern California in 1987, one year before a car accident where I was injured and experienced first hand the healing benefits of liangong. With pain in my neck and lower back, a lawyer advised me to visit a chiropractor rather than treat myself solely with exercise and qigong as I would have in China. I got chiropractic treatments three times a week in the beginning. Later I only went twice weekly. After six months, there was still pain.

I decided then to try using liangong to restore my health. It was painful at first but I continued to practice liangong everyday. In a couple weeks, the pain was gone. By experiencing for myself the healing properties of liangong, my confidence to teach it in the U.S. became strong.

People who desperately needed relief from pain came to me to learn liangong. In the summer of 1992, I met Tina Chin, a real estate agent who suffered from nerve pain caused by a car accident. After seeing about 20 doctors over two years, the pain continued to be debilitating. It woke her every night and any touch upon her body was painful. I taught her the first liangong movements. In a couple weeks, she felt better. A few months later after learning more of the exercise, she was like a new person.

Donna Honings, now a nationally known taijiquan practitioner, approached me the following year. She wanted help recovering from a knee injury caused by years of incorrect kung-fu practice. After about three months of liangong practice, her knee felt restored.

I began to see how liangong could benefit many people in the U.S. So many experience pain and other ailments from stressful lives. Liangong can relieve pain acquired from repetitive movements, hours of sitting at computers or in offices, and awkward body positions such as using the shoulder to hold a phone against the ear. People can find relief from sports and work injuries caused by overuse, improper alignment and posture, and inadequate conditioning.

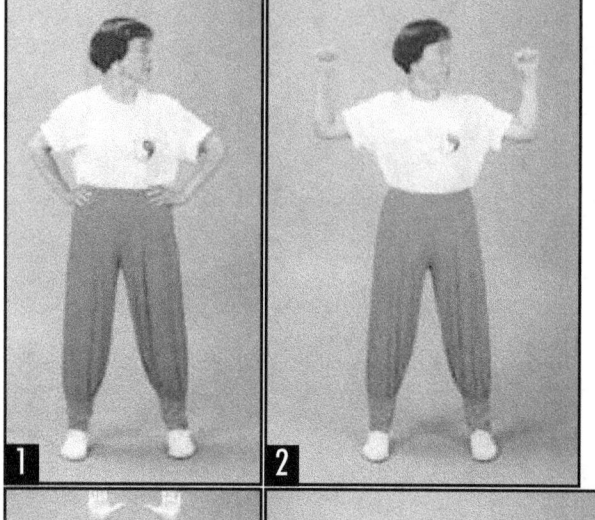

I want to share the benefits of liangong with people everywhere. At workshops across the U.S. and in Europe, people are enthusiastic about the benefits they feel almost immediately. Many later tell me about long-term improvements in their health and well-being after continuous practice.

The exercises are simple but the health benefits increase as more of its details, like the alignment of the arms with the body and the straightness of the neck, are practiced with precision. To help people learn and remember the correct form, instructional videotapes of liangong were produced.

History of Liangong

Dr. Zhuang Yuan Ming, the creator of liangong, is a chiropractor and tui na (Chinese massage and acupressure) doctor in Shanghai, China, who treats many patients daily. Chiropractic and tui na treatments usually provide some immediate relief from pain and symptoms of illness, but multiple treatments are often needed for a complete recovery and health maintenance.

Rather than relying on medical practitioners for continuing care, Dr. Zhuang contended that people could help themselves recover and remain healthy through exercise. He knew that ancient Chinese health exercises used movement to open channels and meridians for the proper qi flow needed to promote health. Dr. Zhuang studied these old therapeutic movement forms, the oldest created 2,000 years ago, taught to him by noted

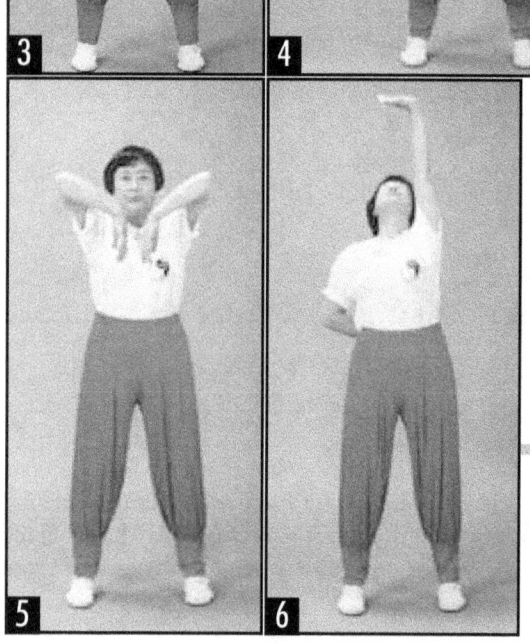

Exercise One
Turn neck (1), draw a bow on both sides (2), stretch arms (3), spread chest (4), spread wings to fly (5) and lift single iron arm (6).

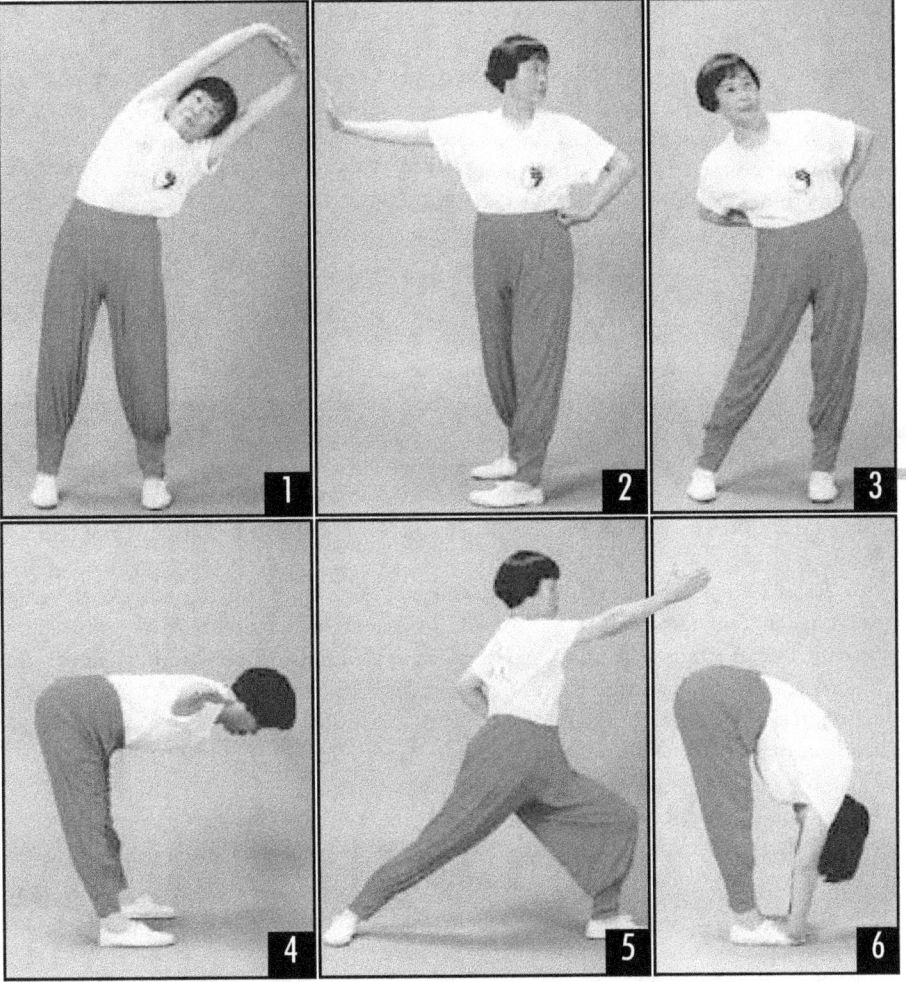

Exercise Two
Hold the sky with both hands (1), turn waist and push palm (2), circle hips (3), stretch arms and bend waist (4), thrust palm in bow stance (5), and place palms on feet (6).

internal Chinese martial arts practitioner, grandmaster Wang Zhi Ping.

Grandmaster Wang had created an exercise made up of 18 movements to help his students more easily learn and gain health benefits from the often esoteric old sports therapies. Such therapies included dao yin (breathing exercises); wuqinxi (five animal game); baduanjin (eight section exercises); and yinjinjing (changing muscles).

To create liangong, Dr. Zhuang systematized these therapeutic movement forms and made them accessible to today's general public. He combined grandmaster Wang's exercises with his clinical expertise, an understanding of the nature of common ailments, and the curative methods of Chinese massage, tui na.

Dr. Zhuang recruited me in 1974 to test the first 18 movements of liangong, which became Series One. I taught these movements to the public, reported my observations, and sought feedback for Dr. Zhuang. I was part of an advisory group composed of doctors, sport professors in physiology and kinesiology, and other exercise instructors enlisted by Dr. Zhuang to help him refine the exercise. Dr. Zhuang also used this process to develop Series Two. Our work resulted in liangong's current form.

The first classes had 50 students. More people joined the classes as word spread of liangong's benefits. People liked the exercise and found its benefits easy to obtain. Relief from neck and shoulder pain was quickly noticeable. Liangong was easy to practice, it wasn't too long and doesn't require much space.

Liangong has become popular in China. It was selected, along with two other exercises, by China's Ministry of Health, National Sports Committee, and the All China Federation of Trade Unions, for popularization in 1980. One thousand coaching centers were established across the country.

In the 1980s, China encouraged skilled practitioners of its cultural arts to teach abroad and pass on an appreciation of Chinese culture to people around the world.

What is Liangong?

Based on ancient Chinese movement therapies, liangong is a modern set of exercises developed to prevent and relieve health problems. It is divided into two parts—Series One and Series Two, each with three sections. The six exercises in each section focus on a specific area of the body such as the neck and shoulders or a type of body part like the joints. The exercises are generally simple and repeated to the left and right.

Series One systematically works down the body from head to toe as it strengthens, stretches, and increases the range of motion of specific areas. Section A is made up of six exercises that relieve pain in the neck and shoulders. The exercises in Section B focus on back problems. The hips and legs are strengthened in Section C.

Each section in Series Two works the whole body while focusing on joints, tendons, or internal organs. Problems with joints are remedied in Section D. Section E provides relief from pain in tendons and connective tissue. Section F features self-massage of acupressure points and areas of the body, along with exercises, to prevent and heal internal disorders.

Although the time required to practice liangong can vary depending on the degree of individualization applied to meet particular health needs, it generally takes 20 minutes to do the entire set of exercises.

Little space is required to practice liangong. In many of its exercises, the feet remain stationary while the arms and body stretch in all directions. A few exercises require a wide step to the left and right of the stationary point. One takes two walking steps forward.

The Liangong Difference

Liangong applies the methods used in qigong to strengthen qi flow and open the channels, meridians, and acupuncture points. But unlike qigong, liangong uses a technique of tightening then relaxing the muscles in coordination with a holding and release of breath to push the qi through areas of stagnation. Along with a precise alignment of the body, this method produces specific sensations that indicate the production of internal energy. Practitioners usually feel health benefits quickly.

In contrast, most qigong forms stress relaxation to improve qi flow. Very few qigong sets have periods of muscle tightening and release. The movements of taiji, a high level of qigong, are always relaxed and continuous. They have martial applications that require a difficult coordination of the upper and lower body together with the arms and legs. Perfecting the proper coordination of taiji's complex movements must be achieved before the relaxation required to attain the intended health benefits can be summoned. Taiji demands dedicated practice.

Unlike the continuous movements of taiji, liangong is divided into separate exercises. They are simple movements focused on promoting the health of one part of the body. The exercises are completed one at a time, unconnected to the others.

Taiji and qigong forms promote health throughout the body. Liangong's set of 36 exercises, when practiced in its entirety, does the same. But individual liangong exercises, developed to prevent or heal problems in specific areas, can be singled out to create an individualized program that meets a person's particular needs.

MARTIAL ARTS

Exercise Three
Turn knees (1), turn body in reverse stance (2), bend, squat and stretch legs (3), keep one palm on knee and lift the other (4), hold knee to chest (5), and ramble through the impregnable pass (6)

Qigong systems have specific requirements for when they may be practiced. Practicing more than one qigong form within a 12- or 24-hour period can cause health problems because of the particular flow of qi produced by each form. Not being qigong, liangong may be reviewed any time, even as a warm-up to performing qigong or taiji.

Benefits of Liangong

Liangong was created to prevent and relieve pain in the neck, shoulders, back and legs. Repetitive strain, overuse, trauma, disease, stress, or a combination of these factors is often the cause of pain. Liangong prevents and reduces pain through gentle stretching controlled by the practitioner, increasing range of motion, improving balance, increasing muscular strength, and the developing of internal strength.

It also develops internal strength by restoring and maintaining the proper flow of qi, generally defined by traditional Chinese medicine as fundamental life energy. As a result, people also claim success in the control of chronic illness after daily liangong practice. Where pain and health problems exist, liangong provides healing relief. For healthy people, it maintains vitality and prevents illness. The exercise may be practiced safely any time of day, as often as desired while monitoring excessive strain and fatigue, and in combination with other movement arts or therapies.

Liangong features four approaches to obtaining health benefits:

• Each exercise in liangong is designed for a specific purpose.

Liangong's six sections, each with six exercises, were developed to relieve pain in a particular area of the body by examining its anatomic and physiological characteristics. Unlike other Chinese therapeutic exercises that provide benefit to the whole body in general, liangong practitioners can individ-

EXERCISE FOUR
Push palms in horse stance (1), push palm in cross-leg seat (2), flow the qi from top to bottom (3), turn body and head (4), heel kick on both sides (5), and shuttlecock kick (6).

ualize their practice based on the location and severity of their health problems.

Practicing liangong in its entirety builds overall good health and fitness while preventing pain and illness. When relief is sought from pain in specific areas, sections may be selected for sole practice or repeated while practicing the whole liangong set.

In the three sections that comprise Series One, the first treats problems in the neck and shoulders. Back problems are addressed in the second section. The third section strengthens the hips and legs. Series Two begins with a section focusing on joints. Its middle section relieves pain in tendons and connective tissue, while the last section is designed to prevent and heal internal disorders.

- Relief from health problems and maintenance of good health are achieved by developing internal energy.

Smoothly flowing qi, generally defined as fundamental life energy, is the basis for good health in traditional Chinese medical theory. Liangong works to strengthen qi flow along channels and meridians through precise body alignment, breath control, and the contraction and relaxation of muscles.

The traditional Chinese medical diagnosis for pain in the neck, shoulders, waist, and legs is usually "retardation of qi and stagnation of blood." Its symptoms include spasm, adhesions, and tightness in muscles, ligaments, and tendons. When practicing liangong, qi is strengthened and pushed out to the extremities, causing stagnant blood to circulate and the generation of internal energy.

Each liangong exercise produces specific physical sensations when internal energy is generated. These sensations signal the proper execution of liangong exercises for therapeutic results.

- Combining liangong with other traditional Chinese medical treatments, enhances the health benefits of all the therapies.

Liangong provides a treatment for pain and illness through exercise. Incorporating acupuncture, acupressure, and Chinese herbal therapy along with exercise into a complete treatment plan enhances recovery. Multiple types of treatments employ different methods to strengthen and store qi while expelling negative factors. This increases resistance to disease and injury, strengthens the body overall, improves the therapeutic effect of the medical treatments, shortens treatment time, and prevents recurrence.

- Liangong's most important feature as a health exercise is its ability to prevent future problems.

Respected physicians in ancient China not only examined and treated patients, they taught them exercises to practice at home to control the development of existing diseases and prevent the occurrence of future problems. They followed the old saying, "A veteran doctor treats before the disease occurs, an inexperienced one treats after the disease occurs." Dr. Zhuang Yuan Ming developed liangong according to this medical principle.

Pain is prevented by regulating and repairing overworked muscles, activating inactive muscles, maintaining normal function within the body by combining motion and rest, and improving balance and coordination. By maintaining vitality, liangong is said to postpone the general decline and weakening of bodily processes caused by aging.

As a general health maintenance and preventative set of exercises, liangong may be among the greatest, yet least-known systems ever devised.

Wen Mei Yu's videotapes on liangong practice are available through Unique Publications at cfwenterprises.com.

Big "D"

Forget About Offense, Tang Soo Do Fighters Score Big with a Strong Defense

Doug Jeffrey

"Sandy pitched a no-hitter."

"Great. How'd he make out?" For years, baseball fans have chuckled at Don Drysdale's response to the news that his teammate [Sandy Koufax] had pitched a no-hitter.

The 6-foot 6-inch right-hander asked if Koufax won the game because the 1965 Los Angeles Dodgers weren't known for their scoring ... or hitting. As crazy as it may sound, it wasn't inconceivable for Koufax to throw a gem and lose. Baseball fans can remember tons of L.A. victories by the score of 1-0 and 2-1. On most occasions, the Dodgers couldn't muster more than a few hits.

Needless to say, the anemic Dodger offense didn't win a World Series for them that year. Instead, it was all defense.

There are some teams in modern sports that are just like that old Dodger team. A perfect example is professional football's Pittsburgh Steelers.

Offensively, these boys aren't quite as inept as Maury Wills, Lou Johnson, Jim Lefebvre and the rest of L.A.'s Boys of Summer. Defensively, however, the gridiron gladiators from Pennsylvania are very similar. These guys are stingy. You don't see many of their opponents dancing in the end zone. And that's exactly why the Steelers won the American Conference's Central Division. Tough defense.

Defense does more than just win baseball's World Series and the NFL's Super Bowl. It also wins fights. Just ask Chun Sik Kim, president and founder of the International Tang Soo Do Federation.

"*Tang soo do* sparring philosophy always focuses on defense," says Kim, a two-time Korean tang soo do champion. "Defense is more important than offense. Regardless of how good your offense is, you won't be that effective if your defense isn't good."

STRONG FUNDAMENTALS

To be effective defensively, the tang soo do stylist needs solid fundamentals. Therefore, Kim engrains in his students the importance of holding their hands close to their body and face.

"We always want to be ready for a block," says Kim, whose federation has more than 20,000 members.

There are a number of blocks at their disposal, including the high "X" block, side block, low-trapping block and many others.

Of course, blocking is not the only line of defense. Evasive techniques also come in quite handy. When appropriate, the fighter may step to the side or out of range from an opponent's strikes. The type of technique dictates his response. For example, the fighter will move to the side if his opponent throws a front kick.

COUNTERS AND COMBINATIONS

Whether the tang soo do fighter has executed a crushing block or evaded the bad guy, he is immediately looking for a chance to counter with a lethal weapon because this is when the opponent is vulnerable.

"In some ways, you might say that our defense is also our offense," says Kim, who was the U.S. Team Coach at the First World Championships. "We might fall back or move to the side 45 degrees. When we do this, we can see if our opponent has exposed a target that we can strike."

Thus, the crafty tang soo do fighter is looking for an opening on his opponent's body, low hands or a certain body position. When he sees the opportunity, he strikes swiftly.

Striking swiftly is worthless, however, if he doesn't hit the right target. Thus, he aims for the solar plexus [because it's a weak, soft area], and he also put a bull's eye on the nose area and throat.

The traditional tang soo do stylist has a variety of counterattacks at his disposal. While he may be known for his kicking expertise, he has more than legs in his bag of tricks.

"I teach traditional tang soo do, which means that we use a 50/50 ratio of hands and feet," says Kim. "After we block with our hands, we can punch or use our feet. They both work together."

One of the most effective is the back kick. Kim favors this weapon because it's short and fast.

"Let's say that your opponent throws a kick," he says. "You can block the technique and throw a jump back kick."

They also utilize a front kick. One is short and the other is long.

"The short kick, which is like a snake, is quick," he says.

Of course, it's always wise to bolster your arsenal with a variety of combinations, he notes.

"The important thing is that combinations must have good balance, and you get that balance from traditional tang soo do forms," he notes. "If you block and punch and lose your balance, you won't be able to follow up with a third move."

FIRST MOVE

When facing an opponent—whether it's in the ring or on the street—the tang soo do practitioner is always conscious of his adversary's first move.

"On the street, if you encounter a troublemaker, he's going to come first," he says. "More than likely, he's going to have a knife, gun or stick and make the first move. Sparring is the same way. When your opponent makes his move, he usually comes with his favorite technique. Right away, we

Master C.S. Kim and his partner square off (1). Kim throws a front snap kick to the stomach of Joseph V. Bruno, who steps into a back stance and blocks the kick with his right arm (2). Bruno counters with a right hammerfist to the head, which Kim defends with a high right hand (3). Bruno follows with a middle punch, Kim blocks it with a middle knifehand (4) and then grabs Bruno's arm (5) and strikes it with a vicious elbow (6).

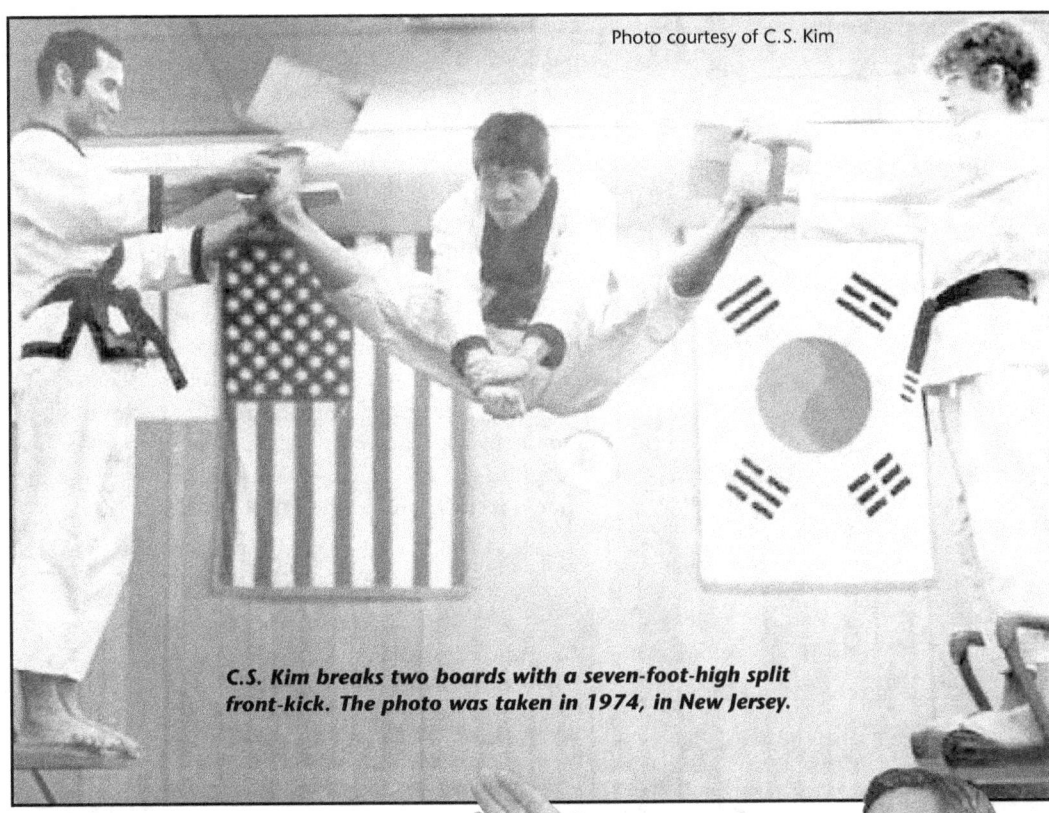

C.S. Kim breaks two boards with a seven-foot-high split front-kick. The photo was taken in 1974, in New Jersey.

know what he likes to do. We can then anticipate the move, be ready for it, block it and follow up."

STAYING READY

Watching an opponent's face is another key line of defense. An opponent's eyes can reveal personality, attitude and intentions. The experienced fighter can read that.

"If you watch your opponent's face, you will know 99 percent of the time what he's going to do," says the 61-year-old martial artist.

RARE OCCASIONS

While Kim stresses defense, there are occasions when they switch things up ... like a fastball pitcher who throws a

C.S. Kim Up Close

Age: 61

Years training: 50

Entrepreneur: Owns 15 schools in such places as the United Kingdom, Denmark, Chile, Argentina, Panama, Korea, Puerto Rico and Portugal.

Value of training: In addition to teaching him how to make friends and build relationships, tang soo do has also taught him patience, discipline and understanding.

Early ambitions: As a little boy, Kim wanted to become a lawyer. He gave that up, however, when his father died because he needed to make money for his family.

Quote: "Tang soo do has taught me many good things. Otherwise, I would be bad. I was a tough guy with a bad attitude."

curve. When they throw their version of their "breaking pitch," the tang soo do stylist attacks first, creating an element of surprise.

"Usually, we wait for our opponent to make the first move," says Kim. "When we do move first, however, we give a little fake and look for our opponent to open up. If he puts his head down or backs up, then we follow up. In essence, we are trying to make the opening."

When the fighter sees the opening, he has to close the gap quickly. To facilitate the move, he might fake, *kiai* (yell), switch his feet or turn his body. The yell is a critical element of this process. Yelling not only shows confidence, it can scare the opponent or make him hesitate for a second, says Kim, adding that the kiai should come from the abdomen for added power.

The fighters assume the ready position (1). Joseph V. Bruno steps back with his right leg (2) and launches a high punch (3), which Kim blocks (4). Kim then follows that with a front snap kick to the ribs (5).

FISH OUT OF WATER

Besides attacking first, there is another way Kim introduces the element of surprise. Believe it or not, even in a traditional art such as tang soo do, his fighters can handle themselves on the ground. These guys are not like fish out of water when they find themselves off their feet. His students not only practice takedowns, they also prepare various techniques for the ground.

"Of course, we learn how to avoid going to the ground," he says. "If, however, we end up there, we have techniques."

The Future of Training

Within a few short years, tang soo do training in Washington, D.C., is going to take on a whole new look. C.S. Kim intends to open a training and meditation center on 300 acres that will encompass 20,000 square feet. The non-profit facility, which will cost about $5 million, will include a temple, a museum and a training hall. Kim also intends to hold championship tournaments at the site.

To be sure, every situation is different, so what they do depends on the situation and what the opponent is trying to do. To make his students as prepared as possible, he teaches a variety of techniques, including how to attack and throw kicks from the ground.

"If your opponent mounts you, you can free your legs and kick his face," he says. "If he tries to choke you, you can grab his clothes and push your thumb into his throat."

Before they even get to the techniques, however, they have to adopt a new mindset.

"When most people go to the ground, they are scared and give up easily," he says. "That is why I teach people not to give up. When a person gets you down, you have to be ready to go down, too."

JUST DO IT

On many occasions during that sweltering summer of '65, the Dodgers found themselves down a run or two. But they never gave up. They continued to play tough defense and chip away with the offense. Eventually, they won the pennant and then the World Series.

So, if you ever doubted the importance of defense, think about that old Dodger team or the 2002 Pittsburgh Steelers or C.S. Kim, who was undefeated in sparring in 1970.

Classic Jackie—10 Chantastics That Will Never Die

Some observers think his early films provide the greatest glimpse of Jackie Chan's brilliance.

Ric Meyers

Talk about timing. Jeff Yang (Jackie's official biographer) and I had just finished recording the audio commentary track for Columbia Tristar/Destination Home Entertainment's re-release of *Drunken Master (Drunken Monkey in a Tiger's Eye)* when an editor sends me this e-mail.

"Interviewed a young female martial artist today," it read, "who said she got into the arts by watching Jackie Chan movies as a child. She loves all of Jackie's movies, but still prefers his 1970s and '80s standards. How about a story on Jackie's top ten old movies?"

Well, perfect, I thought. That would be easy. I'll just rattle them off the top of my head.

Wrong. "If I had known how successful my movies were going to be in America," Jackie recently told me, "I never would have sold them." Or, as he literally cried out at the after-party of *Operation Condor's* New York premiere: "What have they done to my movie?!"

So now, instead, with all the different versions of Jackie's movies coming from so many distributors, what was great in the theaters might be just okay on DVD, and what was okay in the cinemas might be great on home video. Just remember the martial art movie maniac's mantra: wide-screen, subtitled, original score is always best.

We'll start with the first films Jackie made as a full-fledged star, under the contractual control and, often times, direction of the man who took credit for making Bruce Lee a superstar. These are the Lo Wei films, also known as both the "Lo, Why?" films and the "No Way" films—11 movies

Movie posters courtesy of Ric Meyers

produced in about three years which effectively made the then-named Jacky virtual box-office poison. But in the fullness of time, a few emerge as interesting viewing for a variety of reasons.

SHAOLIN WOODEN MEN (1976)

Co-starring: Kam Kan and Lung Chung-erh

Director: Lo Wei

This was Jacky's second film under No Way's control, which many consider the best of the bunch ... for what that's worth. Following *New Fist of Fury*, with Jacky

Jackie's first try at "drunken boxing" in Drunken Master.

looking extremely uncomfortable doing Bruce schtick, this film allowed a little of his growing charm to come through, since he played a kid who takes a vow of silence until he avenges his dad's death. Therefore, all his character must come through his movements and expressions. And what movements. In his early 20s and at the height of his youth-

BEST OF CFW — VOL.1
MARTIAL ARTS

ful strength following ten grueling years training in a Peking Opera school and five more doing potentially deadly stunts in major motion pictures, Jackie pays off on his oft-stated promise of "showing the audience what I can do." As long as you're ready for "old school kung-fu" stylings, and don't expect any of Chan's trademark humor, this will serve as a fascinating introduction to the star's formative years.

SNAKE & CRANE ARTS OF SHAOLIN (1978)
Co-starring: Nora Miao and Kam Kan
Director: Chen Chi-hwa

Jackie himself considered this Lo Wei-produced effort his first dream project since he was given more freedom in character and choreography. He considers it a true harbinger of things to come, since it was here he showcased his use of everyday objects as weapons. Although the No Way films are not nearly as fight-filled as they should, or could be, there was no faulting the plot. A book of secrets from eight styles of kung-fu falls into Jacky's hands and everyone's willing to kill him to get it.

DRAGON FIST (1978)
Co-starring: Nora Miao and James Tien
Director: Lo Wei

After all this time, this one's impressive not just for the locations, but for Jacky's choreography and kung-fu. Even though there are too

This scene from Snake in the Eagle's Shadow was "borrowed" for the movie, Mask of Zorro.

161

many dramatic scenes, the film sparks whenever he starts to fight. And when he finally realizes how he's been fooled and double-crossed, the climatic battles practically buzz.

SNAKE IN THE EAGLE'S SHADOW (1978)
Co-starring: Simon Yuen and Hwang Jang Lee
Director: Yuen Woo Ping
Take a movie star who was then considered "box-office poison," lend to another studio, team him with a young kung-fu choreographer of such sizzling little thrillers as *Bloody Fists* and *The Bastards*, then add the novice director's venerable father, and what have you got? You've got a huge box-office hit and a film that changed the course of Asian cinema. Lewd and crude? You bet. Even so, watch this free-flowing, fight-filled, humor-soaked romp and see how it was a combination of *Animal House* and *Enter the Dragon*.

The Young Master.

Jackie's 10 Best Early Films
1. Shaolin Wooden Men (1976)
2. Snake & Crane Arts of Shaolin (1978)
3. Dragon Fist (1978)
4. Snake in the Eagle's Shadow (1978)
5. Drunken Master (1978)
6. Fearless Hyena (1979)
7. Young Master (1980)
8. Project A (1984)
9. Wheels on Meals (1984)
10. Police Story (1985)

Honorable Mention
Half a Loaf of Kung-fu, Fantasy Mission Force, Spiritual Kung-fu, Dragon Lord, Winners and Sinners, My Lucky Stars, Twinkle Twinkle Lucky Stars, and *Heart of Dragon (First Mission)*

The kung-fu is really superb, the spirit is infectious, and the energy of two young turks finally able to shoot the works are pervasive. You can even see how Jackie and Yuen inspired each other to greater heights.

DRUNKEN MASTER (1978)

Co-starring: Simon Yuen and Hwang Jang Lee

Director: Yuen Woo Ping

One good hit deserves another, and while many thought that *Eagle's Shadow* was the initial film in which Jackie portrayed heroic HK cinema icon Wong Fei Hong as a mischievous rascal, this was actually the first. According to Chan it was based on his own idea to differentiate it from the previous effort. It was a great risk (since Kwan Tak Hing had played the character as a beloved Confucian healer in dozens of films before then), but also made a great deal of sense since the rest of this movie is very similar in structure to its predecessor. Only this time there was even more humor and acrobatic kung-fu. Although Jackie and Yuen went their separate ways afterward, I hear they've both done all right. Sixteen years later, at about the time Jackie was doing the delightful *Drunken Master II (Legend of Drunken Master)*, Yuen had directed *Iron Monkey* and *Wing Chun*, supplied the choreography for *Once Upon a Time in China* and *Fist of Legend*, and would soon do the same for *The Matrix* and *Crouching Tiger, Hidden Dragon*.

FEARLESS HYENA (1979)

Co-starring: Yen Shi-kwan and Li Kuan

Director: Jacky Chan

A superstar's a superstar, but a contract is also a contract, especially in the dog-eat-dog HK cinema. And, according to the fine print, Jacky owed Lo Wei another movie. At least this time Lo let Chan creatively control it, and the result was the first (and last) true "Jacky Chan Film." The patterns established with "Eagle" and "Drunken" are still evident here, only with Jacky's full range of emotional touches. In fact, he maintains that he created the central concept of "Emotional Kung-Fu" specifically for the film. It also afforded him a chance to give full range to his comedic sensibility—allowing him to dress up and fight in a variety of amusing guises. Imagine if Jim Carrey was a killer kung-fu master and you get a flavor of Chan's assault on audience preconceptions.

"*Drunken Master, Snake In the Eagle's Shadow* and *Fearless Hyena* are commonly regarded as the beginning of the true Jackie Chan style," Michael Stradford, executive director of DVD Marketing at Columbia Tristar Home Video (Entertainment), said. "As such, CTHE believes that the only way to present these films to the viewing audience were in the best possible condition. Since they've been available for years in relatively poor condition, we wanted to clean them up as best we can, present them in their original aspect ratio, use original audio where possible, and hope the consumer feels our effort was worth it." Well, here's one consumer who does.

YOUNG MASTER (1980)

Co-starring: Yuen Baio, Shih Tien, Lily Li, and Whang In-sik

Director: Jackie Chan

This was Chan's first film in his long-running string of hits for Golden Harvest (which managed to wrest the star away from the Lo Wei labyrinthine contract clutches), so he wanted to prove that his hits with Yuen and Lo were no fluke. He set out to make his ultimate statement in the kind of knockabout kung-fu comedy he, Woo Ping, and Sammo Hung had developed—and many people think he succeeded. Whether juggling fans, swords, skirts, and pipes; cleverly beating or getting totally beaten; lion dancing or tumbling daredevil style, this has got everything but the kung-fu kitchen sink.

BEST OF CFW ——— VOL.1
MARTIAL ARTS

Jackie rehearses a stunt for his sequel to The Young Master.

PROJECT A (1984)

Co-starring: Sammo Hung and Yuen Baio

Director: Jackie Chan

This film revolutionized HK cinema, all but dragging it, technically and intellectually, kicking and screaming into the 20th century. Jackie brought a sophistication to the plot, characters, dialogue, and action unprecedented in his country. In its original, wide-screen form, it was a true classic, worthy of standing alongside the finest works of screen comedy legends Harold Lloyd and even Buster Keaton. Even its original soundtrack by Michael Lai set new standards for HK screen music. Compare it to Jackie's almost equally brilliant *Project A 2*, and see classic kung-fu cinema at its '80's best.

WHEELS ON MEALS (1984)

Co-starring: Sammo Hung and Yuen Baio

Director: Sammo Hung

The success of *Project A* emboldened the "three brothers" to do a film on location in Spain under the skilled hand of Sammo, whose humor and martial arts style was more marginal than Jackie's family friendly approach. The result is a great yin/yang of kung-fu viewing, whether you liked your action sweet (Jackie) or savage (Sammo). Arguably the best-structured of Sammo's efforts with Jackie and Yuen, this modern-day tale of a private eye and two fast-food purveyors saving a beautiful damsel in distress from an heir-hungry relative has plenty of fun as well as mucho macho martial arts. Unarguably its highlight is a bout between Jackie and undefeated martial arts champ Benny "the Jet" Urquidez, which many feel is one of the best and most realistic kung-fu fights ever filmed. Shot in 48 hours straight, it featured full-contact and some remarkable work on everyone's part.

POLICE STORY (1985)

Co-starring: Brigitte Lin and Maggie Cheung

Director: Jackie Chan

What *Project A* did for period kung-fu films, *Police Story* did for modern martial arts movies. Except for some extremely rare instances, HK action films set in the present day were crude, polyester-laden turkeys. *Police Story* changed all that. It won the Best Picture and Best Action Design Awards at the Hong Kong Film Awards. It was nominated in five other categories. It was a worldwide success, especially in Japan, which screened the best, and longest, of its many edits. In its original wide-screen subtitled American cut, it was the closing-night hit of the New York Film Festival. Jackie himself considers it his favorite. By any criteria the version Jackie lovingly wrote, directed, choreographed, starred in, edited, and scored is still the sun from which all other modern kung-fu sagas are rays.

And even that's not all. There's even some kung-fu fun to be found in such runner's-up as *Half a Loaf of Kung-fu, Fantasy Mission Force, Spiritual Kung-fu, Dragon Lord, Winners and Sinners, My Lucky Stars, Twinkle Twinkle Lucky Stars*, and even *Heart of Dragon (First Mission)*. After you see the Chan man strut his stuff in these early efforts, you'll also know why he led the charge in the Hong Konging of Hollywood.

"Project A revolutionized HK cinema, all but dragging it, technically and intellectually, kicking and screaming into the 20th century."

MARTIAL ARTS

What's in a Xing Ming

Trying to decipher the meaning behind some of China's most important xing mings (names) could take a lifetime.

Peter Gryffin

To many American kung-fu practitioners, sifu (shifu in Mandarin) is the appropriate term for "master." This is the Chinese equivalent of the Japanese term shihan. It is perplexing then, and to some, maddening, to view the growing abundance of "sifu" who are in their early 20s.

How, they wonder, is it that such a young person has already attained the rank of master? Surely this is fraud of some sort, or outright lunacy! The answer though lies not in self-aggrandizement, or devious deception, but rather in the confusing complexities of the Chinese language, and in the changes and turmoil of time. It seems that in modern China sifu has come to be used for both "teacher" and "master"—the equivalents of both sensei and shihan in the Japanese language. So a 60-year-old master of the martial arts is called sifu, as is a 20-year-old martial arts teacher.

According to Caroline Chen, the Asian Pacific Resource Center librarian for Los Angeles, and various Chinese language dictionaries, the word sifu translates as a teacher of both knowledge and skill. A carpenter teacher would be a sifu, as would be a music teacher or any other teacher who teaches a subject involving skill and knowledge. A teacher who instructs only in areas of knowledge (such as an English or math teacher) would be called "lao-shi." Further confusing the matter is the differences in regional dialects and word usage.

Why then do many American teachers insist that the word sifu means master? This is because in large part from whom they learned kung-fu. Many teachers of the martial arts in China, until the last few decades or so, were masters. So it is perhaps natural, upon hearing these masters addressed as sifu, that foreign visitors assumed the word itself meant "master." More troubling is that turning to Chinese-English dictionaries does little to alleviate the matter. Pick up any dictionary and you will find some defining "sifu" as teacher, while others say that "sifu" means master; one dictionary even defined "sifu" as craftsman.

So what then do you call a kung-fu teacher in America, and what do you call his master? Some suggest using the Chinese word "jow-lin," common among many wushu teams in China. Jow-lin translates as coach, appropriate for wushu perhaps, which is considered a sport in China. But is "coach" the best term to use for a kung-fu teacher in America? Many think not.

Some have suggested just using the Japanese word "sensei," stating it has become so common that it is now "Americanized," and as such can be used for a teacher of any martial art. As you might guess, this suggestion is also rather unpopular with many kung-fu teachers. Which still leaves us with the question—"What do you call a kung-fu teacher?"

Sean Liu, a 31st-generation disciple of the Shaolin Temple, also noted that the term for a kung-fu teacher could vary considerably. He stated it is common to use the term jao-lin for the coaches or teachers of professional wushu athletes, that a teacher of kung-fu in a university might be called

MARTIAL ARTS

As an art that develops self-discipline, kung-fu, or "excellence through effort," seems an apropos term, particularly during stance training. ("Lao-shi" Gryffin is shown correcting stances, to use the term for an instructor at a college, mentioned by master Liu.)

Dictionary

NAME	MEANING
Sifu	Chinese for teacher or master
Lao-shi	Educational teacher
Jow-lin	Coach, as in wushu
Sensei	Japanese for teacher
Dashi	Roughly grandmaster
Shi-yei	Grand teacher
Si-gung	Grandmaster
Wushu	Martial art or fighting method
Kung-fu	Working man, excellence through effort
Kung	Skill
Fu	Time
Quan shu	Fist art
Guo shu	National art
Chi	Oxygen
Yin/yang	A principle of duality

"lao-shi," as a term of respect, and teachers operating out of commercial schools or in parks tend to be called sifu. Liu clarified, however, that if you go to China and ask people where you can find a good sifu, they will have no idea what you are talking about unless you clarify a sifu of martial arts.

"In China," Liu explained, "a sifu could also be a writing or cooking teacher." One final note: Liu said that in traditional shaolin kung-fu (Buddhist in origin), a teacher would be called "dashi," roughly translated as "grandmaster."

Duke Cheng, a 57-year-practitioner and third-generation kung-fu master, also stated that sifu can mean teacher in several senses, from martial arts to cooking or business teachers. A more senior teacher could be called "shi-yei," or "grand teacher." Jian Li, a teacher in Scottsdale, Ariz., and kung-fu brother of Jet Li, stated that shi means father, and that in many respects his teacher was like a father to him. In that respect a master or grandmaster would be shi-yei, or grandfather. Li added that this was more common in the old days, and in modern usage sifu mostly just means "teacher" and is used across the board.

American-born instructor Ken Edwards, an eagle claw disciple of Shum Leung, explained that his school uses sifu for teacher, but as the head authority of the school his students and other teachers could call him si-gung, or grandmaster, which is also what he calls his teacher, who is the head authority of the system.

Another American teacher, Steve Herring, said that most teachers, including grandmasters and masters, just use sifu, meaning a teacher of knowledge and skill. He stated that si-gung is the appropriate term for master, and the creator of a style would be called si tai gung, but that those terms are rarely used.

So if it is possible that a sifu is not necessarily a master, then what other well-known Chinese words and terms may not mean what we think? As it turns out, kung-fu is not (just) martial art, chi may be more (or less) than some mystical energy and the well-known "yin/yang" symbol may be—yes, you guessed it—not the "yin/yang" symbol.

Kung Fu—A Work in Time

You may have noticed the growing use of the word "wushu" among Chinese martial arts. Possibly with good reason. Wushu literally means "martial art," or "fighting method." What then does the word kung-fu mean? Chinese dictionaries offer a bewildering array of definitions, ranging from "working man" to "excellence through effort."

Yet peruse much of Chinese literature and you find statements made of various martial artists that they "have good kung-fu," or, "your kung-fu is good." And then there are the endless onslaught of "kung-fu" movies that abound in Hong Kong and Taiwan. So the word kung-fu obviously has some connotation with the martial arts. According to Caroline Chen, the word kung-fu can be literally translated as Kung = skill and Fu = time. So what you have is skill developed over time or the essence of the martial arts. In this respect you can have kung-fu, or skill developed over time, in any art or skill. You can have good kung-fu in being a doctor, a painter, or any other skill or art.

The concept is to find self-perfection by developing a high level of skill in one area (such as martial arts) that translates over into all areas of life. This is similar to developing the spirit in Japanese arts through kendo (the way of the sword), kyudo (the way of the bow), or chado (the way of tea).

How the word kung-fu developed its Western meaning as a Chinese martial art is anyone's guess. One possible story might be during the initial contact Westerners had with Chinese culture, particu-

"Yin/yang" or "tai chi?" This symbol is most well-known in America as the yin/yang symbol, painted as a dragon on a Fullerton College Martial Arts room wall.

Steve Hearing states that most teachers of kung-fu in America use the word sifu for teacher, noting that it is the closest equivalent to sensei used in the Japanese arts.

larly during the turn of the century and the famed Boxer Rebellion. Perhaps on seeing the incredible feats of martial skill, Western bystanders asked what it was they were seeing and Chinese interpreters replied "kung-fu." The Chinese interpreters meant "skilled men, masters of the martial arts," while Westerners interpreted it as "fighting art."

Regional and social differences may also play an important role in word usage. Prior to the 1950s Chinese martial arts were called guo-shu, or national art. Sean Liu stated that in Taiwan and Malaysia many people still use the term, while for the general public they still use kung-fu, and in other areas the term quan shu (fist art) was used.

Duke Cheng attributes the popularity of David Carridine's "Kung Fu" television series in the 1970s as a major contributor to the use of the term to describe the Chinese martial arts. Jing Li stated that these days more people in America are calling Chinese martial arts wushu, but that because of Western influence in China, more people there are starting to call it kung-fu!

Ken Edwards explained that he prefers the term kung-fu since the word is more familiar to the general public. If he told people that he is a wushu teacher, they would say "What's that?" His teacher, Shum Lueng, uses kung-fu and defines it as the hard work it takes to master or excel in anything.

The Chi We Breathe
"Chi," a term growing in common everyday usage, tends to be thought of by most people in America as some kind of mystical energy permeating the universe. Although to some degree chi can mean something along these lines, most people would be surprised to learn, as was this author, that after much reading into various translated Chinese texts, the most-common usage for the word chi was quite simply—"oxygen."

Runners-up were energy, blood, mental energy, inner strength, and vital life force. Although it is romantic and intriguing to think of chi as some sort of spiritual energy that can be developed and utilized in mysterious ways, the more mundane usage of chi simply as "air" is also revealing, and for the ancient Chinese, very perceptive.

Our body's energy is derived from the use of oxygen, or air. We take in air, where the oxygen is transferred to the blood stream and carried throughout the body to be used by the cells to create energy. Developing chi in this sense is roughly equivalent to developing aerobic capacity. The greater aerobic capacity (chi) we have, the greater our capacity for energy. The better you utilize oxygen in the body, the stronger, faster and more endurance you have.

Liu agreed that chi most commonly means air, but that sometimes the word chi can have deeper meanings, such as good essence and the energy of the body. A person with good writing is said to have good essence or good chi, and from a medical perspective chi might be looked at as a combination of bioelectric energy, hormones, endorphins, and a person's genetic make-up.

Duke Cheng also confirmed the general translation of chi as breathing or air, but also elaborated that the term can be used to describe internal power or energy, and the energy of emotions—an angry person has bad chi, or energy; a happy person happy chi; a mad person might be said to have chi madness; and an energetic person is said to have a lot of chi. Jing Li defined chi as energy from oxygen carried through the blood, and that it is not spiritual. He noted that improving your chi through various exercises is essentially improving blood circulation. He compared it to a clogged water pipe. Blood can't get through, so energy is low. Keep the channels open and blood circulation goes through better, so you have better chi.

When is a Yin/Yang not a Yin/Yang?

When it is a tai chi! Some time ago, while teaching English to a group of Chinese high school students, I tried to make a point by comparing opposites to the yin/yang symbol. I received confused looks. Finally I drew a picture of the yin/yang symbol on the board and their faces lit up in recognition. "Aahh," they exclaimed. "The tai chi symbol."

I was amazed to discover that people in China (at least in their region) know the yin/yang as the tai chi symbol. Tai chi loosely translates as "the grand ultimate principle of the universe." It is a principle of duality, and yin/yang is one example of it. Tai chi is physical and spirit, man and woman, good and evil, positive and negative, night and day, land and sea, for example. It is the basic and ultimate principle that nothing exists in a vacuum, everything contains the seeds of its opposite, and every thing has an opposite. Yin/yang is but one of the more powerful and common examples of soft-hard, and sometimes represents woman-man and other representations of the soft-hard concept.

Jing Li knows it as the yin/yang symbol, but agreed that terminology can vary by region. He stated that the symbol is used as a medical symbol to represent a balanced body. He doesn't associate yin and yang with female and male, but rather more in balances such as a balanced diet of meat and vegetables, or balancing work and rest.

Despite discussions with a wide range of individuals, as well as exhaustive literary research, no final authoritative definition seems to emerge for any of the terms mentioned above. The matter is further compounded by differences in methods of translation and dialects. Perhaps only time (as is traditional in kung-fu) will tell.

Peter Gryffin is a Southern California-based martial artist and freelance writer. He last wrote on Yoko Tanabe in the February 2002 issue.

Chin Na—The Art of Fighting Without Fighting

Chin na uses quiet strength and dynamic circular motion to control or subdue an opponent.

Brian M. Brinkman

(Editor's note: Some of the techniques described in this article are deemed extremely dangerous. They should only be practiced under the direct supervision of a trained martial artist.)

Chin na, meaning to seize and control, is best described as, "The style of fighting without fighting," to use a famous quote from the late Bruce Lee. Although not considered to be a complete style of martiat arts, there are aspects of chin na in nearly every style.

Chin na uses quiet strength and dynamic circular motion to control or subdue an opponent. This concept of self--defense is most closely related to the modern martial art of aikido, founded in the early 1940s. Some believe that aikido founder master Morihei Ueshiba most likely fused principles already present in much older Chinese arts, such as bagua and shaolin chuan-fa, with his nasive "budo" or "martial" systems to create aikido.

Adhere, Seize and Control

The concept behind this ancient way of self-defense is to control the opponent while expending little energy or force. A chin na stylist's skill exists adhering to an incoming attack, while redirecting the opponent's energy and allowing the opportunity for control. The fundamental building blocks of chin na, much like aikido, revolve around the use of "chi" energy. By understanding chi flow and performing techniques that redirect or subdue an opponent's attack, a chin na practitioner can render an attacker helpless and off balance.

Reality Check

Contrary to most action movie fight scenes, it is nearly impossible to grab the fist or foot of an incoming attacker. In reality, it is necessary to first slow or redirect the momentum of the attack; when that is accomplished, true chin na can be applied. A practitioner must have a solid understanding of weight distribution to use chin na in a fight.

Understanding how to move with an opponent is important and knowing whether to yield to an

This technique shows the accuracy and focus of the lunging eagle claw. Notice how Brian Brinkman has solidly clutched the attacker around the neck. With sufficient pressure, this movement could easily render an opponent unconscious.

attack or root into the ground will become an automatic response with sufficient opponent practice. To avoid being hit and to apply chin na, the practitioner should also be proficient with basic parrying and blocking techniques. To achieve a foundation of effective blocking and countering applications, a beginning student must learn to adhere to the attack through chi sao. Also called sticky hands, chi sao is the two-person practice of sensing energy and potential strikes by remaining in constant contact with the hands and forearms of a partner.

Much like aikido or tai chi, the practitioner can generate tremendous force through slow and mindful practice. The movements will seem light, even soft in appearance. With proper instruction, a student of chin na will develop the accuracy and finesse needed to perform this gentle art.

Shaolin Chin Na

Chin na techniques were used by kung-fu masters to subdue an opponent without causing permanent injury or death. Today, chin na techniques are used by professional bodyguards, police officers and military personnel throughout the world. The history of chin na can be traced to the Shaolin Temple as early as A.D. 960. General Yueh Fei, a famous military leader known for his martial prowess, is credited with originating the shaolin eagle claw system as well as the concept of chin na.

The four components of chin na are:
- **Separating the muscle**—Seizing various muscles on the body and applying pressure.
- **Misplacing the bone or joint**—Applying pressure or torque to bones and joints. If done too forcefully, dislocation and even breaking may occur.
- **Sealing the breath, artery or vein**—Certain types of striking and pressure applied to energy meridians, veins and arteries can cause unconsciousness, paralysis and even death.

In this sequence the man in the black uniform grabs Brian Brinkman's wrist (1). Notice how Brinkman holds the attacker's wrist at an upward angle, making it difficult for the attacker to escape from his lock (2). As Brinkman turns the wrist to add more tension (3), the attacker relieves his tension by flipping onto his back (4). Brinkman controls the attacker, flowing with the flipping opponent and re-applying pressure to the wrist by driving his elbow into the ground (5).

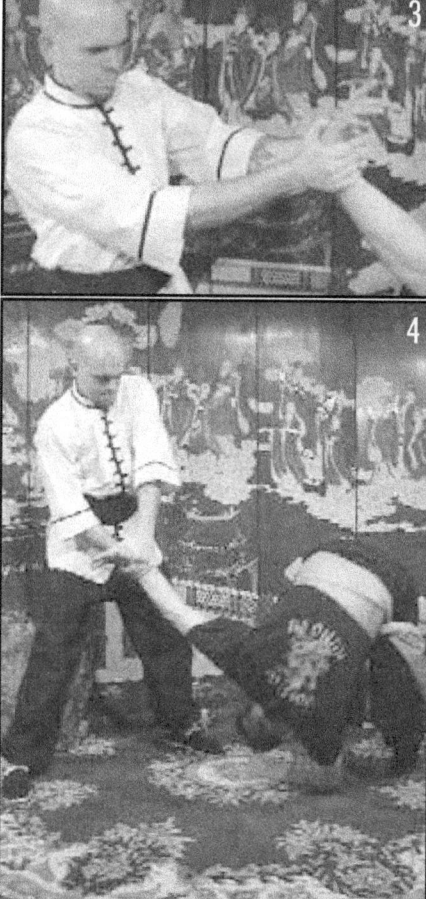

- **Cavity pressure points**—Techniques of this nature involve pressure or striking in such a manner that can cause various internal dysfunction.

Chin Na Applications

Seizing the opponent at the outset of an attack is the most important aspect of chin na, without which there can be no application of leverage or control. The most common and applicable techniques involve the fingers, wrist and elbow. However, we will limit our analysis to techniques involving wrist-seizing techniques.

Strengthening the hands and forearms is paramount to becoming proficient in any chin na technique. Since the vast majority of chin na techniques involve counters to grabs and striking, you must learn to apply pressure to various points on the arm. Seizing the hand to apply pressure to the wrist is the most commonly used form of chin na.

Seizing the Wrist

To practice basic wrist chin na, begin by having an opponent grab your left wrist with his right hand (**as seen in the first sequence accompanying this article**). Cross your right hand over your left and seize the opponent's right or (grabbing) hand. This can be accomplished by placing the thumb of your right hand firmly between the tendons of the opponent's middle and pointer finger, just below the knuckles, digging your remaining fingertips into the palm and gripping your opponent's hand. Now swiftly turn the opponent's wrist clockwise while driving the opponent's hand down and away from you. At this point circle the seized

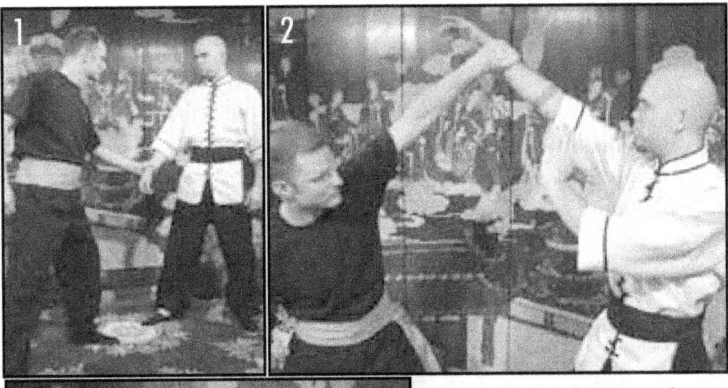

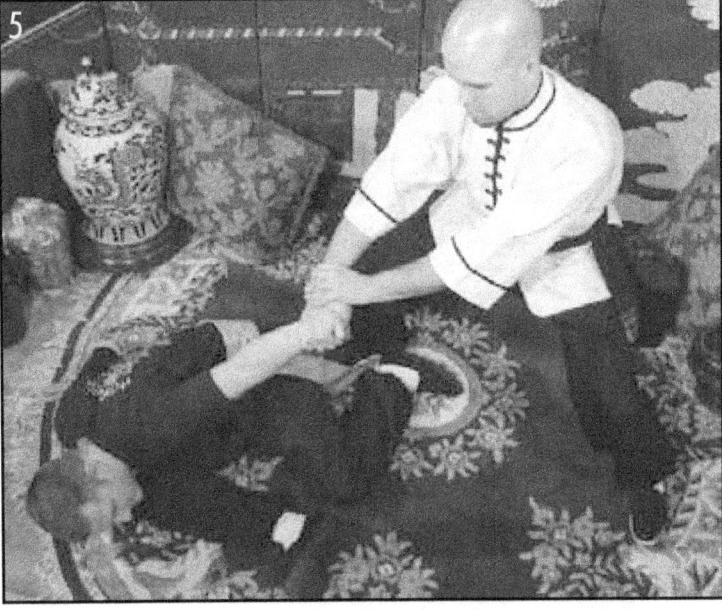

Here, sifu Brinkman makes a large upward circular motion with his arm to put the opponent off balance (1). Brinkman immediately clamps down onto the attacker's grasping hand (2-3), generating tremendous tension in the attacker's wrist. Notice how the attacker's elbow remains locked out as Brinkman forces him to the ground (4-5).

wrist sharply back up and away from the ground. Done correctly, you should be able to flip your opponent onto his back.

But say your opponent grabs the opposite wrist. In this case, you will administer a slightly different type of pressure on the wrist. Have a partner grab your right wrist with his left hand (**as seen in sequence 2**). Draw your arm above you in a circular fashion so both you and your opponent's hands are above your head. Place your left hand firmly onto the opponent's gripping hand and apply pressure. At this point your opponent's hand will be locked onto your right wrist. Now pull your right forearm down toward your chest, keeping the forearm parallel to the ground, and roll his hand away from you. Continue to apply pressure on the opponent's left hand. His motion should cause the arm to lock out and will generate tremendous tension on his wrist and elbow if done correctly.

In this sequence, Brinkman applies the same wristlock as in sequence 1. In this case, however, the attacker is positioned behind Brinkman (1). Brinkman shoots his arm through to block an incoming strike, then takes advantage of this arm placement to control the attacker's left arm (2-3). This position puts much greater tension on the attacker's wrist. Brinkman easily throws the attacker over his hip by twisting the attacker's wrist clockwise (4-5).

MARTIAL ARTS

If your opponent struggles, you may have to widen your stance and pull your opponent toward you. This will force his seized hand toward the ground.

Heady Technique

You can also apply chin na while being subdued in a headlock. Assume the attacker grabs your neck from behind with his right arm. In that case, the attacker can easily strike you with his free hand. You can avoid the strike by shooting your arm up toward the attacker's face, providing the option of stunning your opponent with an elbow strike to the chin or neck. Seizing the opponent's left hand or wrist will drive him to the ground. You may also be able to throw your opponent over your hip (**as seen in sequence 3**). Remember: unless there is sufficient tension in the wrist, your opponent will have no trouble resisting. Practice these techniques slowly and carefully; if these techniques are executed too forcefully, damage to the wrist is possible. Also, keep in mind that every chin na technique should be practiced from both sides.

Strength Training for Chin Na

You don't need a gym full of expensive exercise equipment to become more proficient in chin na. Simply incorporate strength and accuracy drills into your regular training regimen.

Strength training for hands: Begin by squeezing a tennis ball with your fingertips and then with the hand. Switching between the two exercises will give you greater seizing power by increasing your hand strength. As a plus, these exercises will also benefit forearm strength.

Strength training for wrists: High repetition and diversity of exercise technique is the most beneficial approach to strengthening the wrists. Alternating hand positions while performing push-ups will increase flexibility in your wrists and inevitably improve their strength. This can be accomplished by resting your body weight on the backs of your hands and doing as many push-ups as possible. Another great chin na exercise is the tiger claw push-up, which are push-ups on the tips of your fingers. Making these exercises part of your daily training program will improve seizing power and make your hands and wrists more powerful.

Training for Accuracy

Next to strength training, accuracy and proper hand placement are the most important aspects in chin na. A straight punch to the face can be deflected and countered with a lunging eagle claw to the throat. This simple, yet potentially dangerous technique requires both accuracy and hand strength. One way to improve strength and accuracy as it applies to eagle claw grasping is with a common red masonry brick. First, grab the brick with your thumb and fingertips. Now flip the brick into the air by snapping your wrist and grab it before it hits the ground with your fingertips. Imagine an eagle using its talons to snatch a fish from the water. As your accuracy and strength improves, move on to larger objects with greater weight.

As with any martial arts concept, chin na requires hours of practice and plenty of patience. The basic seize-and-control concepts illustrated in this article will increase your confidence and improve your self-defense skill. A chin na practitioner can defend himself and avoid serious injury by learning to adhere, seize and control his opponent. Once accomplished, you have truly mastered the art of fighting without fighting.

Brian M. Brinkman is a 3rd-level black sash/head teacher and founder of the House of KungFu in Olympia, Washington. He can be reached at www.houseofkungfu.org

MARTIAL ARTS

Planting the Seeds of Hung Gar

Lam Chun Fai's tour of the United States re-established his family's hung gar roots.

Donald Hamby

My visit to Hong Kong last year was such a rewarding experience I wondered how enlightening it would be if the American hung gar practitioners could experience a rare opportunity to train under the watchful eye of Lam Chun Fai, current grandmaster of the Lam Family kung-fu system.

Even though grandmaster Lam Chun Fai has visited the United States several times and has held seminars all over the world, this was the first time a member of the Lam family offered a seminar in the United States.

> "Expression and intent play a major role in one's performance. Each animal has its own characteristic—there are sporadic sounds that resonate to express the power and nature of each animal."

Seminar Tour

Master Lam Chun Fai's itinerary took him first to Bellingham, Wash., then to Oakland, Calif., where two of his disciples, George Kikes and Ben Hunter, received him respectfully, and finally to Boston, Mass., to the Calvin Chan Hung Gar Kung Fu Academy. Chun Fai tantalized the audience with a combination of the tiger crane (fu hok shong yin) and gung gi fu hu that left them yearning for more. Expression and intent play a major role in one's performance. Each animal has its own characteristic—there are sporadic sounds that resonate to express the power and nature of each animal.

Master Chun Fai is a master performer whose tour was both successful and rewarding. Chun Fai was pleased to see that hung kuen has such a large family with schools throughout the world. The seed that was planted in the 1600s in the heart and mind of master Hung Hai Gung, founder of hung kuen, by his master, monk Gee Sin, truly demonstrates that he was the master planter.

According to an old saying, you can tell the tree by the fruit it bears. The fruit of grandmaster Lam Cho consists of five sons and two loving daughters, all of whom were imbued with the tradition and the rich legacy of Lam Sai Wing Hung Family tiger and crane kung-fu. Chun Fai is the eld-

est and began his training at five under the guidance of his father. His training regimen consisted of running for 15-to-20 minutes prior to each kung-fu practice session. After running, his father would train him in the kung-fu forms. This daily training regimen continued for many years because his father did not want him to be idle.

According to Chun Fai, "My father was very strict. The forms had to be played correctly; every little minute point was critical to him." Chun Fai said his father could look at a form being performed one time and copy it. "He was a genius," he explained.

Chun Fai attended kung-fu demonstrations with his father, where he was required to observe a person's performance and tell him of his weak points. "If my observations were correct, he would okay them, if not he would explain them to me," Chun Fai noted.

Chun Fai began teaching when he was 18 and opened his own kung-fu school and dit dar (bone-setting) clinic in North Point, Hong Kong. He also helped teach his brothers and sister. He believes the main benefits of kung-fu training are improving one's health—both mentally and physically—confidence, self-defense, and the courage to stand up against one's enemy.

From the on-guard position (1), the attacker goes after grandmaster Lam Chun Fai with a right punch to the midsection (2) and a left roundhouse to the head (3). Lam Chun Fai defends with a chopping right-hand block and an upper tiger claw block (4), then attacks the chest with a left knifehand (5).

From a ready stance (1), the attacker leads with a left mid-section punch (2) and a right roundhouse punch to the head (3). The grandmaster counters with a right cutting hand block and a left forearm block. He then presses downward to break his attacker's arm with a water-casting hand technique by swinging upward (4). The form that corresponds to this technique is shown below.

Chun Fai also made reference to a phenomenon called "gang," which is an inner power developed through a long period of practice (i.e., punching and kicking associated with the use of the hips, waist, shoulder action, and mental focus).

From a young age, master Chun Fai has been active in representing the Lam family's hung gar tradition. He has appeared on Hong Kong television on many occasions and is so highly revered for his skill and knowledge of the hung gar system that teachers and practitioners from all over the world have sought his advice.

From all the hung gar masters around the world, the honor of unveiling the statue of the legendary master Wong Fei Hung during the opening ceremonies of the Wong Fei Hung Museum in China was bestowed upon master Lam Chun Fai. Housed in the Museum is a repository of information depicting the life of Wong Fei

From a ready stance (1), the attacker opens with a strong right reverse punch (2). The grandmaster counters with a tiger claw grab and finishes with a powerful right sidekick to the midsection (3).

From an on-guard stance (1), the attacker leads with a right front kick to the groin. Lam Chun Fai uses a left scissors stance and right forearm block to stop the rush (2). He then steps forward to lift and throw (3).

Hung and his most-prominent student, Lam Sai Wing. The Museum also has on display information about the great Lam Cho and the reigning grandmaster, Lam Chun Fai.

Because of the love and respect he has for his father, as well as the physical dexterity and mental fortitude required to endure the training, Lam Chun Fai now sits on the right hand of his father. The virtues needed to be grandmaster—righteousness, justice, fairness, love of humanity, respect for life and perpetuation of family tradition—are building blocks that help establish the foundation of a true martial artist.

Chun Fai can truly be proud of a tradition that dates back to the Shaolin Temple. He hails from the following line of great masters: Wong Ki Yin, the father of Wong Fei Hung, who was the teacher of Lam Sai Wing, who was the uncle of Lam Cho, and who is the father of Lam Chun Fai.

You can contact Lam Chun Fai at www.hungkuen.com/

Gut-Wrenching Plyometrics

Better Speed, Power and Strength Mean Better Kumite, Kata and Kicking

Doug Jeffrey

Are you an ordinary Joe? You know ... the type of guy who can kinda jump. (When you were playing in that pick-up basketball game, you drilled that jump shot over that 10-year-old kid). You know ... the type of guy who can sorta shuffle his feet. (Remember when that bee swooped toward you while you were leaving the grocery store? Like Muhammad Ali in his prime, you smoothly shifted out of the way ... and knocked the grocery bag right out of that woman's arms).

You know ... the type of guy who has got his fair share of speed. (You left your car in a no-parking zone for just a moment while you ran over to the ATM. When you noticed the black and white parked right behind your SUV, you motored over there ... just in time for the cop to personally hand you a ticket).

If you're tired of being an ordinary Joe, it's time to undergo a transformation. How'd you like to become a superhero? A superstar? Superman? If so, step into the phone booth.

NO ORDINARY JOE

There's one and only way for this to happen. And that's the following plyometric drills. These exercises will make you so good that you'll forget what it's like to be ordinary.

"When I first started in the martial arts, I had no jumping ability or coordination," says Roland Osborne, the 25-year-old owner of Red Dragon Karate of Covina, California. "I was just an average kid."

Now he is anything but average. He flies through the air like an actor on a wires and jumps like he bounced his 165-pound frame off a trampoline.

"These plyometrics have enabled me to do all the advanced techniques that I can now do, such as the hardest kicks you'll see on the tournament circuit to a back flip gainer kick," says Osborne, who was rated No. 1 on the West Coast in forms, weapons and sparring from 1992-1996. "These drills will enable you to excel to any level you want."

Of course, you won't get one inch off the ground without good, old-fashioned determination.

Remember, these babies aren't easy. Mustering up a little determination shouldn't be a problem for any of you guys, though. Like most martial artists, you've not afraid of hard work or challenges.

WHAT TO EXPECT

If you've never done anything like this, you're in for quite an experience. To prepare you for what it's like, close your eyes momentarily and imagine …

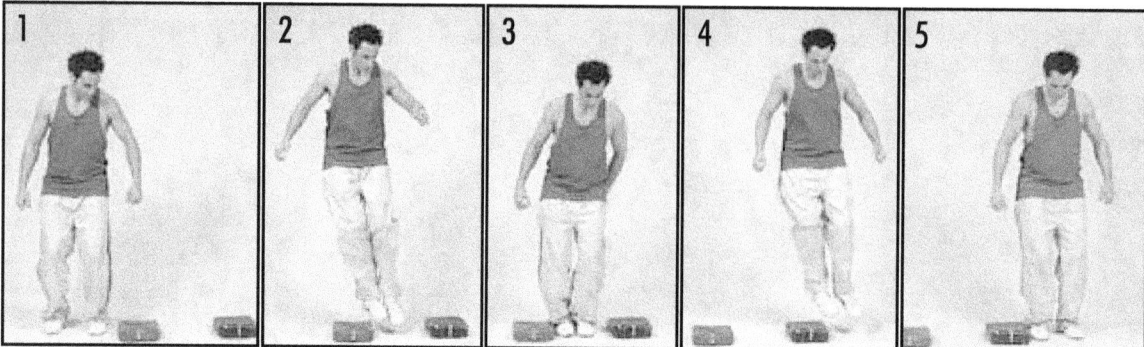
Double Pad Jump

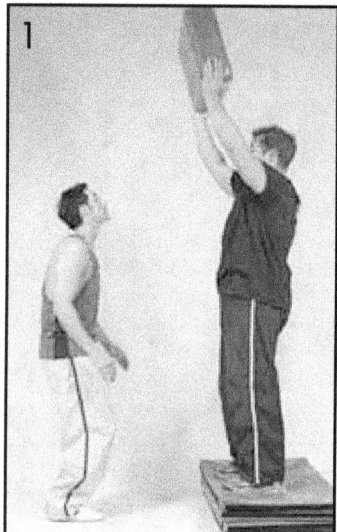

RIM JUMP

You've waded into the salty, blue ocean and a large wave has just clobbered you. Just as you figure out which way is up, you get drilled again. And then again. You frantically open your eyes, hoping to figure out which way is up so you can scratch through the murky, brown water to the surface. You're tumbling helplessly through the water when you finally burst through to the light. You stand up, gasping for breath and walking like a drunk, hoping you can make it to shore before Mother Ocean strikes again.

Got the idea? Good. Now you know how you'll feel after doing plyos for the first time.

"[Regardless of what type of shape you're in], you're going to feel tired and out of shape," says Osborne. "These are difficult. You have to have the mental strength to push through them."

Now, let's imagine something a little more pleasant. Pretend like you just won an Olympic gold medal. You're on the victory stand, the national anthem roars over the public address system and you start to cry. Eight years of incredibly hard work just paid off. Imagine the feeling.

Got the idea? Good. Now you know how you'll feel after you do plyos for awhile and you notice your speed, jumping ability and coordination improve.

"These will turn you into a complete athlete," says Osborne, adding that he's been doing them for about six years.

MARTIAL ART BENEFITS

Not only are these drills going to improve your speed, jumping ability and coordination, they will help you in all facets of your martial arts training. Let's start with sparring.

First, you'll move more efficiently ... in all directions.

"When you move forward, you'll have more speed going into the pocket when you try to score or hit your opponent," he says. "You will also be faster on the way out."

Balance is the next benefit. Whether you're kicking or moving or doing forms or doing weapons, balance is critical. Plyometrics will enhance this critical skill, he says.

Kicking power and speed are next. A regular routine of plyometrics will enable you to kick faster, jump higher and give you more explosiveness. On your jump kicks, you'll get back to your stance faster.

"You will excel," says Osborne. "You will spin faster and kick a lot higher. And that means more excitement."

SPECS

These are hard-core, gut-wrenching, sweat-flowing, you-wish-you-were-done exercises. They are definitely exciting, but they definitely aren't easy. They are demanding on your body. So, start by doing them twice per week. If you're really dedicated and determined to improve quickly, try three times per week. Whatever you do, make sure you leave a day of rest between plyo workouts. Your body needs time to recover. And, of course, warm up before you begin.

THE WORKOUT

Exercise: Run Up

Benefit: This will increase your front kick chamber speed.

How To Do It: Place a mat on the ground. You're going to step onto the mat as quickly as possible, step off and repeat.

Duration: A set is one to three minutes. Beginners should do three sets of 25, intermediate should do three sets of 40 and advanced athletes should do three sets of 50.

Notes: Keep your legs in tight and concentrate

Squat Jump Front Kick

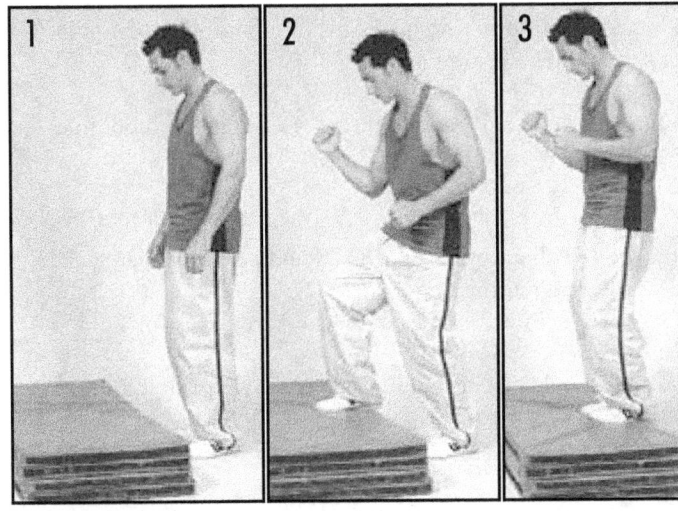

Run Up

Safety, Performance Tips

- When performing these exercises, think of the floor as hot coals and immediately jump as soon as your feet touch the ground.
- Elevated surfaces give your body increased downward momentum, increasing the stress to your leg. It will take more energy and strength to stop this momentum, reverse it and jump back up.
- When jumping down, be sure to use your muscle strength to stop your momentum — not your knee joints. This will reduce the likelihood of injuries.
- Don't use ankle weights while doing plyometrics because they can increase the chances of an injury.
- Older athletes should use discretion in the drills they choose to do.

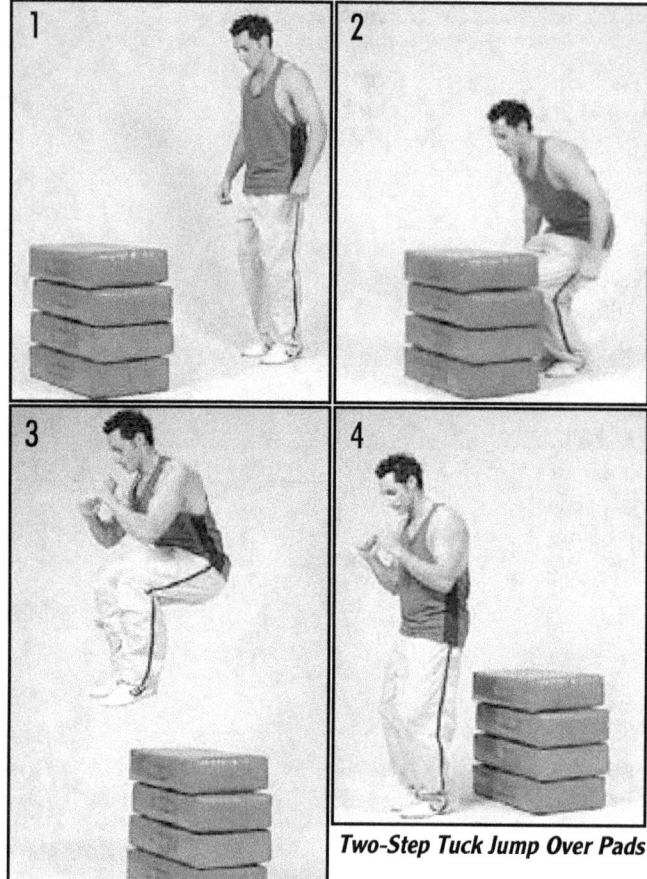
Two-Step Tuck Jump Over Pads

on lifting your knees quickly and straight up.

Exercise: Low Squat Jump
How To Do It: Squat in front of a mat, jump onto the pat, jump off and immediately jump back on.
Duration: Beginners should do three sets of 15, intermediate should do three sets of 25 and advanced athletes should do three sets of 35.

Exercise: Elevated Side Jump
Benefit: This will improve your side-to-side speed.
How To Do It: Stand perpendicular to a mat. Jump onto the mat, quickly jump off, land, jump back on, jump off to the other side, land, jump back on and repeat.
Duration: Beginners should do three sets of 20, intermediate should do three sets of 30 and advanced athletes should do three sets of 40.
Notes: Explode quickly from side to side.

Exercise: 30-45-60 Second Drill
How To Do It: Stand perpendicular to a mat. Jump onto the mat, quickly jump off to the other side, jump back on, jump off to the other side and repeat.
Duration: Do this for 30 seconds.
Notes: Your goal is to land on the pad 30 times in 30 seconds, 45 times in 45 seconds and 60 times in 60 seconds.

Exercise: Double Pad Jump
How To Do It: Place a pair of pads on the ground about one foot apart. Stand perpendicular to the pads, jump into the middle, jump to the far side and return.
Duration: Beginners should do three sets of 15, intermediates should do three sets of 25 and advanced practitioners should do three sets of 40.
Notes: Do this as quickly as possible. The pads should not be that high, so try to keep a fast line and level jump.

Exercise: Squat Split Jump
How To Do It: Place a pair of mats on the ground about two feet apart. Squat in the middle, jump,

spread your legs and land on the mats. Immediately drop down and repeat.

Duration: Beginners should do three sets of 15, intermediates should do three sets of 25 and advanced practitioners should do three sets of 35.

Exercise: Two-Step Tuck Jump Over Pads

How To Do It: Place four kicking shields on the ground. Stand about three feet from the shields. Accelerate forward with one leg, bring your back leg forward to meet the front and jump. Tuck your knees to your chest and land on the opposite side. Turn around and repeat rapidly.

Duration: Beginners should do three sets of 7, intermediates should do three sets of 12 and advanced practitioners should do three sets of 20.

Notes: Using the pads will give you measurable height to use for setting goals and seeing results. The pads also force you to lift your legs higher.

Exercise: Rim Jump

How To Do It: Have your partner stand on some mats and hold a kicking shield above his head. You should stand about two feet away from your partner. Bend your knees slightly, jump up, slap the pad, land and repeat.

Duration: Beginners should do three sets of 30, intermediates should do three sets of 40 and advanced practitioners should do three sets of 50.

Notes: When you jump up, concentrate on pushing your toes down and using your calf muscles. As your legs become stronger, you will be able to jump faster and higher.

Exercise: Squat Jump Front Kick

How To Do It: Have your partner stand on a mat and hold a focus mitt straight out. You are going to squat about two feet away from the mat, jump and throw a front kick at the target. Land and repeat as quickly as possible.

Duration: Beginners should do three sets of 10, intermediates should do three sets of 15 and advanced practitioners should do three sets of 20.

Notes: When you jump up, concentrate on pushing your toes down and using your calf muscles. As your legs become stronger, you will be able to jump faster and higher.

Exercise: Power Squat Jump

How To Do It: Stack several mats on the ground. Squat in front of the mats. If you like, you can support yourself on the mats. Explode up as quickly as possible, straighten your legs and try to land on the mats with your knees slightly bent. Hop down, rest one second and explode back up.

Duration: Beginners should do three sets of 12, intermediates should do three sets of 15 and advanced practitioners should do three sets of 20.

Notes: As your power increases, elevate the surface higher and higher.

> ### Did You Know?
> Your plyometric workout should consist of 10 to 15 minutes of warm up and stretching and 20 to 30 minutes of exercise.
>
> Plyometric exercises are anaerobic; therefore, you will need more time for the muscles to recover between sets. Experts recommend a 1-5 to 1-10 rest ratio. Thus, for every second performing an exercise, you should allow five to 10 seconds of rest. If a drill takes 30 seconds, you should rest at least 150 seconds.
>
> ### Seminar Info
> If you'd like to contact Roland Osborne for a seminar, call (626) 339-8885 or reach him through e-mail at **rddrgn55@aol.com**.

MARTIAL ARTS

Vision-Airy

The great Andy Cheng gladly puts his life on the line every day so moviegoers can go away satisfied.

David Tadman

A member in good standing (and flying) of the infamous Jackie Chan Stunt Team, Andy Cheng has spent a lifetime proving that movie action is only limited by the imagination of the choreographer. Cheng's stunts are equal parts daredevil and visionary, which is no surprise considering the man he's worked for and with has been pushing the envelope of martial arts movie action for almost three decades.

Trained in tae kwon do, wushu and Chinese weapons, Andy has parlayed his traditional training into a movie art he now calls "Hollywood-do."

"Whatever the scene requires I will adapt my skill accordingly," he explains. Adapt he has done, moving and jumping and twisting in some of the most-popular martial arts movies ever made. Here is his story.

INSIDE KUNG-FU: Tell us your martial arts background.
ANDY CHENG: My background originates from tae kwon do. I represented Hong Kong in an Olympic-style competition. I was a four-year champion in Hong Kong. I have also trained in wushu, judo and karate. I use most of these arts in films that I do. In fact, I call it "Hollywood-do." Whatever the scene requires I will adapt my skill accordingly.

IKF: Describe your typical daily workout.
AC: I do gymnastics, stretching and a lot of cardiovascular exercises like running, rope jumping and basic martial arts movements.

IKF: How did you get into stuntwork?
AC: When I was in Hong Kong, there was a television promotion that was advertising for martial artists/ actors for work in films and television. I sent my demo reel in and because of my popularity in Hong Kong with my championships in tae kwon do, etc., I got the job. I started training with the company. For months I trained in wushu and Chinese weapons. I also had to learn wire works, because in

Andy Cheng hangs from wires in Rush Hour 2.

Photos courtesy of Andy Cheng

Hong Kong there are a lot of wires used in films. I mostly did small acting parts backed up with a lot of stuntwork.

IKF: While growing up in Hong Kong, did you have a favorite martial arts star?

AC: I would have to say that Jackie Chan was my favorite martial arts star. Others like Bruce Lee were great but something about Jackie made me like him the best. His comedy and movements mixed with great creativity had me hooked.

IKF: As a child growing up in Asia, did you aspire to be involved with films doing martial arts action?

AC: No, not really. It was when I grew older and trained in tae kwon do that I got interested in that type of thing. I can remember going to the movies and seeing Jackie Chan in Police Story and thinking to myself that this is something I want to do. Jackie is amazing and I was attracted to that. For me, Jackie Chan was a hero and I wanted to be like that.

IKF: It is well-known that you are one of the most sought after martial arts stuntman in the world. What does this mean to you on a personal level?

AC: Of course, I feel flattered and appreciated. I have to thank Jackie Chan for the exposure in films like *Rush Hour* and I worked with great people like Sammo Hung on "Martial Law" as well. I feel very fortunate that I have had a chance to work with some great people that furthered my reputation as being one of the top stuntmen in the business.

IKF: Can you tell us some of the films you've been in?

AC: I have done a lot of films in Hong Kong that people would not recognize here, but the most popular ones are, *Rush Hour 1* and *2*. I worked on *Charlie's Angels, Wild, Wild West, Shanghai Noon* and recently I've worked on *Scorpion King*. I have worked on countless other films as well and have also worked seven years in Hong Kong in television doing stunts including wires and some acting.

IKF: Do you have a personal favorite?

AC: I would have to say all of them. No matter what project I do, I try to put my heart and soul into it. I have something special I take with me from all the films I do.

IKF: Do you have any film projects coming out in the near future?

AC: Well, I have *Scorpion King* coming out and then there is *Tuxedo* with Jackie Chan. I trained the actors for this project.

IKF: If you were to do your own film, what would it be?

AC: Well, I would do a film that is action-oriented that follows the same type recipe that Jackie Chan's films have, but I would use my own flavor so to speak. I would also love to do an emotionally touching story someday. When I see a film that makes me sad and moves me, then I know there was something special that happened that included me, even if it was just for a few moments. It is very important to include the individual who is sitting in the theater. He or she needs to be touched or your work was not worth doing.

IKF: What do you try to get across to the audience?

AC: I want the audience to appreciate the pain and sweat that goes into a stunt. Stuntmen risk their lives to entertain the audience. I love what I do and it makes me proud when I execute a dangerous stunt or martial arts move on film and the crowd goes wild with excitement. That shows me that the audience has an appreciation for the actor on screen. There is nothing more satisfying than that.

IKF: Have you experienced any injuries or close calls while filming?

AC: Well, when I was in Hong Kong filming *Rush Hour 2* I had a scene in which I was fighting and I fly off the back of a yacht. I did the stunt and went into the water. The next thing that happened was the most frightful experience of my

Profile
Name: Andy Cheng
Birthplace: Hong Kong
Hometown: Los Angeles
Birthdate: Dec. 23, 1966
Siblings: 3 sisters (he is the oldest)
Started Martial Arts: At age 14
Arts Studied: Tae kwon do
Belt Level: Black in 1984; also trained in Hollywood-do or movie-do
Current Work: Untitled martial arts television pilot for ABC-TV
Outside Loves: Plays golf, has started to snowboard
Career Goals: "I want to direct a SAG movie, one which makes people laugh and cry. I have done too much action; I'd like something different."
Facts: Did six Jackie Chan movies, including *Rush Hour 2*. Also trained Jennifer Love-Hewitt in *Tuxedo* and performed location scouting.
10 Years From Now: "If I'm lucky I'll be a rich man and will be directing a movie. I also want to be able to pick my projects. But that's too long. In 10 years I'd like to be retired.
Contact: andykccheng@aol.com

life. I was sucked under the boat and the water was like a whirlpool that kept me going around and around under the boat. I was stuck there for what felt to be a lifetime. I was swallowing water and I hit my head under the boat. I kept thinking to myself that I hope I don't go into the propeller. I tried, but could not get out from under the boat. After what seemed like an eternity this hand reached down and pulled me up. That hand was Jackie Chan's. At that time there were many people in the water looking for me in the wrong places and Jackie saw part of my jacket. He pulled me up with the help of others. I will never forget that. He saved me.

IKF: What's the funniest thing you have experienced while filming?

AC: What's funny to me is that I go around the world and I don't have to pay a dime. It is all paid for and the only time I spend my own money is when I buy little things for my family and myself. I am very fortunate for that, but it is humorous at the same time.

IKF: What is your favorite action film?

At top, Andy choreographs a fight with fellow actors on the set of U.S. Seals 2. Above, Cheng in the early '90s shows his high-kicking tae kwon do form. At left, after a hard workout, Nicky Li, left, Andy Cheng and Jackie Chan find time to relax.

MARTIAL ARTS

AC: I would have to say that *Drunken Master II* is my favorite. I was working in Hong Kong at that time on a television show and I was truly upset that I did not get a chance to work on that film. That film had all the elements and to this day is my favorite.

IKF: In the last five years, Hong Kong action cinema has become mainstream here in America. Do you feel it is more difficult to express yourself on film to the American audience compared to the Asian audience?

AC: I feel that the American audience is open to new things and Hong Kong action cinema is one of those things. For people in Hong Kong, films have always been packed with martial arts and action. It is daily life there. Sometimes here in America, the audience does not believe some of the Hong Kong stunts, like flying through the air or flipping and spinning while fighting. I say, "What about Superman or Batman? They are doing the same thing. The cultures are different but there is always a common ground. The American audience is open and very accepting; this is a good thing for all Asian actors.

IKF: Do you feel that the American audience expects more or less than the Asian audience?

AC: I feel lately that the American audience is crazy for more Hong Kong action. The doors here in America are pretty much open for action cinema. This is also good for many stuntmen in Hong Kong, because they have the chance to come here and work. There are many talented people there that want to entertain America.

Above, Andy Cheng choreographing on the set of Scorpion King. *At right, hanging from wires in* Rush Hour 2. *Below, Andy poses with four-time Olympic gold-medal gymnast, Li Ning, in the television show* Shaolin Temple, *which was filmed in Hong Kong in the early 1990s.*

IKF: Do you feel that the stuntmen from Hong Kong are restricted in what they can do on film here in America?

AC: Here in America you have a union that oversees the safety and rules for the stuntmen. In Hong Kong, a lot of the rules that apply here do not apply there. You can say that you are judged a lot on your word in Hong Kong. If you say you can do something, then you better do it or you won't work again. Here in America, there are many rules to follow. There are many issues about safety here and that is a good thing. You have a lot of freedom to do certain things in Hong Kong that you can't do here and that is also a good thing. I feel that Hong Kong and America complement each other.

IKF: Do you feel that today's Hong Kong stuntmen have evolved from the days of making *Enter the Dragon*?

AC: Yes. I feel a lot of the stuntmen from the past looked at stuntwork in films as a job for money to survive. Today, I feel stuntmen in Hong Kong look at it as a career. The training is different now and more intense. You can say there is more of a structure to follow now, and the young stuntmen of Hong Kong are in better shape, keeping up on all the new health-conscious ideas, as opposed to the past, where a lot of the Hong Kong stuntmen partied too much or gambled a lot. We seem to be more focused now and have taken control of our own path, so to speak.

IKF: It is well-known that you are one of the key stuntmen on the Jackie Chan Stunt Team. What does it take to be considered for such a prestigious spot?

AC: First, I have to say that Jackie Chan is a very smart man. He also is a charming man and he knows a lot about people. I started to work with Jackie slowly. He used me here and there and slowly we built up the trust that was needed to take it a step further. I am very lucky that Jackie picked me to be part of his team. He meets many people that have great talent, but he is always cautious about who he lets in. He has a lot on the line, so he picks the people he can trust and knows they will go the extra mile for him. It's like a family that eats together and lives together; there is a relationship there and that is very important to him. I am truly lucky and grateful for all he has done for me.

IKF: Do you feel that the Hong Kong stuntmen have a code or certain philosophy they follow?

AC: Yes, Asian stuntmen believe in friendship and trust. We take care of each other and look out for one another. When doing stunts in Hong Kong we always look out for each other to make sure we are safe. That takes a lot of trust. I believe this to be true here in America, but the difference in Hong Kong is, it's much smaller, so the circle is not that big and everybody knows each other. Therefore, trust and looking out for one another is a matter of survival in the industry there.

IKF: How do you feel about the job you do?

AC: I have been injured many times in my career, but I keep pushing myself to do bigger and better stunts that will entertain people. I hope people will understand the work that goes into what we do. Blood, sweat and tears are part of a stuntman's make-up. To entertain is to share part of yourself with others, and if one person walks away from seeing one of my films and says excitedly, "Wow, how did he do that?" then, it is all worth it to me.

David Tadman is a frequent contributor to Inside Kung-Fu.

Shin Lin, Warrior-Scholar for the 21st Century

Shin Lin is trying to change the way the world views martial arts.

Ric Meyers

"Take two kung-fu classes and call me in the morning." Think it's impossible for doctors to ever say that? Not if Shin Lin, associate vice chancellor for Biomedical Initiatives at the University of California (UC), Irvine, can help it. He has spent the last 40 years preparing to do what some people have said was impossible: scientifically prove the health benefits of kung-fu and qigong.

And he's just the man to do it, too. Rarely has an individual been so prepared to accomplish his life's work. The concept of the warrior-scholar goes back hundreds, if not thousands, of years, but it's hard to imagine even the greatest of history's warrior-scholars matching the combination of ancient martial arts and modern science the way Shin Lin has. His training in each is equally impressive.

An Early Start

Starting as a teenager in Hong Kong, he trained with grandmaster Chan Hak Fu at his White Crane Kung Fu Institute and became a senior student of sifu Lin Shu Fan of the Tai Shing Pek Kwar School of Kung Fu. After immigrating to the U.S. with his family at age 16, he received his bachelor's in chemistry from the University of California at Davis, his master's in chemistry from San Diego State University, and his Ph.D. in biological chemistry from UCLA.

But coming to America did not end his kung-fu education. Not by a long shot (or punch or kick). In America, he trained extensively with sifu John Clayton and had advance lessons with grandmaster William Cheung at the World Wing Chun Kung Fu Association. Meanwhile, after three years of post-doctoral training in the Department of Biochemistry & Biophysics at the University of California at San Francisco, he was appointed a professor of Biophysics at The Johns Hopkins University in 1974.

Not only is this just scratching the surface of his accomplishments in both science and kung-fu,

it merely sets the stage for what he is doing now. Incredibly, it all started with a single book and a single Chinese boxing bout.

"I was born in Hong Kong, and, like many teenagers I used to read a lot of Chinese kung-fu novels," Lin relates. "Most people stop at that, but I went beyond.

"There was a very famous kung-fu novel by the premier novelist Jin Yong. Loosely translated, it's *The Story of the Book and Sword*. The main hero is very unusual: he's a young kung-fu expert who is also an excellent Chinese scholar. Very early on, a grandmaster trained him in a unique style of kung-fu synthesized from many different schools. Ever since then, that has been a direction of my life: to be a top scholar in the scientific world—writing papers, publishing, teaching, holding high positions at universities—while learning many different types of kung-fu from many different teachers."

A Fight for the Ages

For Lin, the pen is truly mightier than the sword. But it may not be as mighty as tai chi and white crane.

"I first started to learn kung-fu when I was about 14," he explains. "Because, back in the mid-1950s, there was this famous duel between a tai chi master, Wu Kung Yee and a white crane master, Chan Hak Fu. They signed documents relieving the other of responsibility if anyone got killed. Hong Kong wouldn't allow the match, so it was held in Macau.

"It was a defining moment for kung-fu in the Far East. In the end, it was a draw. That really got me to become serious as a martial arts student. But as a 14-year-old I didn't want to get into tai chi. That seemed like a sissy thing to do. So I went to the white crane master and started training with him. From that point on I started to get more and more interested in different things and wherever I went I learned different styles."

He trained in the wing chun butterfly (bak jarm dao) knives and dragon staff; the pek kwar broadsword, straight sword, and spear; the shaolin jill jow (9-provinces) staff; the bagua jui fung (chase wind) double broadswords; the Chen Family iron fan, iron flute, liu hur (6-combination weapon) umbrella; tsi moo (son-mother) butterfly swords, nunchaku, 3-section staff, and sai; and sash/belt fighting techniques. Everywhere he went, his mind was seemingly insatiable—not just for martial arts but also for science.

"I got my Ph.D., then a professorship at a top university, served on national panels, and established a com-

Dr. Shin Lin performs Chen family iron fan and silver flute at his home in Baltimore.

Train With Shin Lin
You can personally train with Dr. Lin in China. He will be participating in "The Heart & Mind of Martial Arts" tour in China Sept. 12-21. For more information, call (203) 348-2356 or smgemail@aol.com

pletely separate career," Lin says. "The reason you may never have heard of me is that many other people know me as a leading expert on biological drugs that affect cellular movement in normal and cancer cells. As a hobby, at least until four years ago, I used scientific principles, like principles of biophysics, to try to understand the strength and weaknesses of each kung-fu style. There's no such thing as the best style, otherwise the whole world would be learning that. So every style has different advantages and disadvantages, and I tried to analyze this in terms of biophysics and the human physiology of the different styles. Luckily that has now become part of my profession. I'm doing research and using scientific principles to explain a lot of these things."

Kung-Fu Goes to School

That all started more than a decade ago, when he was Chairman of the Biophysics Department, a position he held for more than a dozen years. "When I was at Johns Hopkins I had less responsibilities than I do now," Lin explains, "so I started a kung-fu club and taught my students the scientific basis as well as the moves themselves. Then I turned 40, and I had a reawakening of sorts. Because of my academic work, I had to go to Taiwan repeatedly for weeks and months at a time.

"There I met a sifu who said, 'You know, you are getting into your middle age. And all this training in the hard styles are not going to be good for you anymore. As a professor you're never going to get into the ring and fight for championships. What is more important is your health.' So I started to really get into the soft, internal styles: tai chi, bagua, hsing-I, and qigong. I'm not going impress people with the size of my biceps, I have to impress myself with how healthy I am."

> "Oh, I don't think of myself as a warrior-scholar. Just as a nerdy professor who really knows how to fight."

By the early 1990s, Lin had attained the highest degree black sash from the Chinese Martial Arts Training Center in Taiwan; was named honorary president of Tai Sing Pap Kar Martial Arts Association in Hong Kong; and was awarded a ninth-level gold sash at the Wing Chun Academy of Maryland. Meanwhile he was lecturing worldwide, doing scientific research, serving on national advisory boards, publishing in scholarly journals, and helping found the Krieger Mind/Brain Institute, the Institute for Biophysical Research on Macromolecular Assemblies, the Cardiovascular Mechanics Research Center, and the Intercampus Graduate Program in Molecular Biophysics at The Johns Hopkins University.

It seemed as if Lin would continue to train in martial arts while serving as Associate Dean of Research and Graduate Studies for Johns Hopkins' School of Arts and Sciences until retirement. But in 1997, it all changed again. It was then that he was recruited to be the Dean of the School of Biological Sciences at UC Irvine.

"I feel for the next ten years, Irvine is going to be the place for some real unique opportunities," Shin Lin maintains. "I say that for two reasons. One, the University really believes in Oriental medicine while a lot of other medical schools 'poo-poo' this kind of thing or just give it nominal lip service. But here, Oriental medicine is fully accepted and promoted. In fact, we have a multimillion dollar Susan Samumeli Center for Complementary and Alternative Medicine. More importantly, there is a whole cast of characters here, professors who are on the cutting edge of different types of technology, which are quite applicable for studying qigong. They are all interested in what I want to do and so I was able to organize them into a team. In terms of collaborative studies on the science of qigong and soft style kung-fu such as tai chi, this is the perfect place."

Progressive Approach

In January 2000, the "perfect place" got even better when Lin was named Associate Vice Chancellor for Biomedical Initiatives.

"Here at UC Irvine our College of Medicine is very progressive. They want to promote complementary and alternative medicine, which gets into qigong, acupuncture, pressure point massage, herbal drugs and those sorts of things. So it gives me a legitimacy to combine my two careers. As a scientist and professor I'm teaching and doing research on qigong and tai chi.

"I have also been formally educating myself in Chinese Medicine," he adds. "I've now completed medical school courses in Oriental Medicine, in Manipulative Therapies, and I'm in the midst of finishing up a course on dietary supplements and herbal drugs. For the past several years I've also been studying the scientific literature on qigong research and visiting the top research places in China, Hong Kong, and Taiwan."

So what started in his 40s with training in southern sung tai tsu emperor qigong/kung-fu with master Chan Shui Tsai at the Chinese Martial Arts Training Center in Taiwan, and in sum yi qigong with master Yew Ching Wong of the Y.C. Wong Kung Fu Studio in San Francisco, continues into his 50s and beyond as a member of the China-U.S. Wu-Dang Qigong Association in Los Angeles, doing advance training with master Zhou Ting-Jue.

"While I've continued to train in the hard styles, particularly wing chun, the soft styles, particularly tai chi and qigong, have become a passion," he understates. But rather than simply using his kung-fu for his personal balance, energy, and health, Lin has a greater goal.

"Now my interest is not so much studying the biophysics of the hard styles such as white crane and shaolin, but explaining the beneficial effects of qigong and tai chi in scientific terms. I'm shifting over more than half of my laboratory resources to it.

"People have obviously been studying qigong for years in Asia, so before I even started I visited a lot of the key places and established collaborative relationships, like with the Qigong Research Institute in Shanghai, which was not taken seriously in the United States because they don't publish their findings in English, they work out of a center dedicated to promoting qigong, and they have no previously established stature in the eyes of American scientists. So I see myself in a unique position, where my long-standing interest in the martial arts, fluency in Chinese, and international stature as a scientist could really help."

So "take two kung-fu classes and call me in the morning" doesn't sound so far-fetched anymore. What's even more impressive is that it could all happen sooner than you might think.

"It's quite simple," says Lin. "The five-year plan: make qigong training and therapy as acceptable as acupuncture in California. In California, acupuncture is covered by many insurance companies. That's a high standard. But I believe qigong can be viewed as acupuncture without needles. Recent studies at UC Irvine and elsewhere are suggesting that both tai chi and qigong involve activation of specific parts of the brain, which then send signals to regulate or heal different parts of the body.

"If we can provide biomedical evidence on how qigong, tai chi, etc., affect specific mind, brain, and body functions—using high-tech equipment not readily available anywhere else but here at UC Irvine—it would go a long way to convince private foundations and the government to provide funds for large-scale clinical studies on healthy people as well as those suffering from different diseases.

"But one thing I can assure you of: the whole next generation of doctors coming out of UC

MARTIAL ARTS

Dr. Shin Lin (above) assumes a tai chi style "low stance single whip" move in a bamboo forest in Central Taiwan. At right, Dr. Lin teaches students how to use a piece of hi-tech biomedical research equipment at Johns Hopkins University.

Irvine will know Chinese medicine, because we are incorporating this field into their medical school education."

And if anyone can do it, it is this truly remarkable warrior-scholar who, with every study, lecture, article, conference, committee, advisory board, guest lecture, scientific forum, and martial arts class is showing just what a human being can do.

"Oh, I don't think of myself as a warrior-scholar," Lin says, modestly. "Just as a nerdy professor who really knows how to fight."

For more detailed information on Shin Lin's accomplishments and future goals, see the following web sites: http://www.faculty.uci.edu/scripts/UCIFacultyProfiles/ BioSci/alphaprofile or http://www.jhu.edu/~jhumag/ 0997web/photo2.html

Ric Meyers is a former Inside Kung-Fu *"Writer of the Year."*

Strike First

The Offensive Assault of Kung-Fu San Soo

Bill Lasiter

You hate to do it, but you've got no choice. It's almost 11 p.m., and you've got to run over to the grocery store, which is just a mile or two from your home. You rush in, grab what you need, pay and head back to your car.

As you approach your shiny, new SUV, you glance up and notice three men badly beating a man in the back of the lot. They turn and see you.

"Hey, punk!"

Your heart races. Before you know it, they are on top of you. You drop the bag at your feet and...

a) Try to convince them that fighting is a bad idea?
b) Hope that they will run right past you?
c) Or, as my instructor used to say, "It's time to use yourself."

The answer, of course is C. In a circumstance like this, you've got no choice.

GO TO WAR

Offensive techniques. When do you use them?

Without a doubt, you should put them to work when you know for sure that the bad guys are going to try to hurt you first, especially when they make it obvious that they will do whatever it takes—including using weapons—to accomplish their goal.

Therefore, the first thing you need to do is stay calm and focused, so you can execute your techniques.

Second, try to make him feel that you are not ready to fight. Don't clinch your fists or puff up like some angry men

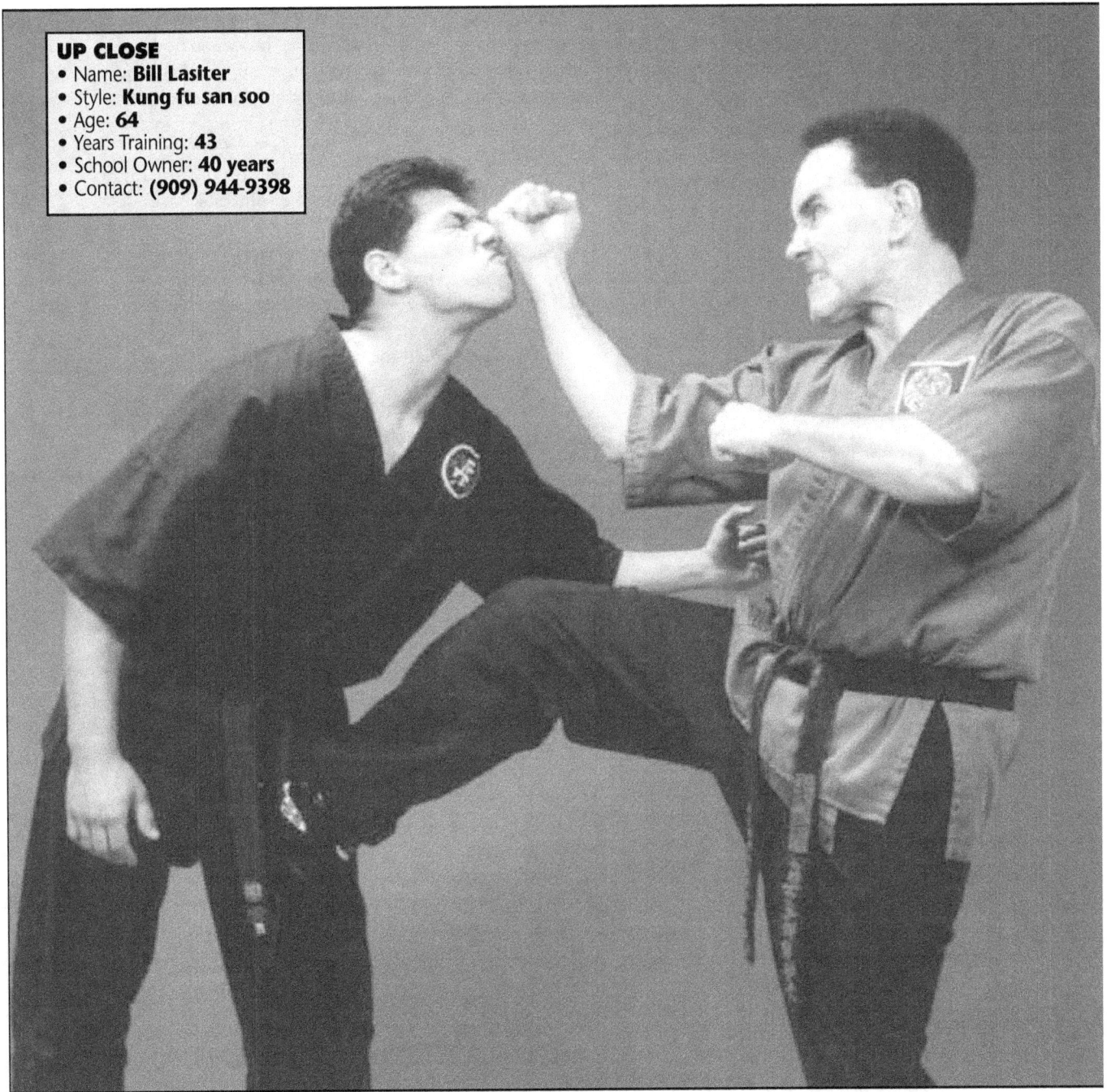

UP CLOSE
- Name: **Bill Lasiter**
- Style: **Kung fu san soo**
- Age: **64**
- Years Training: **43**
- School Owner: **40 years**
- Contact: **(909) 944-9398**

do. These are tip-offs to them that they are in a battle, and this will enable them to prepare themselves for your attack.

To deceive your opponents and distract them, shift from one foot to the other. Move your arms when you are talking. Get him used to your movements so that your strikes blend in with one of these movements.

BEST OF CFW — VOL. 1
MARTIAL ARTS

> ### 8 WAYS TO BOLSTER YOUR SKILLS
> Following are some other items you can't afford to ignore.
> - Footwork. Learn to be light on your feet. Try moving on the balls of your feet.
> - Sometimes your opponent's strike may come at you so fast that you won't have time to move your feet, so you have to develop blocks from a stationary stance.
> - When delivering a hand strike, try not to take the hand backward if you want to strike forward. Place your hands in different positions and develop the power to strike straight to your opponent.
> - The instant you feel a strike, you've got to move with it.
> - There are many good video tapes and books out there on the market that may bolster your self-defense skills. You may not agree with some of them, so take what you need to make yourself a better fighter.
> - With a good foundation to build on, there is no limit to the growth you can attain.
> - If you see anything in the martial arts world that can help you as a fighter, use it.
> - Just remember. In self-defense, there are no rules or regulations. There are no judges or referees. You fight for your life. So learn everything you can because the one thing that doesn't feel important to you as a fighter could cost you your life.

Third, lower your eyes to his solar plexus. By using peripheral vision, you'll be able to see his whole body. If you are looking eye to eye, you may not see his foot moving at you. You also need to be able to use yourself offensively—whether you are standing, sitting or in the prone position. Let's look closer at this last point.

While standing, you should be able to move to any angle that enables you to strike to the vulnerable areas of your opponent's body.

If sitting, you may be able to lean forward and slap or punch your opponent's groin. If you are in a chair, try grabbing the sides of your seat, lift your butt and throw a front kick to that target.

Finally, if you are in the prone position, following are some things you might try:
- Try to hurt his ankles or knees as you roll onto his legs and take him down.
- Become adept at kicking while on the floor. Targets could be his legs, groin and head, if he leans over.
- Learn how to block his kicks if you are the floor and he is standing.
- Practice different ways to stand from the prone position. For example, you can roll upward, kip up, etc.

Next, quickly assess the situation and devise a little strategy. For example, let's say you're faced with two attackers and that one of them is substantially larger than the others.

In this case, it might be prudent to take the biggest man out first. That, in itself, may stop the other one or two attackers. If not, you have to hurt them, too. Therefore, go for the vulnerable places on their bodies. Targets such as their eyes, nose, throat and groin are good.

The front snap kick to the groin is a good technique if your opponent has his legs fairly close together. A straight leg instep kick up into the groin works well if his legs are apart. Straight punches are good to use because they blend in with your body, making it harder for your opponent to see and block the punch.

In the meantime, keep moving around so it will be harder for your opponents to come at you at the same time. Practice blocking and striking in different directions because you may have to block one man while you are striking another. You might not have the time to strike a man more than once, so it's got to be a good strike. Make it count.

You have to learn how to kick or strike your opponent even if he is behind you. Learn how to shuffle backward and close the distance on your opponent so that you can strike him before he strikes you.

You should also try putting them on the ground by kicking their knees and ankles.

If he goes to the ground, there are some things to consider. First, do you have time to get away while he's down? If not, try to move around to a position where you can kick or strike him to a vulnerable position of his body. If you strike him with your hands or fists, make sure you squat to strike instead of leaning. Your balance is not as good if you lean, and he may be able to take you down with him. Practice different ways of using leverages on his arms and legs without going to the floor with your opponent.

CHECKLIST

If you ever do find yourself in a confrontation, following are some of the things of which you should be aware.

- How is your opponent positioned in front of you? Are his shoulders square to you, making it easy for you to attack his centerline? Or is he in a boxer's stance in which a front kick to the groin might not work, but a modified roundhouse kick to the groin might work better?
- Where are his hands? Are his hands high, enabling you to go low to his body with kicks or strikes? Does he have his hands behind him or in his pockets, indicating he may have some sort of weapon?
- Which way is he leaning—away from you or toward you? It's faster for him to move in on you if he is leaning forward. If he is leaning slightly backward, he may be ready to kick you.
- Is he in constant motion or is he stationary? You should be able to see and feel his strike

The fighters square off (1). When his opponent throws a left punch, Bill Lasiter steps diagonally to the right and executes a left out block catch (2). While holding his opponent's left arm near the elbow, Lasiter takes a small left step and drops to his right knee. Meanwhile, he brings the inside knife edge of his right forearm up into his opponent's groin (3). Lasiter then slides his hand down and grabs his opponent's ankle (4). He stands up and lifts the ankle while pushing down on his opponent's left arm (not shown). He finishes with a right heel kick to the kidney, ribs or spine (5).

The opponents square off (1). Anticipating a left punch, Bill Lasiter (right) slides into a right kick stance and throws a right back knuckle to his opponent's right eye (2). He follows that with a hammer fist to the groin (3) and finishes him off with a left knee to the left eye or nose (4).

coming at you faster when he is in the stationary position.

- What kind of shoes is he wearing? If he is wearing boots, it's hard to stomp his foot. If he's barefoot, it's easy to hurt his food by stomping. Running shoes? He may be able to move around pretty fast. In this case, trying to run from him may not be a good option.
- What kind of clothes is he wearing? Loose clothing is easy to grab and manipulate. If his clothes are tight, it's going to be harder to grab him so it's better to grab his body or strike him.
- Does he have a weapon? It is important that you understand how he could use that weapon against you. The more you understand the movement of that weapon, the easier it will be to protect yourself from it. The bottom line … practice your weapons defense.
- Does he have hair? If he does, grab it and take him down.
- Are you facing more than one opponent? If so, how are they positioned around you? Train yourself to be able to strike two or three opponents in one movement.
- If there is a bright light in the area, try to have your back to it. If the light is in his eyes, he may not be able to see you as well.
- Be aware of the things around you. Is there anything you could throw or use to block a weapon he may have? Is there a car antenna you could use as a whip? Is there dirt that you could pick up and throw into his eyes?

> "You have to learn how to kick or strike your opponent even if he is behind you."

LEGAL RAMIFICATIONS

Of course, anything that occurs on the street may have ramifications later in a court. To make matters worse, it may take all of one second to find yourself fully engaged in a life-and-death struggle. So you have to think fast.

The main thing to remember is that if you feel a man intends to do you bodily harm, you can restrain him from hurting you. Of course, it's not going to be easy to hold down a 300-pound man down without hurting him first.

Regardless of how big your opponent is or how many you are facing, you may only have a fraction of a second to decide what you are going to do. Your life or the lives of your loved ones may depend on that split-second decision. Think fast.

About the author: Bill Lasiter is owns and operates a school in Rancho Cucamonga, California.

Ready for Battle

Bunkai Kata Prepares the Goju-Ryu Student for Combat

Thomas J. Nardi, Ph.D.

Originated by Chojun Miyagi, *goju-ryu*—one of the most popular forms of Okinawan karate—is a blend of Chinese *kempo* (soft, flowing, circular-yielding movements) and the indigenous Okinawan art of *naha-te* (hard, linear power movements). Indeed, "goju" translates as "hard, soft (yielding)" to denote the synthesis of these two martial influences.

For the traditionalist, kata is considered the heart of karate. For the Okinawan goju-ryu practitioners, bunkai kata is the life-blood that surges through that heart. In Okinawa, *bunkai* training is much more widely practiced than sparring. Indeed, bunkai kata training is considered to be superior to sparring as a preparation for actual combat.

KATA, REAL FIGHTING

Domingo Llanos is a leading practitioner of goju-ryu. Having trained and competed in Okinawa and mainland Japan with some of the highest ranked goju-ryu masters in these countries, Llanos' credentials are impressive (see sidebar). Additionally, his teacher and mentor during his 30-plus years in goju-ryu is hall of fame instructor Chuck Merriman, who once said, "Anyone who thinks kata is unrelated to real fighting does not understand kata or real fighting."

It is within the bunkai that the real understanding of both kata and fighting is developed.

BUNKAI DEFINED

"Bunkai refers to an analysis of the kata and the application of its technique," explains Llanos.

There are 12 kata in the goju-ryu curriculum (see sidebar) and each has its own bunkai. The student progresses by learning the individual kata and its accompanying bunkai. Each kata teaches different fighting concepts, principles and techniques.

Some kata mimic the fighting mannerisms of animals—like the tiger and crane—reflecting the kata's Chinese roots. Some kata simulate fighting multiple opponents or armed attackers. Each kata also expands upon and complements the others. They are all interrelated and provide a lifetime's worth of study if one is to actualize all their benefits.

KIHON BUNKAI

There are three levels to bunkai training, and beginners start with *kihon* bunkai. The "kihon" (basic) application of the kata includes the more obvious interpretation of techniques. The kata's

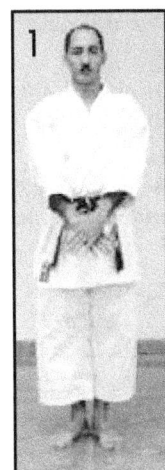     

Domingo Llanos demonstrates a sequence from saifa kata. He assumes the ready position (1), steps off diagonally (2) and shifts his position as he pulls his arms across his body (3 and 4). His left hand crosses his right (5), and he executes a right back fist (6). Llanos shows the application (7).

LLANOS UP CLOSE
- In 1982, Domingo Llanos earned a silver medal at the World Union Karate Organization (WUKO) in Taiwan.
- Llanos was also a member of the AAU National karate team from 1977 to 1982. He was also a four-time AAU all-around champion (weapon, forms, sparring).
- A student of Chuck Merriman, Llanos has schools in Haverstraw, New York and in the Dominican Republic.

basic blocking, striking and kicking are easily seen and understood by the beginner. At this point, things are as they appear to be.

For the novice, the more sophisticated application of the kata's techniques would be lost. Therefore, simple, straight forward and obvious applications of the kata are taught and drilled. This gives the student a clear understanding of the basic foundation of the kata.

At this stage, the individual techniques of the kata are practiced in isolation. For example, a high block and mid-level thrust could be performed over and over to assist in learning the movement. In isolation, the movements may not resemble a flowing kata.

RENZOKU BUNKAI

As the student progresses, he will next learn *renzoku* bunkai. This is considered the intermediate level of understanding of the kata's true function.

"Renzoku is the continuous two person form of the bunkai," Llanos explains. "One student, in effect, performs the entire kata in the proper sequence while the other student provides the attacks that would elicit that particular response found in the kata."

Although prearranged, this practice assists in the development of timing, proper range appreciation, focus and speed. And, of course, it helps in the mastery of techniques.

The student learns to flow with the attacks of another person and to respond swiftly and correctly. Advanced students deliver their techniques with full speed, focus and power.

The rhythm of the bunkai simulates and matches that of actual combat. Indeed, the choreographed movements give the appearance of an actual combative encounter.

There are two levels to the renzoku bunkai. There is the basic continuous flow and an advanced, much higher form of continuous flow. The more advanced form teaches fairly intricate techniques

Llanos begins with his left hand overhead and his right hand at his midsection (1). He changes stances (2), withdraws his front leg (3) and does what appears to be a double strike (4). The goju-ryu stylist shows the application against an opponent who attacks with a front kick (5). He scoops him up (6) and then can crash him to the ground.

that would be considered too difficult for novices to master. At this stage, the student begins to realize that there is much more to the kata than first meets the eye. The more subtle, less obvious applications now start to manifest. What once was taught as a high block and mid-level strike, for example, may now be discovered to be a joint lock and throw.

OYO BUNKAI

> **SANCHIN & TENSHO KATA**
>
> Twelve kata of goju-ryu blend opposites (hard and soft, closed fist and open hand, fast and slow, linear and circular). In addition to these, there are two breath-control kata: sanchin and tensho.
>
> Sanchin symbolizes the "go" or "hard" and tensho the "ju" or "soft" aspect of goju-ryu's unique deep abdominal breathing techniques.

The pinnacle of kata understanding can only be achieved with many years of dedicated training and concomitant advancement in the art. After years as a black belt and the attaining of teacher's credentials, the practitioner is now expected to develop what is known as the oyo bunkai.

This refers to the goju-ryu stylists own unique insights, experiences and personal analysis of the kata. It derives from his own research, gained in part from years of devoted practice of the kata and the renzoku bunkai, as well as from awareness gained from teaching others. It also includes the oral teachings of his own instructor, often shared privately and reserved for true disciples of the art.

During oyo bunkai training, the practitioner often achieves an awakening. Suddenly, a very familiar move will take on a totally new meaning as he discovers an application that was always there but hidden in plain sight. It is what many old masters referred to as "coming out of the dance" and can be likened to a flash of creative insight.

REAL FIGHTING

Goju-ryu, as a blending of hard and soft, has within its kata many different techniques.

"One often hears how all 'real fights' go to the ground," smiles Llanos. "Well, within the kata are techniques to prevent that from happening."

As discovered in the bunkai, there are many ways to redirect an opponent's attack. A true and deep understanding of kata also reveals methods of either controlling, disabling or destroying an attacker. Bunkai teaches how to hurt to an appropriate degree. Although often associated with other martial arts, trapping is to be found in the goju-ryu bunkai. So, too, are joint locks and throws.

"You cannot always depend on a strike or kick to end a fight," explains Llanos, "but a broken leg will certainly stop an attacker."

THE PARADOX OF GOJU

The paradox of goju-ryu's philosophy of synthesized opposites is also found in the bunkai. A very basic white belt kata may contain very advanced—albeit hidden—techniques; and, a very advanced kata may have hidden within it very basic techniques.

Advanced students and teachers are encouraged to return to the elementary kata and discover new meaning with them. Perhaps the goju-ryu philosophy can best be summarized by Western poet T.S. Elliot: "We shall not cease from exploration;

And the end of all our exploring,

Will be to arrive where we started;

And know the place for the first time."

Versatile Taekwondo

With Its Arsenal of Takedowns and Locks, The Korean Art Proves That It's More Than Just High-Flying, Fancy Kicks

Terry L. Wilson

"No way, man." "Impossible." "You're crazy." "Get outta here." If I told you that *taekwondo* featured takedowns, kicks, locks and scissors moves, those are some of the nicer things you'd probably say. Well, I hate to be the one to break it to you, but you're flat-out wrong.

Sure, you might associate this Korean art with high-flying, fancy kicks, but it's more that that. Much more. Young Bo Kong, a former national champion who now operates a school in Pennsylvania, is the man who is going to ably demonstrate the versatile moves of taekwondo.

SHOWCASE THE ART

He begins by defending against a gun-wielding man. First, Kong spins to the side, knocking the weapon away from his head. He then wraps the attacker's arm into a behind-the-back bar while forcing him to the ground with a leg trip.

Next, looking more like a *jiu-jitsu* master than a taekwondo expert, Kong executes a series of wrist-lock takedowns against a knife attack. As the weapon is swung toward Kong's head, he executes an upper block, then steps into the attacker while simultaneously wrapping his adversary's wrist, forcing him backward and onto the ground.

Next up ... another knife attack. Using expert timing and blinding speed, Kong swiftly takes the attacker down with a flying scissors maneuver.

The next move looks very much like an *aikido* move. He deflects the blade and steps to the side while wrapping the attacker's arm against his chest. He breaks the arm at the elbow while simultaneously pulling the bad guy's head backward in a neck break.

And he's just getting started. Kong has a wide variety of combinations that feature his famous kicking techniques in tandem with locks, throws and takedowns. Add his incredible breaking skills into the mix and you have a man who knows how to use everything around him as a weapon in a self-defense situation.

"I believe in using what works," says Kong. "Many of

our (taekwondo) techniques incorporate locks, throws, and other moves that are also found in other martial art styles. I believe that taekwondo should have a variety of self-defense techniques. In addition to our kicks, I teach boxing, locks, throws ... anything that can be effective. Martial arts should be taught to cover every aspect of life, not just tournaments."

MARTIAL ARTS

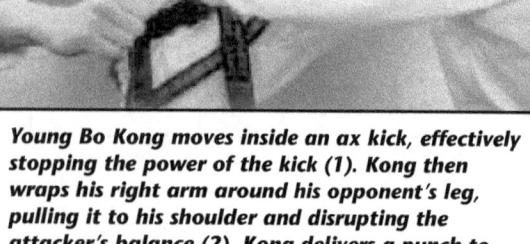

ON THE STREET

On more than one occasion, Kong's martial arts skills have been put to task when his very life was on the line. Whether fighting for trophies or his personal safety, Kong's martial art skills have put him in the winner's circle when push came to shove.

Of course, there are obvious differences that separate a street fight from a martial arts tournament. According to Kong, just because an individual is good enough to take home a first-place trophy doesn't necessarily mean that he will be the last one standing when the fur starts flying for real.

"If someone fights in the street the same way he would fight in a tournament, I don't think he would win," says Kong. "Things happen fast in a street fight and a person must be able to use any tool available at the time to win. A street fight requires a different kind of mind-set. In taekwondo, every part of your body should be used as a weapon. In a tournament, they don't use knees, forearms and throws. Subsequently, many students only train for tournament fighting. When they are faced with a real fight, they don't have the mind-set or

Young Bo Kong moves inside an ax kick, effectively stopping the power of the kick (1). Kong then wraps his right arm around his opponent's leg, pulling it to his shoulder and disrupting the attacker's balance (2). Kong delivers a punch to the attacker's solar plexus (3), the force of which drives the attacker to ground (4).

knowledge necessary to put their adversary down."

There are, however, some similarities between mock combat and the real deal. According to Kong, keeping a cool head and controlling the attack is imperative in the ring and in the street.

"It's important to stay calm in a fight," he says.

Your mind must work in a calculated manner. When you are in control of your thoughts, you are calm. Even in the midst of battle, if you can allow your mind to work in harmony with your fists, you will stay ahead of the aggressor.

Set Up Your Opponent

Following are some ways to set up your opponent.
- Fake an attack to the upper body. This will often give you an opening to attack low.
- The eyes are also a an effective tool for setting up a move. By looking off, you can often distract your opponent for a split second, which should give you enough time to make your move.
- You may even want to "give" your opponent an opening to attack in an effort to "sucker" him into making a move, which you are prepared to counter.

The two fighters square off (1). When the man lunges at Kong with the knife, he steps to the outside while trapping the knife hand by guiding it over his wrist (2). Kong applies a knife hand strike against attacker's radial nerve (3) and then grips the attacker's hand with both of his hands (4). He pulls his adversary's hand above his chest (not shown), setting the attacker up for a kick. To conclude, Kong executes a hooking kick to head of attacker while continuing to twist the knife hand in a downward circle, away from his body (5).

ALWAYS PREPARED

You must also know how to defend against all kinds of attacks, says Kong.

"For example, when someone throws a roundhouse at me, my favorite counter is a spinning back kick. I spin in the same direction as the person who is attacking me and my back kick will land while his roundhouse kick is still in the air. He cannot move back or to the side, making the roundhouse vulnerable to a spinning back kick counter."

You might also have to deal with an inside and outside crescent kick. Let's say you block your opponent's punch. Your opponent is going to think that you are open to a crescent kick or an ax kick, says Kong. If he starts to throw either one, step into the attack. Of course, this requires good timing, but it's effective.

"I like to grab the attacker by the shoulder and sweep the leg out from underneath him or to strike him hard with a punch or heel palm," says Kong.

THE IMPORTANCE OF STRATEGY

In addition to being prepared for anything, it's also important to think a couple of shots ahead of the game. Positioning the opponent should not be a game of chance; it should be a matter of strategy. Setting up your opponent requires a balance of gamesmanship, technical knowledge and the courage to commit. Thus, in some ways, fighting is like a game of billiards.

Kong follows a tried and true adage for setting up an opponent: Hands set up the feet and feet set up the hands. Calling upon a potpourri of punches such as hooks, upper cuts and ridge hands, Kong is an expert at using his punches to set up his kicks and vice versa. Although the backfist isn't widely used in taekwondo, it is a strike that Kong uses with great effect to set up his strongest kick.

"I like to use a backfist to set up a side kick," says Kong. "Even if the backfist doesn't land, it makes my opponent back up, and it is deceptive because it appears that I am too far away to kick. That's not true. As I throw the backfist, I close the gap by sliding up with my back leg, giving me the opportunity to land a sidekick. I can also easily change up to a hook kick."

"I also use my legs to set up a punching attack," says Kong. "I pretend that I am kicking with a left leg back roundhouse kick. When he moves in to jam my leg, I come over the top of it with a power punch and follow it up with a hooking kick. This is a fast and effective move in the ring or in the street."

The Korean stylist went on to explain that should your opponent back up instead of attempting to block the "fake" kick, merely set your leg down and change the attack into a back kick.

"To be successful in a fight, you must stay agile and be prepared to change your direction and your attack in response to what your opponent is doing," says Kong. "Ideally, you want to make your opponent fight your fight and set him up then score on his mistake."

SWEEPS AND LOCKS

Now, let's say your opponent attacks with a high round kick. While Kong has an arsenal of techniques to counter such a technique, one of his favorite moves is to take the attacker down with a leg sweep and wristlock.

"If someone comes in with a right leg roundhouse kick, I will step parallel to the attack with my right let," he says. "I avoid the impact of the kick. With my left hand, I'll catch him underneath the leg then sweep his left leg with my right leg. His body will impact the ground with great force, stunning him."

It's important to keep your legs spread for the follow-up technique, he notes. To do this, turn your foot to the outside and downward, applying a sort of ankle lock, making it difficult for the opponent to rotate his legs.

Next, quickly drop your shin or knee into his groin, all the while maintaining a tight grip on his legs. If you let his legs loose, you are in danger of being countered with a scissors move, so slide your arms down the length of his leg as much as needed to apply the knee to his groin, he says.

At this time, additional pressure may be applied to his leg by twisting his ankle in a circular manner with both hands, turning the toes down and ankle up. Once this lock is applied, you can break his leg by merely leaning forward and pressing his locked ankle against your chest.

TAKEDOWN TIPS

If you're going to take your opponent down, timing is a critical factor.

"Your body must 'flow' with your opponent's energy," says Kong. "If you move in harmony with your opponent, you will be able to use his energy against him."

To practice this, select a technique and break it down into three moves as if you were "dancing" with your opponent. Use the first two moves to get the feel of your opponent's movement. On the third movement, "flow" or execute the takedown.

Once you have mastered the three-step takedown, shorten the steps to two and then one. By practicing your techniques in this manner, you will improve your timing while training your reflexes to "go with the flow of your attacker's momentum."

WRIST LOCK VS. KNIFE

When faced with an attacker using a knife, the kind of defense you use depends on how he attacks, says Kong. For example, if he thrusts at your chest, turn in the direction of the thrust, while deflecting the weapon by grabbing his hand (over the top of his thumb) with your left hand, pulling it down and toward your belt.

If done properly, this will pull the attacker off balance, even if it's only for a moment. It's vital to support your left hand by gripping under the attacker's hand. At the moment when the attacker is most off balance, make 180-degree move to the outside of his attack while turning his knife hand like a doorknob. If possible, keep his hand and weapon close to your body.

It's also important to drop your hips when you turn and when you twist his hand. This action will add power to your technique. More than likely this will break his wrist, but maintain the grip as he hits the ground and pull his hand tight to your body.

Next, with your right leg, step around the attacker's arm at the elbow, and twist it against your left leg, breaking his elbow.

WELL-ROUNDED

Things aren't always as they seem, are they? You've now probably got a little different opinion of taekwondo. Sure, it's got some of the most dazzling kicks you'd ever want to see, but it should now be obvious that it's a well-rounded art.

About the author: Terry Wilson is a freelance writer and martial artist who lives in San Diego, California.

Defense Against a Punch

The Concepts Behind the Way Karate, Judo, Aikido and Kendo Handle An Empty-Hand Assault

Dan Ivan

Dan Ivan, a black belt in four styles, has virtually devoted his life to training in the martial arts. That 53 years entails military experience, operating his own school and training with some of the biggest names in the martial arts.

In the following story, Ivan, who now lives in the Palm Springs area of Southern California, explains the concepts behind the way karate, judo, *aikido* and *kendo* practitioners handle a punch.

NO. 1 KARATE

In its various forms, karate is generally a hand-and-foot fighting art that is designed primarily to deal with counterattacks. Interestingly, however, street fighting in Japan many years ago was for the lower classes, thugs and criminals. The Japanese considered karate as the lowest

> **Dan Ivan's Career Highlights**
> - Likely the first non-Japanese martial artist to get black belts in four martial arts (karate, judo, aikido, kendo)
> - First director for the American team in the first world championships in Tokyo in 1970
> - Started Japan Karate Federation of America in 1962 or 1963
> - Brought topnotch martial artists to America, including Fumio Demura
> - First USA director for the International Martial Arts Federation in Tokyo (1986)
> - Entered military in 1945 at age 15
> - While in the Army, served in criminal investigations and military intelligence.
> - Discharged from military in 1960 and opened first martial arts dojo in Orange County. Also became police instructor to various departments in Orange County.

form of martial arts. On the other end of the spectrum, there was kendo, *iaido*, judo and aikido.

Since the average Japanese rarely engaged in street fighting, except for those mentioned above, karate was not needed. As time went on, including to this day, top sensei in Japan have worked hard to elevate karate to a sport and include it in the curriculum of universities so the public would accept it better.

SELF-DEFENSE

Of the four major Japanese arts, karate is best suited to defend against punches and street attacks. Unlike karate, the other arts—judo, aikido and kendo—really do not allocate training specifically for defenses against punches and street attacks.

MARTIAL ARTS

KARATE

Dan Ivan (left) and Alan Godshaw square off (1) for a karate demonstration. Notice how Ivan is out of striking range, his hands are ready to block, his knees are slightly bent and he is ready to counter. When Godshaw throws a lunge punch, Ivan shifts sideways and executes a sweep block with his open hand (2). He then grabs the attack arm and chambers for a round kick (3) and throws it (4). He snaps his kick back and maintains his balance (5). He places his kicking leg on the ground, assumes a forward stance and uses a forearm smash to drill his opponent's elbow (6). He turns his hips toward Godshaw and delivers a face blow (7).

BEST OF CFW — VOL. 1
MARTIAL ARTS

To add power to their counters, karate practitioners use a body bag or *makiwara* (wooden training device). Those who work diligently at this can toughen their arms so much that it's like getting hit with a 2-by-4. And that's the intent of strengthening their arms. They want to be able to block a punch with enough force so that it disables their opponent's arm.

In addition to this, karate stylists will use other defenses against a punch, including sweeps, parries, strikes and kicks. They also may simply maneuver out of range of an attack.

NO. 2 JUDO

Judo, as Dr. Jigoro Kano envisioned it, wasn't intended to be used for fist fighting. Kano *sensei* came from an era that held the samurai in the highest esteem. The jiu-jutsu arts evolved from the samurai era, so Kano brilliantly conceived techniques from the jujutsu arts and invented sport judo.

I trained at the kodokan in Suidobashi, Tokyo. This is probably the original of Kano sensei's pub-

JUDO In this judo demonstration, Ivan leans toward his opponent and prepares for a leg sweep (1). He lifts his leg behind his opponent's knee and simultaneously pushes him with both hands, as he pulls back and upward on his leg (2). His adversary lands on his back (3). At this point, Ivan could then execute a submission (4).

MARTIAL ARTS

lic dojo. He intended for people of all ages to enjoy judo training. And it was so. It's a beautiful art to practice and to watch two skillful participants as they vie for the throw or sweep. It includes both stand-up throws and takedowns and comprehensive takedown pins and submissions.

SELF-DEFENSE

Self-defense is clearly not the intent or goal of judo. You are only going to practice against attacks in *judo-no-kata*, which is part of earning rank in judo. Otherwise, no one practices blocking and punching or street fighting.

That certainly doesn't mean judo students aren't tough. There is throwing and falling. Mat work. In many cases, these guys are stronger than the karate and stand-up fighters.

As far as self-defense goes, it's a mindset. You have the abilities, so add the determination to use your skills if you are attacked.

When using judo to defend against a punch, rush your opponent and jam him. Go for a takedown or body dive. Go in with your arms up, but don't neglect your groin. You may get hit, but it doesn't mean you are going down. Remember, your body is tough from judo training, so you can take a lot more punishment than you think. Nullify an attacker by grabbing him, shoving him off balance, jam him and work in close where you have an advantage.

NO. 3 AIKIDO

The founder, Morihei Ueshiba, developed this art from jujutsu and the sword arts. In its original and pure form, aikido students do not train to defend against punches. However, they do train to defend against open-hand attacks that simulate a sword.

But it is possible to defend against

AIKIDO *Ivan and Godshaw square off for an aikido demonstration (1). Notice Ivan's defensive stance is similar to a swordsman. His hands are open, as if he were holding a sword, and he's facing his opponent. Ivan evades the punch by pivoting and bringing his leg around in a semi-circle (2). He executes the block with both hands and ends up facing almost the same direction as the attacker. He has misdirected the attack, which is a major principal of aikido. Ivan then counters with a distracting blow (3), and then he grabs Godshaw's attack hand (4). As Ivan twists Godshaw's wrist, he swings his back leg around for better leverage (5). He then throws his opponent (6) and finishes with a submission hold (7). This close-up shows the proper hand position for the wrist leverage (8).*

a punch in aikido. That's not an issue. The only question is does the pure aikido practitioner want to? Most prefer to keep their art pure, and some even emphasize that the art is not for self-defense. However, remember that aikido was developed from arts (jiu-jutsu and the sword arts) that were designed for self-defense.

SELF-DEFENSE

Whether it's the pure art or the eclectic that adapts punching and kicking, aikido still has many outstanding self-defense techniques. Even the pure art teaches blocks, parries and counters. Furthermore, there are countless takedowns, throws, joint locks and submission techniques.

Compared to the disabling and damaging techniques of karate, aikido is considered humane self-defense. The goals are to evade and discourage an attacker. Sometimes the aikido stylist will even try to restrain his opponent.

KENDO Note how Ivan is upright, he's on the ball of his back foot and his hands are held as if he were holding a sword (1). When Godshaw throws his punch, Ivan blocks it quickly and precisely, using his wrist (2). He then raises his arm as he prepares to throw a downward chop (3). He strikes his opponent between the eyes with the bone edge of his palm (4). This technique simulates a kendoist who would parry and counterstrike.

A close-up of the kendo-style strike between the eyes with the edge of the palm.

To be sure, aikido has some of the best defensive footwork and evasive movements in the martial arts. Older aikido sensei in Japan always referred to the art's escaping techniques as "attacking a shadow" because of the evasiveness.

Strikes are used but only to distract an attacker while you apply one of their locks or restraints. Kicks are for the same reason—they are just a distraction.

Keep in mind, though. An aikido stylist can do some damage if he wants. Instead of just applying a joint lock, he can break the joint or wrist. Instead of making a clean throw, he can slam his opponent to the floor.

Whether the purists agree or not, every movement in aikido was born of a self-defense technique.

> **Street Smart**
>
> If you have trained in the various arts we discussed, what is the best way to handle an attack on the street? We posed this question to Dan Ivan. Following is his answer:
>
> "Most altercations on the street are explosive, spontaneous and don't give you much time to prepare, mentally or physically. If it's a matter of a couple of guys who mouth off first, you have to make a quick decision. Will this end up in a fight or they just letting off steam? At least if an argument precedes an attack, you do have some time to prepare.
>
> For the spontaneous attacks, regardless of what art you train in, your reactions will take over. With no time to think or prepare, the knowledge that is drilled into your system dictates what you would normally do.
>
> Don't expect a clean technique as you have practiced it in the dojo. Maybe if it's a pushover fight, and it might happen that way. But I always teach that every technique should be practiced with the thought that your opponent is bigger, stronger and tougher. Then you will try harder and learn better.
>
> The bottom line is that you should avoid situations and areas that might lead to fights."

NO. 4 KENDO

Kendo is the martial art of the elite in Japan. Along with iaido, kendo is the most revered art in the universities. These two arts have a rich heritage and are born from the samurai era. In fact, many of the high-ranking politicians and business executives in Japan have a background in each. Among the Japanese population, kendo stylists earn the most respect of all the different types of martial arts, simply because it is derived from centuries of samurai tradition.

SELF-DEFENSE

It is offensive to kendo and iaido practitioners to think of their art in terms of self-defense. They think of them as cherished arts. In the case of kendo, it's even a sport. But it's never for street self-defense.

Nevertheless, following are some vital facts that kendo training offers that can be a big benefit to coping with punches.

- When you practice kendo, you stand upright and utilize the reach of your *shinai* (bamboo sword).
- Your targets are your opponent's head, neck, wrists, body and throat.
- With only a few months training, you will find your forward momentum and speed vastly improved.
- Your eye-and-hand coordination skill level probably improves beyond all the other arts because of the speed. Therefore, even if you have never thrown a block or punch, you have the speed to do it much faster than the average person.

There aren't any techniques in this art are intended for street self-defense. It's a noble art and should be practiced as such. Moreover, there are tremendous benefits. Not only is it great exercise that will build your heart and lungs, it will enhance your ability to concentrate.

About the author: Dan Ivan is a freelance writer who lives in Southern California.

MARTIAL ARTS

Zhuang Gung—Back to Basics

Get a jump on the Olympic competition by mastering these basic wushu training exercises.

Kenny Perez

Among the most basic and important wushu gung-fu training techniques are exercises designed to improve the style's "foundation." This training is perfect for anyone preparing his body for the rigors of more-advanced training. Once a practitioner has a firm hold on the ground, he can expand on his level of expertise from both an offensive and defensive standpoint.

"Zhuang gung" training instills the virtue of patience into the beginner and weeds out the good from the bad student. After a year of horse training, only the most serious of students will remain.

Zhuang gung exercises develop an "iron horse" by rooting you to the earth, which is vital to successfully delivering techniques, controlling your body, and handling your adversary. When grounded, you are in a better position to neutralize your adversary, unleash devastating counter-techniques or remain calm and in control should your opponent attack with punches and kicks.

Zhuang gung or "pole skill" refers to remaining steadfast against attacks, as though you were a pole driven into the ground. Zhuang gung is divided into two categories: zhuang gung in motion and zhuang gung in stillness. Both sections require some degree of chi gung and physical body response. Zhuang gung in stillness is a method of standing meditation, while zhuang gung in motion are moving drills incorporating stances.

After an extended period of training, the practitioner will see a difference in his foundation, body and balance, as well as the force released with each technique. Standing in a horse is time consuming

MABU Horse Stance.
Requirements: The back should be straight, yet the hips should be drawn slightly in rather than protruding backward. The legs should be parallel, knees open and in line over the feet (not too wide), and the feet should be pointing straight ahead. The toes should be used to grip the ground, which will help to root the stance. Balance is held between the ball of the foot and the heel.

ZOU PAN (Crossed-Leg Sitting Posture.
Requirements: The legs are crossed and the knees should be squeezed tightly together. Do not curve the back; keep it extended with the chest up. Develop the ability to rise from the ground without using your hands.

and may be boring to the beginner, but this time-honored tradition remains a mainstay in many gung-fu studios around the world. Its impact should never be under-emphasized or neglected. In today's commercialized gung-fu systems, many sifu pass over this exercise and move right on to fighting and defensive techniques.

Many martial arts practitioners have found a way around the boredom by combining more training exercises. A common drill used by martial artists incorporates zhuang gung's horse stances with punches and blocking drills. There also is a variety of training aids such as standing on blocks, plum

MARTIAL ARTS

> "Zhuang Gung" or 'pole skill' refers to remaining steadfast against attacks, as though you were a pole driven into the ground."

GAO XU BU (High Empty Stance).
With flash palms. This is a distinct wushu posture used in routines to show poise and dynamic body alignment. Requirements: The body should be extended, the chest lifted, the hips drawn in slightly but not protruding backward. The arms and legs should be extended fully, yet not looking tense or tight. The shoulders must be down and the neck should look long and not squeezed out by tight-looking shoulders that are raised too high. The weight is on the back leg with the front toes slightly touching the ground. The palms should be stretched fully to show the bridge, which displays strength and poise. In this posture the body lines and poise are expressed.

GUNG BU Bow Stance.
Side Position. Requirements: The weight distribution is 70-to-30 percent, with 70 percent on the front leg and 30 percent on the back leg. The hip should be rolled forward and sunken.

XE BU (Crossed Crouching Stance) or Twisted Horse.
Requirements: The back knee is tucked behind the front knee. Balance is on the ball or the back foot with the front foot flat. The buttocks should be sitting low.

GOU TWEI BU (Knee Hook Stance).
Requirements: The supporting leg is in a crouching position. The other foot hooks behind the supporting knee. This stance is used to show leg balance and strength. The torso should not lean forward.

flower stumps and balance beams, which help strengthen the legs and develop overall coordination.

Other alternatives include vest weights and leg weights, sprints with a parachute, mountain climbing and trampoline exercises. These exercises not only build the legs, but also help increase vertical lift and increase float time, which are necessary for competitive forms such as chang chuan.

In kung-fu's formative years, beginners were required to practice standing positions for hours on end. Masters insisted this practice not only worked the legs, but also led to a cultivation of chi.

This phase of training would last anywhere from six months to a year depending on the progress of the individual. For example, the one-leg balance or horse stance would be held in a relaxed state for the length of a burning incense or candle. Techniques developed at the Shaolin Temple included the skill to jump high, "ching gung" or hard body skill, iron palm skill, pressure point skill, and the Virgin boy skill known as tong zhir gung.

Taught to young recruits, tong zhir gung consisted of exercises and medita-

In "Standing Firm Like A Mountain," sink the weight like an anchor.

MARTIAL ARTS

"You must first learn to stand before you can walk and run before you can fly."

tive positions to build the untapped power of the Virgin boy strong in prenatal chi. Tong zhir gung was said to keep the practitioner young, strong and flexible into old age. Among these skills, which developed a martial artist both internally and externally, was the daily practice of zhuang gung. These positions resulted from research into chi gung and Chinese medical theories of chi and jing lo, which are the channels throughout the body used to transport chi.

This skill also parallels the technique of testicle strengthening and retraction, which was an advanced skill believed to have been used by the Bai Mei system and other internal styles. However, this skill could only be obtained if

GUNG BU (Forward Bow Stance. Requirements: The front leg should show a 90-degree angle from the thigh to the foot. The back knee should be locked. The chest is forward, with the arms and shoulders kept down to emphasize that the full neck weight distribution is 70 percent on the front and 30 percent on the back.

one started before the male practitioner reached puberty. Since tong zhir gung stemmed from youth and virginity, a practitioner could only excel by retaining the jing or essence of the body. Therefore, the trainee was forbidden contact with girls.

The young monks at Shaolin were required to sleep either on narrow planks no wider than the width of their body or in an upright position, such as the lotus posture. This was to prevent any shifting of the body during sleep that may result in a nocturnal emission. Ideally, retention of the jing combined with chi, shen and yi-mind development resulted in a body linked physically, spiritually, and mentally. Though tong zhir gung exercises may have developed the physical body, tempered the mind, and enlightened the spirit, daily tasks such as fetching water and plowing fields also were part of the training.

These young Shaolin trainees were required to practice zhuang gung positions for many hours to develop their bodies. Some basic positions required strength, balance and flexibility. One position may have featured the practitioner standing on one leg, twisted sideways at the waist and leaning backward with his arms outstretched. Another position might require him to stand on his fingers.

The purpose of these exercises was three-fold: They developed balance as well as arm and leg strength; they stretched specific muscles and organs; and they helped the body secrete fluids and move chi through corresponding channels.

Among the many outward-motion, inward-stillness zhuang gung techniques used at the Shaolin Temple was an exercise called "running the stumps or beams." Those well-versed in this concept could run the stumps as if they were simply moving across the ground.

Absorbed into the training regimen by many martial arts styles, zhuang gung remains a necessity for any stylist hoping to achieve true rootedness. Whether ultimately used for forms or fighting, these training techniques are vital to the improvement of any practitioner and should be performed as often as possible.

Zhuang gung helps instill in the stylist a clear mind and a relaxed state, whether practicing, performing or facing an actual street encounter. Once a solid foundation has been achieved, "like a mountain" your level of gung-fu mastery will grow by leaps and bounds. And you will be ready to discover the advanced levels of wushu's vast repertoire. After all, you must first learn to stand before you can walk and run before you can fly.

Kenny Perez is a wushu instructor in Glendale, Arizona.

The Next Generation

The Young Gracie Guns Are Ready To Rock The Martial Arts World.

Doug Jeffrey

In many ways, the Gracie family is like California's famous San Andreas Fault. This fault system, which entails about 800 miles, runs under much of California and has produced some of the largest recorded earthquakes, including the 8.3 temblor that struck San Francisco in 1906.

Similarly, throughout the years, the Gracies have rocked the martial arts world on several occasions. Consider the magnitude of the following events:

For years, everyone was saying that Rickson Gracie may be the best fighter in the world. His convincing wins in the NHB world made it difficult to believe otherwise.

Left to right, the Gracie boys—Ryron, Ralek and Rener—are ready to rumble.

Enter Rorion. In the early 1990s, Rorion Gracie, the eldest of the brothers and the possessor of a law degree, attracted everyone's attention when he and Art Davie started the Ultimate Fighting Championship (UFC). You couldn't swing a stick without hitting someone who was chattering excitedly about the new fighting sport.

Enter Royce. The younger brother won the UFC three times. What made this particularly interesting was that most of his opponents outweighed him by a significant amount. When he stepped into the Octagon, he weighed about 178 pounds. That's not exactly skinny, even if he was almost 6 feet. However, he was disposing of some brutes who probably outweighed him by as much as 40 pounds.

And, of course, Helio, their father, got it all started years ago with his marathon fights, some of which lasted as long as three hours and 40 minutes.

Oh, and let's not forget some of the challenges they issued. Like the one to Benny "The Jet" Urquidez. Some people interpreted their demeanor as arrogant and distasteful. Others viewed it as supreme confidence. Regardless of what it was, it was excellent marketing.

Like the San Andreas Fault, which hasn't done a whole lot recently, things have been a little quiet

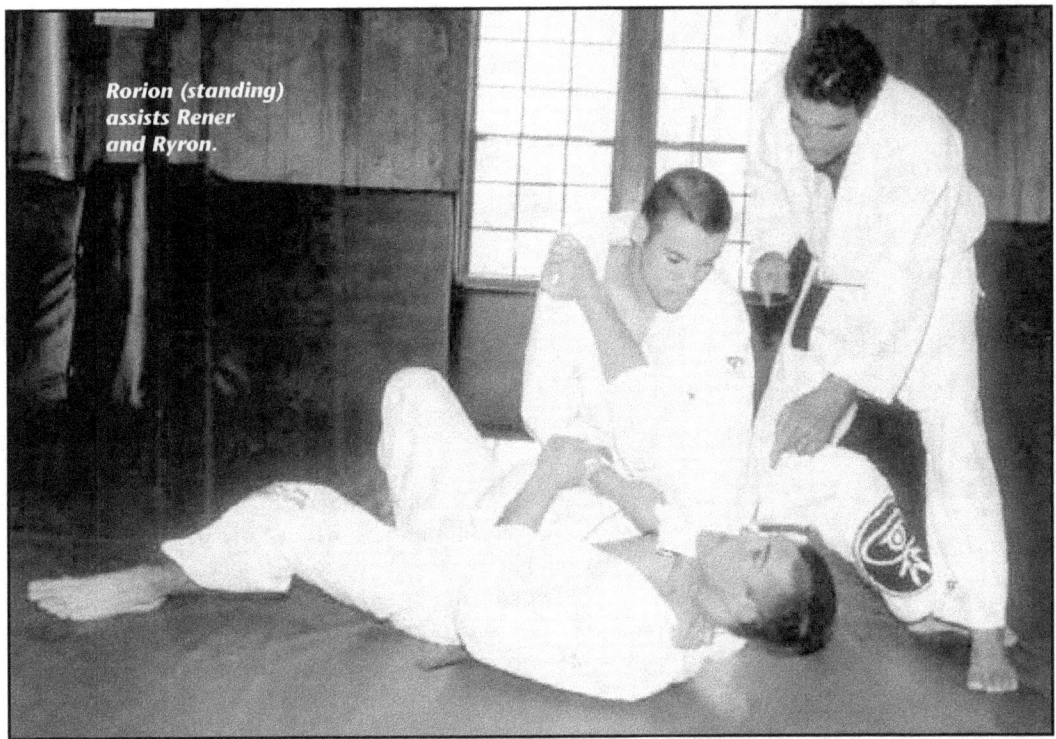
Rorion (standing) assists Rener and Ryron.

in the Gracie world. There have been no fights, no victories and no challenges from the War Horses we've been accustoming to seeing.

After all of their years of success, controversy and publicity, it seems odd that we haven't heard from them. But we know that they are there ... just like the San Andreas Fault. And we know it's just a matter of time before we hear from them again, just as geologists know that the San Andreas Fault will again shake the Earth violently in California.

Well, as you might have guessed, they're back. But we're not talking about Rickson, Royce, Rorion or Helio. No, we're talking about a new generation of Gracies.

THE BIG LITTLE ONES

You might think that the Gracies are small. At least that is the public perception. Compared to a guy like Mark Kerr, that assessment is probably right. In reality, however, they are not exactly small. But perceptions are perceptions.

As most know, Rickson is built like a Mack truck. Royce is close to 6 feet and Rorion exceeds that barrier. But that's nothing compared to Rorion's three oldest sons.

Ryron, 20, is 6 foot 3 and weighs 195. Eighteen-year-old Rener is an inch taller and weighs about 190. Ralek, 16, is 6 foot 1, 180 pounds and still growing. These guys are big, and, according to their dad, formidable fighters who are going to make a name for themselves in the near future.

"They have endless possibilities," says Rorion.

WHERE IT STARTED

As it is for most martial artists, Ryron, who teaches full-time at the Gracie Jiu-Jitsu Academy in Torrance, California, and Rener, who also teaches while not attending high school, the boys started training rather early in life.

Ryron Gracie records another victory.

Rener and Ryron work out at the Gracie Jiu-Jitsu Academy.

And it's paid off. They're taking titles at tournaments left and right. In some instances, they are doing it like their grandfather did. Ryron rolled around for 90 minutes before he defeated one opponent.

"He [his opponent] was a tough kid," he notes.

While the jiu-jitsu tournaments are fun and satisfying and challenging, eventually they want to take it to the next level. The world of NHB awaits them, and they're pounding on the door.

"It's in my blood," says Ryron.

Like his brother, Rener is anxious.

"Definitely, [I want to compete in NHB]," he says. "No doubt. I've had a taste of that life, and it would be a waste not to do it [compete]."

Looking deadly serious, Ralek agrees.

"I want to fight pro," he says. "I'm going to work up to it."

Walking in someone's footsteps is not always easy nor is it always fun. That is especially the case when the predecessor(s) have been topnotch competitors. In the case of the Gracies, topnotch may not be strong enough of a word.

For years, these guys were downright perfect. They had never lost. Royce, simply proving that the family was human after all, ultimately lost two matches, including a 90-minute marathon fight in Japan.

Does the family's success create a little pressure for the newcomers? You might think so, but you don't know the kids.

"Pressure? Not really," says Rener. "In fact, it might create a little motivation."

The guys won't step into the NHB ring until Rorion gives them the green light.

"It's like a guy who owns a thoroughbred that has ponies," he says. "He has the horses to win, and it's just a matter of time before they all get a turn."

THE SIZE ISSUE

In the early days of the UFC, Royce disposed of his opponents because he was extremely skilled on the ground and because his adversaries were proficient on their feet—not on the ground.

"At that time, size and weight were irrelevant," says Rorion.

Now, however, it's a different story. After Royce's victories, the martial arts world realized that they had to broaden their skills. Now, you've got the big guys proficient on their feet and on the ground. It's a new ballgame.

"The fighters are bigger and stronger, plus they know the techniques," says Rorion.

But that's OK. The Gracies are also bigger and stronger, and they already know the techniques.

MATURE BEYOND THEIR AGE

While the kids are packing on the muscle and working on their technique from sunrise to sunset, they are also working hard at keeping their head on straight. All three of them are mature and confident way beyond their years. And they fully appreciate the opportunity to teach.

"It's good to know that the information that I pass along during class can make a difference in someone's life," says Rener. "It's cool to be able to change someone's life."

Things certainly changed for Anthony A. Hurwitz when he started training at the Academy in Torrance, California.

"I'm not the same person I was six months ago," he says.

For example, he notes that he wouldn't trade punches with anyone and he's confident he could take someone down if it was necessary. And he credits the Gracie's teaching for his newfound confidence.

"All three of them are incredibly technical and patient," he says. "Every session is an incredible learning experience."

Rorion is quick to point out, however, the students are learning much more than just self-defense. They also benefit from stress relief, self-confidence and an enhancement of their character.

"Training [in jiu-jitsu] can provide some amazing results," he says.

> ### When the "Old" Is Still the Best
>
> It happened in Huntington Beach, California, at the "Copa-Pacifica de Jiu-Jitsu," where, without a doubt, two of the most anticipated matches of the year occurred.
>
> Ryron Gracie and Rener Gracie, who embrace the "old-style Gracie Jiu-Jitsu," were pitted against Rafael Lavato, Jr. and Mike Rose, both of whom have been practicing the "new style of jiu-jitsu." Featuring Brazilian jiu-jitsu rules (eight-minute rounds for brown belts), this was the kind of match everyone wants to see.
>
> Many people have been saying that Ryron and Rener would not compete under the regular jiu-jitsu rules because they were afraid of losing. Which is not true. The reason they don't usually compete under regular jiu-jitsu rules is because these rules encourage a distorted approach to the essence of what jiu-jitsu is about. After scoring a couple of points, competitors are encouraged to stall so that the time runs out and they may be declared winners. This shows that the rules are not objective. We can't forget that the purpose of jiu-jitsu is to increase one's effectiveness in combat, which in competition translates into chasing victory through submission.
>
> Ryron and Rener, who gave up about 30 pounds each to their strong opponents, stuck to the basics and gave a wonderful performance. Without any "fancy moves" or "hidden, secret techniques," the two young Gracies earned their clean victories by sticking to the basics.
>
> Every professional athlete and/or fighter knows that the "secrets" are in the basics. Unfortunately, many people spend a lot of time learning the "new tricks" to make gains in competition instead of sticking to the basics and mastering those properly. Years later, when they don't compete anymore, they realize that their "basic jiu-jitsu" is lacking a strong foundation.

HAPPIEST MAN ON EARTH

Ryron, Rener and Ralek certainly have some amazing role models to follow ... in and out of the ring.

"I see my father doing the right thing and guiding me in the right direction," says Rener. "And I want to follow. I don't see him smoke, and I don't see him drink. It's easy to follow in his footsteps."

Rorion credits "the old man" (his father) for instilling the good values in him that he has since passed along to his sons. While he would love to see his kids attain the same success that Rickson, Royce and Helio did, Rorion is pretty darn happy with how things are right now.

"I am the happiest and proudest father in the world," says Rorion.

And you can bet that it's just a matter of time before they do something big, real big. Capture an NHB title. Maybe add another UFC belt to the family name. Regardless of what they do, you can be sure that it will be an 8 on the martial arts Richter Scale.

Bringing the Past to Life

Liu Kan-yi is trying to turn back the pages of martial arts time.

Brian Kennedy

"*The smallish figure, covered head to foot in black, hugged the top of the wall surrounding the master's family home. The thief had learned that the quan bu, the book containing the secret methods of the master's style of martial arts, was kept in a chest in the room closest to the northeast corner of the compound. Getting the book would not be easy, but its value as a storehouse of martial arts knowledge made the attempt worth the considerable risk. Driven by that desire, the thief slipped over the wall...*"

Chinese martial arts training manuals are not always this hard to get. Many modern-day teachers of Chinese martial arts have written training manuals that are widely available through the Internet or publishers catalogues. But like the thief in the story, many stylists today are driven by a desire to own copies of older, classical martial arts training manuals.

Worn Pages

Training manuals, quan pu in Chinese, are books or manuscripts that teach the principles, techniques or forms of a martial arts system as opposed to books which discuss the history of martial arts or works of fiction based on the martial arts. Such training manuals have existed in some Chinese martial arts systems at least since the early Ming dynasty.

Their existence, however, can be quite tenuous. Older hand-written training manuals may be lost or destroyed; either on purpose or simply by the ravages of time. Printed manuals become unavailable, go out of print or the publishers close their doors. In every case, the knowledge contained in them becomes lost to modern practitioners.

But these training manuals are being revived. Several publishers in both China and Taiwan are republishing the older manuals, keeping the tradition alive and making the information available to modern readers and martial arts practitioners.

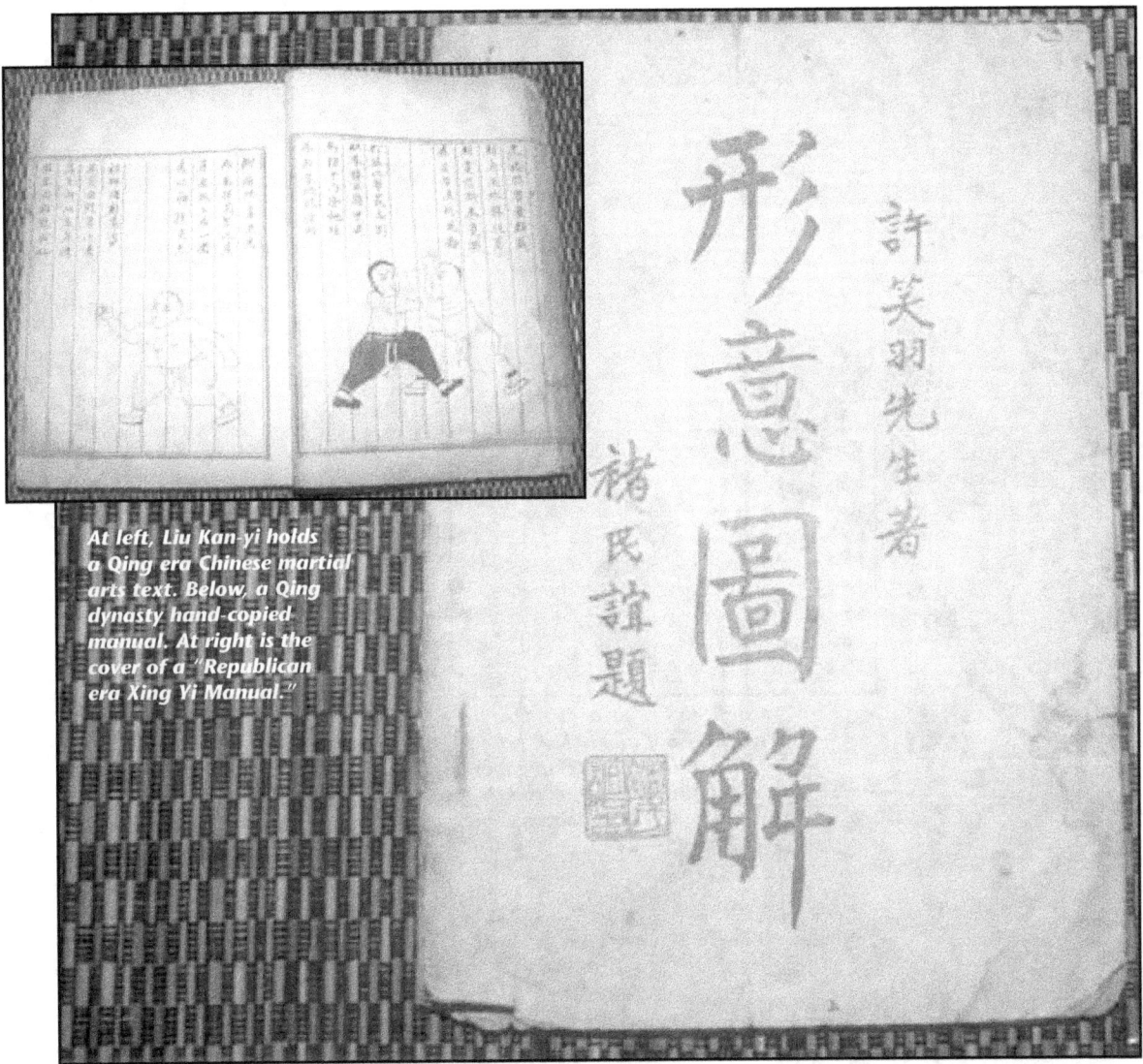

At left, Liu Kan-yi holds a Qing era Chinese martial arts text. Below, a Qing dynasty hand-copied manual. At right is the cover of a "Republican era Xing Yi Manual."

An excellent example of such endeavors is Lion Publishers in Taiwan. Founded in 1995 by Liu Kan-yi, Lion Publishers in its own words, "Seeks to preserve martial arts culture through high-quality reprints available at moderate cost."

"I had been in the publishing business since 1992," Liu explained. "When I started Lion Publishers I hoped to meet the multiple goals of publishing both old and new martial arts books, having a retail outlet, expanding my martial arts book collection, putting out a martial arts journal, and hosting a web site."

Art for Art's Sake

Liu began collecting martial arts books well before he started Lion Publishers.

"I went through all the second-hand bookstores in Taiwan, buying up everything that was available," he related. "And then I later made a survey of what older martial arts books were available in Taiwan. Initially I worked alone collecting the books, but after a time I developed a 'reputation' for

MARTIAL ARTS

Qing dynasty hand-copied manuals.

Profile
Name: Liu Kan-yi
Born: July 25, 1967
Native: Taipei, Taiwan
Profession: Chinese martial arts book publisher, collector of antique Chinese martial arts books.
Martial Arts studied: Long fist and preying mantis
Contact: www.lionbooks.com.tw or lionbooks 200e@yahoo.com.tw

At left, the cover of *Fist Classic; Fist Method*, and below, a page showing Shaolin Temple monk Shen Ji teaching the iron door bar posture.

collecting old martial arts books and people approached me with books for sale or sometimes simply gave me older martial arts books that they were no longer interested in. I then turned my attention to China, where there were far more books available.

"Soon, my collection became so large that I was not able to actually read all the volumes and some of the books were so obscure that I could not understand them even when I did attempt to read them," he added. "I noticed that these older martial arts books usually discussed martial arts in conjunction with broader health programs, Chinese medicine, divination (i.e., such theories as the five elements, the *I-Ching* and so forth), and metaphysics."

Recreating History

Reprinting these older, more holistically orientated Chinese martial arts text was the first goal of Lion Publishers. To date it has republished over 20 of these older training manuals and Liu hopes to keep that process going for many years. There are a great number of valuable Chinese martial arts texts, which have gone out of print and risk being forever lost.

One example has its origins in the fabled Shaolin Temple. The book is titled *Fist Classic; Fist Method* or *Quan Ching, Quan Fa* in Chinese. The edition reprinted by Lion Publishers appeared in Shanghai in 1936. The work is a compellation of two earlier works that date from the Ming dynasty; one of which originated with a

Shaolin monk known as Cheng shi. The work was put in its present form and published in 1784 by Tsao huan-dou.

In its original form, this book was an example of a hand-copied training manual. The earliest training manuals were hand copied either from other hand copies or from notes made of a martial arts teacher's lecture. These early training manuals tended to be quite basic but were sometimes illustrated with line drawings. They were largely useless unless one had already trained in that school; the texts tended to be made up of shorthand notes, mnemonic rhymes and esoteric philosophy. These hand-copied texts were intended exclusively for students of that school. The language used is arcane, symbolic and vague.

Those untrained in martial arts would have trouble learning straight from the book. But for the initiated, the books provided valuable guidance on the advanced aspects of martial arts. These early hand-copied manuals are the real-life "secret kung-

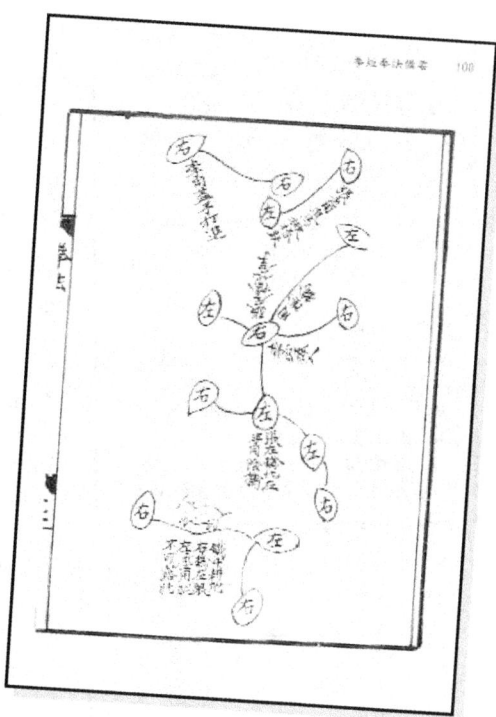

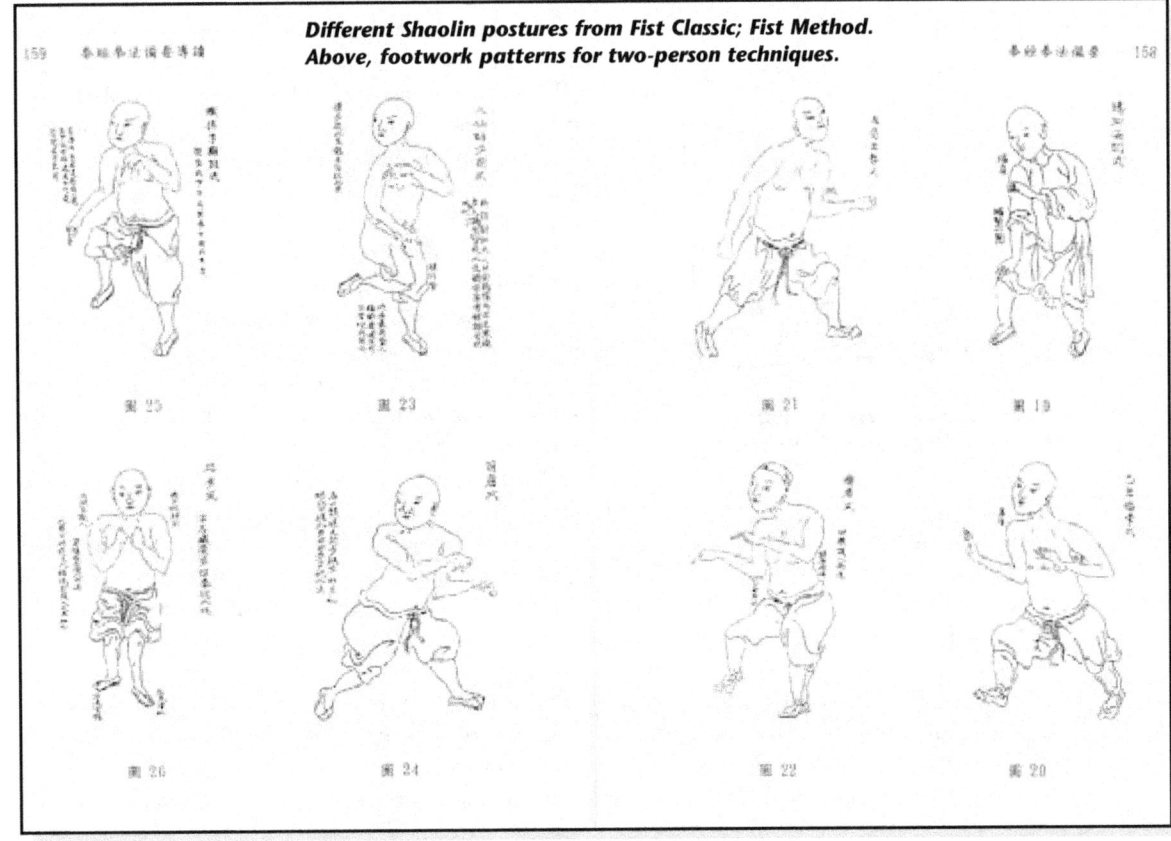

Different Shaolin postures from Fist Classic; Fist Method. Above, footwork patterns for two-person techniques.

MARTIAL ARTS

5 Most Important Chinese Martial Arts Books Reprinted To Date

1. *Xing Yi Quan Training Materials* (1929) by Dien Xie, Gao Hsiao Jen, and Jiang Shen-shan
2. *Chen Family Tai Chi Quan* (1932) by Chen Zi-ming
3. *Fist Classic; Fist Method* (1784) by Chang Kong-jiao
4. *Complete Book of Practical Tai Chi Quan* (1934) by Yang Chen-fu
5. *Swimming Body Linked Form of Pa Kua* (1936) by Du Chao-tang

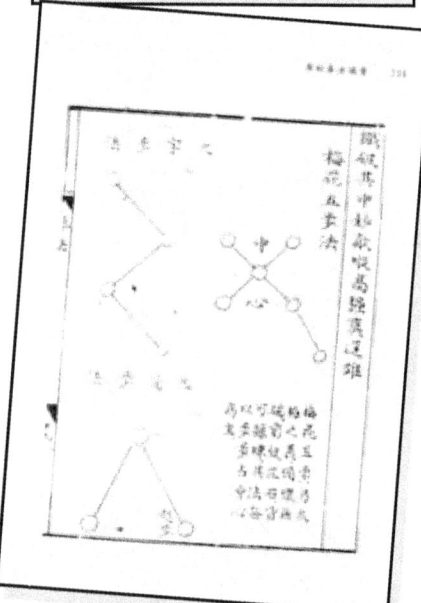

Plum flower five steps method from Fist Classic; Fist Method.

fu manuals" that figure so often in martial arts fiction and movies.

Liu's personal library of Chinese martial arts books now contains over 2,000 volumes that are out of print, as well as over 500 volumes that were published in the early Republican period.

"The major turning point in the expansion of my collection was about two years ago," Liu noted. "The first time I went to China, there were lots of materials available. Because in China there is the 'new martial arts,' which is public-performance orientated, a mix of gymnastics and opera; a show. So they have no use or interest, especially after the Cultural Revolution, in these older materials. Anything old is not worth anything. So the first year I went back I just collected any and all martial arts books that were available."

New "Old" Idea

This wealth of new "old" materials gave Liu an idea for a new direction. Along with reprinting older, out-of-print Chinese martial arts books, Liu intends to begin releasing a new series of training materials. These new training materials will bring together information from a range of older training manuals, integrating the teachings into a format that can be understood and used by modern practitioners.

"In older martial arts books one master will say one thing, use one approach," he said. "We will publish books that draw from all the lineages within a certain system. So it is a modernization of the old books. It is more educational, with more explanations. One old manuscript may make ten new books that explain the one older book." This new series will be available in Chinese, English and Japanese. The new approach will also include a web site.

Liu, who has studied tang long (preying mantis) and chang chuan (long boxing), believes he knows the best way to present martial arts to the public.

"The Western view of martial arts is that it is dissected into discrete units, steps," he noted. "The Asian view is integrated. Qi, by way of example, in my view is a phenomenon that occurs as a result of many things happening. It is not a process with a step 1, step 2, step 3 and then qi occurs. The idea is to go back to the original way of presentation of martial arts, bringing together and integrating ideas from health maintenance programs, martial arts, medicine, fortune telling (five elements et. al.) and metaphysics."

Liu publishes *Taiwan Wu Lin* magazine, considered to be Taiwan's premier martial arts journal, and hosts an annual historical martial arts book and film show, where the public can see many rare martial arts texts, films and videos of past martial arts masters in action.

Liu is working on returning Chinese martial arts back into their cultural context by making available a range of older martial arts texts. Also at risk of being lost is the richness of human development and human ability that can come from martial arts practice, some of which border on the unbelievable.

"One martial arts teacher I knew here in Taiwan told me that 30 years ago he traveled all around Taiwan to visit many old martial arts practitioners," Liu recalled. "One time he met a blind old man, who had been blinded by the Japanese because they thought he was a spy. The old man was a white crane practitioner. He could jump from the ground to the second floor. My friend told me he saw it with his own eyes. Martial arts is beyond your normal conception, martial arts is beyond your imagination."

Brian Kennedy is a Hong Kong-based freelance writer.

Fundamentally Sound

Forget the fancy, secret moves. To win, you need to get back to the basics.

Jose Fraguas

Evolution is one of the most venerated words in the dictionary of mankind. Science, mathematics, medicine, physics, sports, etc. spend billions of dollars researching new methods of improving the old ways.

If we take a few minutes to analyze the evolution of different sports, we'll come to the conclusion that the fundamentals of any athletic activity have been barely altered. Practically, the same ways and premises used in the past are still valid today, although it is true that they have been improved.

Due to the interest of the grappling arts in the last decade, let's focus on a style of martial art that took the world by storm in November of 1993: the *jiu-jitsu* style of the Gracie Family.

To begin, all the Brazilian jiu-jitsu comes from the Gracie Family, although nowadays there are substantial differences in the way a member or associate of the Gracie Family teaches the art and what is called more generically Brazilian Jiu-Jitsu (BJJ). To be sure, it is the same style, but there are more differences than similarities between what is taught and how it is taught at the Gracie Academy in Torrance and what is taught at many BJJ schools throughout the United States.

OLD JIU-JITSU

For the sake of this article and in respect to copyright laws, let's call what is taught at the Torrance Academy "Gracie Jiu-Jitsu" and the rest "Brazilian Jiu-Jitsu."

Why I am making this distinction? Well, for the last nine years and after Royce Gracie opened the doors to many Brazilians to teach the art in the United States, the methods of teaching and practicing the art at the Gracie Academy have been criticized and described as "old jiu-jitsu and an obsolete method, incapable of doing good in modern competitions because is stagnant and has never evolved."

The new [BJJ] approach "is more direct, with more combinations and countless new movements developed after years of high-level competition in every corner of Brazil," they said.

Technical modifications and new and improved "tricks" used by the new champions convinced 99 percent of the jiu-jitsu aficionados and practitioners that they had to leave the "old jiu-jitsu" from the Gracie Academy and go to those places where more "advanced" movements were being taught. The increasing number of Brazilian instructors coming to teach in the United States made it easy for the students go from one school to another in search of a "new" trick that could counter the techniques they learned at their former school.

MARTIAL ARTS

Royce Gracie

TOURNAMENTS AND RULES

These differences also extend to tournaments, which, as you know, are an important part of promoting the martial arts. But when practicing a martial art, we must take into consideration what the real goal of the art is—since ultimately a martial art is something different than a sport. Rules in competition, in any kind of competition, set the direction in which the physical techniques of the art will evolve.

For instance, if you score one point with a high kick to the face and one point with a straight punch to the stomach in karate, why are you going to take more chances with a high kick when you can score the same point with a simpler and less complicated straight punch? It is common sense.

The goal of jiu-jitsu is to control and submit your opponent, and these are the only things that should be recognized and worth points in competition. Why, for example, would a poorly executed side-control or technique receive any point or "advantage?"

Think of it this way. If Oscar de la Hoya punches the shoulder of his opponent instead of hitting the head, the judges won't give him a "half-point" or any type of advantage at all. Either he punches the guy or he doesn't.

Therefore, why would you give an "advantage" to a competitor who gets a half-mount that lasts less than a second? After all, he doesn't fully apply the technique and he barely controls the opponent.

In soccer, you don't get a half-goal when your kick hits the post. Kobe Bryant doesn't get a half-

In this sequence from one of the early Ultimate Fighting Championships, Royce Gracie (white uniform) tangles with Ken Shamrock. While in Shamrock's guard, Gracie throws a palm to the side of his opponent's head (1). Gracie then ends up on the bottom (2). The Brazilian then reverses and ultimately chokes out Shamrock (3-7).

Photos by Holly Stein

point when his shot hits the rim and bounces toward mid-court. He simply didn't score. Period. It is that simple; either it is in or it is out.

Conversely, a jiu-jitsu competitor should be awarded points for either controlling his opponent clearly for a certain amount of time (several seconds) or for making his opponent tap by putting him into a submission. Nothing else should score a point, a half-point or an advantage.

This will not only ensure that the competitors have to train to fully control and totally submit their opponent, but that they will stop playing games that create a bad reputation for the sport and catch the winners by surprise. Sometimes competitors don't even know why and how they have won. With the current rules, the winner is not necessarily the best fighter.

OLD JIU-JITSU

But what happens to the "old" techniques ... such as those taught at the Gracie Academy? Every elite fighter knows that mastering the basics is the "secret" to reaching the higher levels of the game. Does Lennox Lewis have more "modern" boxing techniques than George Foreman and Muhammad Ali in their prime?

If that's the case, is it better to learn from Lewis because Ali or Foreman used the "old boxing"? No way. The techniques used by Tyson (with the exception of the biting skills) are the same as those taught by Dundee to Ali or Ray "Sugar" Leonard. The punches, combinations and principles behind every technique are all the same. Why? Because those are the basics, and the basics help you become a world champion.

How many times have you heard in the last 10 years that a boxer has come up with a "new, improved and modified" version of an "old boxing technique?" None. Of course! Professional boxers know better. They need to win fights for money and have no time to fool the crowd with stupid statements. They know what works and have no time to waste in non-sense talking.

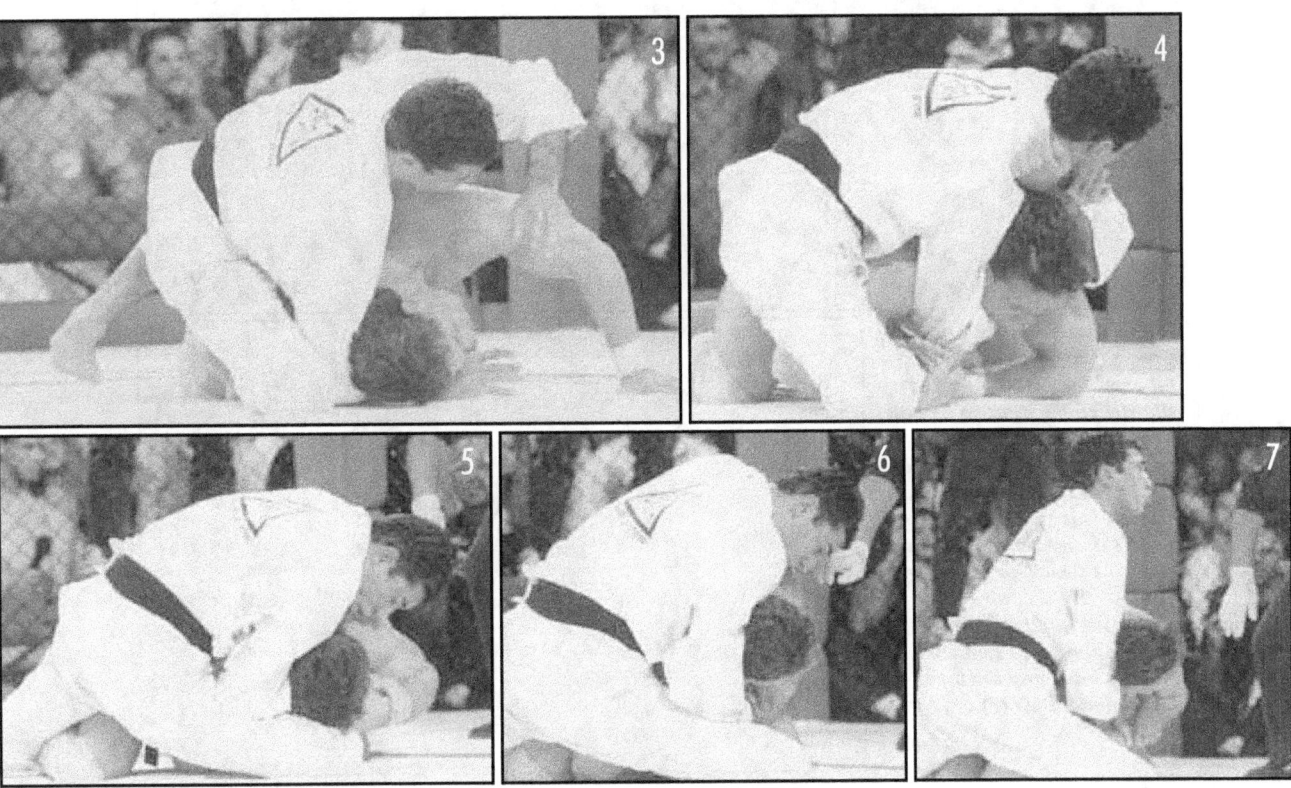

MARTIAL ARTS

If you watch the Los Angeles Lakers practice, you won't see Kobe Bryant or Shaquille O'Neal practicing the latest slum-dunk techniques developed by who-knows-who. They repeat and train the basics shots, the basic footwork, the basic passes and the basic movements. Why? Because when the game is on the line, only these basics will allow the player to score a three-pointer that will win the NBA title—not the fancy movements used for show and to impress the crowd.

The efficiency of jiu-jitsu—like any other fighting art—lies in the mastery of the basic movements. In the long run, you will learn that it is a waste of time to learn 100 different modified techniques [supposedly developed by the champions] because you won't be able to pull these movements off against a decent opponent. Why? Because, instead of spending hours, weeks, months and years working your basics, you skipped those to learn and train the "new" techniques ... those that one day will allow you to beat the old techniques!

What is described as "old" Gracie Jiu-jitsu techniques are no more than pure and simple basics. In the best scenario, the coveted "new" techniques of the modern Brazilian jiu-jitsu instructors are no more than modifications of the basics ... personal modifications developed by competitors who have spent many years training and improving their basic "old" jiu-jitsu techniques.

In the worst scenario, that particular fighter has spent many hours developing new movements for competition as results of his inability to successfully apply the basics [new and improved tech-

In this sequence, Royce Gracie (top) demonstrates an armbar. First, he moves slightly to his right so he can get in position to break his opponent's hold (1-2). Gracie then places his left hand on the left side of his opponent's head (3) and breaks the hold (4-5). As Gracie prepares to execute the armbar (6), he places his hand on the side of his opponent's head. He lays back and finishes his opponent off (7).

nique as result of a lack of basic skill it is not the best example to follow by anyone]. In any case, you won't get any good results by following the wrong path in training.

The techniques Royce Gracie used to win three Ultimate Fighting Championships and the basic techniques that make Rickson Gracie the best fighter in mixed martial arts are not new or modified jiu-jitsu techniques but old jiu-jitsu. So, where are the flaws?

MASTER THE BASICS

There is no flaw. The techniques are the same that are being taught at the Gracie Academy in Torrance. You don't need to know 100 different ways to choke your opponent out. All you may need is four or five fundamental techniques that work from different angles and possibilities—and master those well. The number of variations that you know will be irrelevant if you don't have what it takes to make them work.

The secret is body feel and body mechanics on the ground. By the way, in a stand-up fight these principles apply very differently. These two attributes only will be developed through long sessions of drilling the basics and not necessarily fighting. Drilling the basics is the only "secret" and not necessarily fighting. Professional basketball and football players drill every day and rarely play a full game at practice. That is the same for professional Thai boxers.

Granted, let's say you've been training in jiu-jitsu for a few years. A friend who trains at another school—who may be learning "10 new modified techniques" for competition every day—will make you tap most of the time.

But give yourself eight to 10 years and you'll see the difference. You'll have the experience, skill and ability, and all of these will be built on a good and strong technical foundation. You'll be able to apply the basics, change the angle and modify them at will to suit your game plan. At the same time, you will be able to prevent your opponent from controlling you, simply because you will have more advanced control of the body mechanics and body feel. That is a bit ironic because these are the skills you developed in the first few years of training that you thought were so boring and tedious. Only when you have these attributes developed to a high level, you can apply the basic techniques at will. Hundreds of new movements won't bring this important aspect of fighting.

Rickson Gracie (top), the best mixed martial arts fighter, relies on basic techniques from "old jiu-jitsu."

One of the members of the Gracie family—who also happens to be one of the most respected fighters in Brazil—recently admitted to me just how important the basics are. He said: "To be honest, I don't know all these new techniques, modifications and combinations developed in the last years but nei-

Helio Gracie

Helio Gracie, Royce's father, is the man behind Gracie Jiu-Jitsu.

ther do I care about them. When I'm in the mat with some of my young students, and many of them are champions in Brazil, I can easily stop them and control them. This is all due to my deeper understanding of the basics in jiu-jitsu. Now, at my age, I can truly appreciate how important the basics are and how wrong the practitioners are when they learn all these modifications. They need to work the basics. That's the secret."

Neither Rickson Gracie nor Royce Gracie is any different than Kobe Bryant, Andre Agassi, Mark McGuire or Muhammad Ali. They all learned the basics and developed them without wasting time and energy in searching for shortcuts that—in the long run—will be useless.

When the level of the game increases and your opponents are more knowledgeable and capable of stopping your techniques, you won't need more "secret" techniques and new modifications. Instead, you will need a better game plan, a better understanding of the basic techniques and how they can be used under different scenarios and situations.

THE ABILITY TO ADAPT

The key word here is adaptability. It is not a "new" technique that you need but a deeper understanding of what you have and how to adapt it to a new situation, while maintaining the principles that make the basic technique work. Many people try to "look for" new movements instead of going deeper in the understanding of the fundamental technique. They look for the answer outside while they should be looking inside.

Once again, the secret to making techniques work is the physical attributes developed through many years of drilling the basics. You'll get to the point that you can apply a simple armlock—before the opportunity appears—simply by "feeling" the right opportunity. Believe me, there isn't a "new" technique in the world that will you give you the ability to do this. Instead, it's only tedious repetition of the basics. This will help you to develop the correct body feel.

Unfortunately, it's not human nature to stick to the basics. Instead, everyone is always looking for something more.

MARTIAL ARTS

FORGET THE FANCY, SECRET MOVES. TO WIN, YOU NEED TO GET BACK TO THE BASICS.

Once one has accepted the fact that there are no "secret" techniques, the key element lies in other aspects surrounding the technical training. Physical conditioning, strength training, power training, cardiovascular training, psychological training, et cetera, are all attributes that will make a difference at the end. It is like an iceberg: the tip of the iceberg represents the physical techniques of the art—the basic movements. The rest, all the physical attributes necessary to make that "tip" work in a fight, are the other nine-tenths of the ice. They are under the water where you can't see them.

In the beginning of the Ultimate Fighting Championship (UFC), Royce Gracie defeated bigger opponents by simply using "pure" technique. Nowadays, the fighters are more knowledgeable about the groundwork and technique only is not sufficient to achieve the same results. There is nothing wrong with the old techniques since they are still valid and efficient but now they have to be supported by supplementary aspects due to the fact the game has improved tremendously in the last six or eight years.

In Formula 1 car racing, the basic driving principles used today are the same as those used in the past: you switch to a lower gear before making a turn, you cut the turn in a straight line to save time and you use the same fundamental sport driving principles the old-timers used. The difference lies in the car technology, not in the basic driving principles. The modern aerodynamic shape of the cars, the better engines, cleaner fuel, et cetera provide an advanced support to the old driving techniques that are still valid today because the basic principles are immovable. Once again, the drivers stick to their basics and combine these with the advancements of high-tech research.

FASTEN YOUR BELTS

One of the major criticisms the art of jiu-jitsu has suffered during the last decade is the length of time it takes to gain a color belt (rank) in this martial art. Before making any statements, let's analyze briefly the very nature the jiu-jitsu training in comparison with other systems. In other martial arts methods such as karate, kung-fu and *taekwondo*, the trainees have to develop skills in three different aspects of the art. They are as follows: basic techniques or fundamentals, forms (*kata, kuen, hyong* or *pumse*) and sparring against an adversary. Only one of these three aspects needs an interaction with another live opponent: sparring. The training of the basic techniques and the forms are exercises performed solo, with no opponent involved in the process. This can be described as "shadow boxing." Mastery of any physical activity that involves interaction with another person is twice as difficult to attain than those that require making the movements correct in relation to another's movement. There are simply more elements to control when an opponent is involved in the action than when one person is trying to perfect a physical movement by himself.

Jiu-jitsu techniques—unlike karate-do, taekwondo or kung-fu—must be applied and perfected against live opponents. There are no kata, kuens or hyongs to shadow box. This simple fact makes everything more complicated for the student. It is easy to drive car at 90 mph when there is no traffic on the street. It is a different situation when the street is packed with other cars, cars that move and create a different environment. The level of skill now required to drive at the same speed with cars surrounding us is far more difficult to achieve simply because our driving skill has to be applied in relation to other moving objects. This creates an extremely high level of difficulty. The same thing happens with the art of jiu-jitsu. All the "driving" (training) takes place with other "cars" (opponents) trying to make things difficult for us.

It is then understandable that to achieve the skill level of black belt in jiu-jitsu may take longer than the time required in other arts to get the same rank. Approximately five years of steady training in the other arts (karate, kung-fu and taekwondo) is what it takes to achieve a black belt. Five years in jiu-jitsu will normally get you to a purple belt level, and, as we mentioned previously, a good purple belt knows the most of techniques known by a black belt but lacks more years of additional experience. Additional experience that can be unnecessary in other arts due to the training requirements (forms) is needed in jiu-jitsu because of the need to apply the techniques against moving (alive) opponents. It is not only extremely necessary but mandatory. Imagine just for a moment how many years it would take for a karate-ka to be capable of using (against an uncooperative opponent) all the techniques found in every kata he knows!

After many years of practice, the jiu-jitsu exponent has a higher level of practical application of the technical knowledge he knows as compared to students of most other arts. The reason for this is simple—everything in jiu-jitsu involves training with a partner.

Royce Gracie (right) squares off with an opponent (1). When his opponent throws a right, Gracie moves in and ties up his opponent (2–3). Gracie wraps his arm around his opponent (4), steps forward with his right leg and throws him to the ground (5–9). Gracie finishes by cranking his elbow (10–11).

MARTIAL ARTS

GRACIE JIU-JITSU AND JKA KARATE

To imply that the "old" Gracie techniques taught, for instance by Helio Gracie, are no longer valid because they represent "traditional" jiu-jitsu is like saying the karate system taught by the late Masatoshi Nakayama at the JKA Headquarters is no good anymore and is obsolete because "JKA people do not do well in modern competition." Interestingly enough, in a World Shotokan Cup held in Germany, the top WUKO champions had to face some of the JKA members in *kumite* and *kata*. Well, the JKA exponents, the ones always practicing "boring basics," swept their opponents with simple, straight and powerful tech-

Rorion Gracie (standing)

niques. Many of these Caucasians were European and world champions. Later on, the JKA decided not to compete under these rules because they felt many of the techniques allowed to score didn't represent what a "real" karate technique should have: focus, balance, control and power, all supported by a perfect technical delivery. Masters like Hirokazu Kanazawa, Taiji Kase, Keinosuke Enoeda, Mikio Yahara, Y. Osaka, Hidetaka Nishiyama, et cetera are the result of this "old" form of karate and guess what? They are the best karate masters in the world today! Their basics are almost perfect, their kata precise and clean, their understanding of the principles behind the technique amazing and their teaching abilities second to none. They can easily "play" with many so-called modern world champions. Not bad for being the practitioners of "old" karate! If you have the chance of training at the JKA *Honbu* dojo, you'll see that even the advanced and senior instructors repeat the basic techniques over and over again. They don't waste time in fancy and modified techniques. Instead, they focus on pure and simple basics. They (the JKA masters) know that any advanced technique, to be successfully applied, needs the attributes developed by constant drilling of the basics (balance, accuracy, speed, focus, power, et cetera.) Without the constant training of the basics—even if you are an advanced practitioner—you won't be able to use more advanced movements. But what exactly is an *advanced movement*? Well, for the average martial arts practitioner, an "advanced movement" is a new trick, something he needs to know to impress friends or to keep students interested in case he is an instructor in the school. For a fighter, an "advanced movement" is simply a more sophisticated application of a basic principle or technique. No basic technique, no advanced application. It is a fact that in combat any "advanced technique" can only be countered by a "basic" technique. Simply ask the best fighters in the world regardless of style, from Thai boxing, boxing, karate or Brazilian jiu-jitsu to NHB and you'll see this is true.

Any double spinning high kick can be stopped by a simple and powerful *gyaku tsuki* to your body. So instead of spending hours and hours practicing these modified techniques and advanced

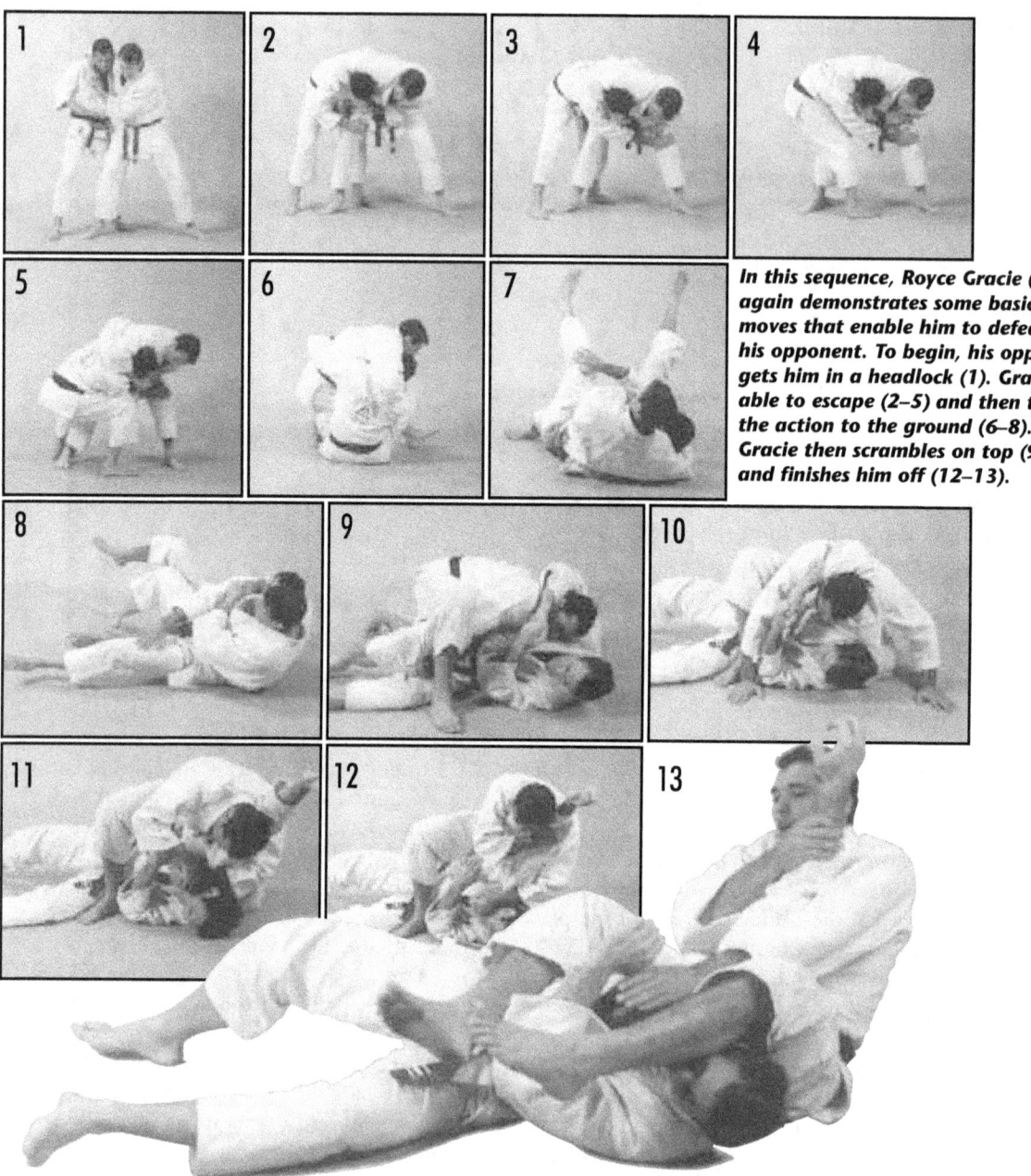

In this sequence, Royce Gracie (left) again demonstrates some basic moves that enable him to defeat his opponent. To begin, his opponent gets him in a headlock (1). Gracie is able to escape (2–5) and then takes the action to the ground (6–8). Gracie then scrambles on top (9–11) and finishes him off (12–13).

movements, it would obviously be wiser to spend time practicing the basics: the "old techniques" many describe as obsolete. After years of practice, you'll have a strong foundation and you'll be able to use the art effectively and not simply being capable of showing some fancy movements to your friends and students.

It is true that the way these great karate masters teach the art is not suitable for modern sport competitions in which a simple touch is scored as a full-point and many other "funny" strategies and tactics are used to win tournaments. Their technique is not modified or changed to "fit" the new rules. These masters are living repositories of the art and their students can be told apart by the way they use the techniques—with power, precision, without compromising the art for the sport. They stress the importance of developing a good foundation in the art. Then, if the student wishes, he will use these techniques in sport competition. The problem arises when the rules change so much that nonsense techniques are valid in competition. That's exactly what is happening to Brazilian jiu-jitsu competitions these days. As a result of this, the instructors, instead of teaching and spending time drilling the students in the basics of the art, teach random techniques that won't allow the student to improve in the art. They may allow him to win a competition scoring five advantages and half-points for doing nothing, but they will never be able to submit an opponent properly with a precise technique.

In the past Copa Pacifica, Ryron and Rener Gracie from the Gracie Academy in Torrance were scheduled to fight two tough opponents who train under relevant instructors in South Bay area. Their opponents exemplified the more modern approach to jiu-jitsu, were well-versed in the "updated" new competition moves and they also outweighed the Gracies by a considerable amount. In the end, Ryron and Rener submitted their opponents making them tap out with a straight and basic "old" choke—the very first choke you learn at any jiu-jitsu school. It seems that the "old techniques" are still valid and important, especially when your opponents spent a lot of time developing the "new" stuff!

THE GOAL

The goal of this article is to bring to the attention of Brazilian jiu-jitsu practitioners and martial artists in general that the direction that they have been heading for the last few years may not be the one that eventually will bring them the best benefits. A top Brazilian instructor visited a well-known Brazilian jiu-jitsu school in the United States to give a three-day seminar. After the first day of analyzing the students' skill levels (many of them brown and black belts), he whispered: "I don't know what I'm going to teach. These people don't know their basics well. They have been wasting their time with competition techniques!" Needless to say, for the next two days the "advanced" group spent six straight hours per day drilling the in most basic jiu-jitsu techniques, the ones some people call "old and obsolete." By the end of the seminar, all of the participants understood how mistaken they were in the direction their training was going. This is similar to what Hirokazu Kanazawa sensei did during a karate-do seminar in England in which he had the complete group of students repeating the *reverse-punch* (gyaku-tsuki) for the whole day because "they didn't have the feeling of it, let alone the right body mechanics." This is particularly embarrassing when one considers that in the group there were many elite fighters—world and European champions from Italy, France, Spain and Great Britain.

Unfortunately, not everybody has the opportunity to train under a good martial arts instructor. This kind of instructor is not only capable of showing the technique and explaining its important points. He also knows how to teach the student to analyze and dissect any other physical technique so a student can find the reason why a movement works or doesn't work without waiting the rest of his life for his instructor to tell him. This kind of instructor is hard to find. If you are lucky enough to find one, don't be silly and leave him for another place where you can learn "cool" stuff. Instead, stick to this instructor like glue and train hard. One day, you'll certainly understand!

MARTIAL ARTS

The 3 Doors of Raymond Wong

Three styles, one great system. Sifu Raymond Wong has opened the door to a brand new kung-fu world.

Ron Quan

When his name was announced to the audience, he was greeted with a hearty welcome from traditional aficionados. And a traditionalist he was. Having recently arrived from Hong Kong and after spending time in both Vancouver, B.C., and San Francisco, Calif., he was drawn to the Southern California area.

Today, he was about to perform the nine-sectional chain whip for the first time in the Los Angeles area. He opens his routine by whipping the chain straight out from his hand and beginning a series of flowing circles followed by another series of circle eights. As he moves about the gymnasium floor whipping the chain in artistic motion, exhibiting control and complexity, at times whipping the chain around his ankles, then his waist, then his neck, the spectators stare in awe at his unique performance. When the artist signaled the end of his routine by whipping the chain around and catching the tip of it in his hand, the audience stood and clapped. The time: 1972. The occasion: the Southern California Kung-fu Exhibition, held in the basketball gymnasium of Los Angeles City College.

Now almost 30 years later, the performer, sifu Raymond Kwok Jung Wong still practices this nine-sectional chain whip weapon.

"This chain is not like the light-metal wushu-type used today to show speed," Wong explains. "The traditional chain whip is made of heavy steel and when one starts learning, it leaves many bruises on the head, arms, and shins.

"But I have always enjoyed this weapon. It was a gift to me from grandmaster Chiu Chi-Kai of the tai chi praying mantis system," he adds. "He wanted me to learn one of his favorite weapons, as he played it often, even into his 70s. It is a type of weapon that still requires practice. If one does not, one loses his timing and the chain, having its own personality, will not cooperate."

Profile
Name: Raymond K.J. Wong
Birthplace: Kwangtung, China
Style: My jong law horn, tai chi mantis and dao ga
Contact: RaymondWong@MJLHKungfu.com

Today, this quiet traditional master teaches this tai chi praying mantis system as well as two other systems—the my-jong law horn (lost track/Buddhist monk) and the Taoist. Beginning his martial art career at the age of eight, Wong now teaches more than 80 single- and two-person fist and weapon routines, traditional weaponry, self-defense techniques, and traditional herbal medicine. Sifu Wong is a walking encyclopedia of Chinese martial arts.

"When I was young, learning traditional routines was easy for me," he explains. "My mind was

Tai Chi Praying Mantis Style. Master Wong blocks a punch and grabs the attacker (1-2). The attacker counters with a wristlock (3-4). Master Wong breaks the lock and traps the attacker (5-6). He finishes with a backfist to the head (7).

fresh and I was enthusiastic to learn. I learned quickly. I could almost watch a routine a few times and after some practice, I would have it.

"I feel lucky to have learned the long-range kicking and jumping techniques of the law horn system," he notes. "And to be able to add the close-range techniques of both the tai chi praying mantis and the Taoist systems made my martial art goals complete."

My Jong Law Horn (Lost Track/Buddhist Monk)

This more than 100-year-old Northern China long-fist system is actually a merger of the my jong (lost track) and the law horn (Buddhist monk) systems. Grandmaster Yep Ye-Ting was originally a law horn specialist from the Hopei province. His life is filled with adventures as a transport security guard, a warlord army instructor, and a Shanghai Jing-Wu Academy instructor, where he added the famous my jong system and became one of the few north China instructors to travel south to Hong Kong to spread northern martial arts.

Both systems are characterized by their low stances, long-arm punching, continuous jumping, lively kicking, and free-flowing movement. There are several routines requiring varying degrees of agility; moving fast, leaping high then dropping low while applying a variety of defensive or offensive techniques. While parrying, striking, and kicking are common features in the routines, grabbing, controlling, and counterrelease techniques are also emphasized.

There are several single-fist, two-person fist, individual and two-person weapon routines in this combined classical system. Beginning students start with the gung lik kuen (internal strength), cheung kuen (long fist), jeet kuen (intercepting fist), and suet fa don do (snow flake single saber) routines. Traditional weapon instruction extends to variations of single and double saber, double hooks, staff, spear, trident, horse cutter, two- and three-sectional staffs, various internal swords, and the Kwan do. The spear is often used in various two-person weapon routines against the single saber, double saber, double hooks, horse cutter, three-sectional staff, two-sectional staff, and a unique single saber/tonfa combination.

Tai Chi Praying Mantis

This system was made famous by grandmaster Chiu Chuk Kai, a praying mantis and tai chi specialist from Shantung province who migrated south where he taught for several decades in both South Vietnam and Hong Kong.

This variation of the northern China praying mantis system is characterized by its close in-fighting hook-and-strike combinations. Its movements are continuous, fluid, and rhythmic. Using hand trapping and quick body shifts, the practitioner strikes quickly to the

Tao Ga Style. Master Wong blocks the punch (1) and steps to the side of the attacker. He traps the attacker's elbow (2), grabs his hair and knees him in the ribs (3). Master Wong blocks a second punch (4) and elbows the attacker's head (5). He follows by throwing him to the ground (6-7).

opponent's eyes, throat, or groin areas. Strikes are made in rapid combinations while the body shifts from high to low positions and clings to the opponent's hand and feet movements. Both mid-body and shin kicks are used in unison with the hand movements.

The tai chi component of this system refers to the routines that resemble tai chi chuan in practice, but are not the same as those practiced in the Chen, Wu, or Yang styles. One of the routines is called "mor wan jiang (opening the clouds) and sifu Wong currently begins each of his practice sessions with this routine.

"The original praying mantis style was an external style where all of the moves were quick and hard," he relates. "But I think that as grandmaster Chiu entered his 70s, he began to rethink his art and began to apply an alternating hard-and-soft approach. One's strikes should not be too hard nor should they be too soft. There is a time to strike hard and there is a time for moving lightly. One can be quick and fast but one should also be light footed and agile. This is the essence of tai chi praying mantis."

Sifu Wong's learning of several individual fist routines, two-person fist and weapon routines, two-person sensitivity exercises, a dynamic wooden durnmy routine, and the nine-link chain all served to make learning the tai chi praying mantis system a true martial art experience. Students begin with bun bo kuen (crushing steps), mui fa kuen (plum blossom), chop chui kuen (trapping punch), and the bok jow kuen (eight elbow) solo routines.

Dao Gah (The Taoist System)

But of the three systems, sifu Wong speaks fondly of his dao gah.

"I learned this soft wudang style from a Chan Ghim, who later left Hong Kong for Brazil where we subsequently lost touch," sifu Wong recalls. "Wudang is generally considered a soft style, yet this form of wudang is both hard and soft—that's why it is also called "leung yhi pai." Leung yi makes reference to the Taoist symbol of yin and yang, the black and the white, and the hard and the soft."

The basis for Taoism is that nature is a oneness composed of opposing but harmonious forces that are always in a state of flux. And while these opposing forces seem to counteract each

My Jong Law Horn Style.
Master Wong grabs the attacker's wrist (1-2). He steps inside and under the attacker's arm, turning and twisting as he moves (3-4). He applies pressure until the attacker drops to the ground (5-6).

other, they also serve to complement each other—resulting in a harmonious balance. The Taoist views life as attempting to achieve oneness with nature by balancing nature's opposing forces while maintaining moderation and simplicity.

Thus, in this soft style, there is a soft component that consists of tai chi-related routines, and there is a hard component called the dao gah.

"I enjoy this dao gah because of its practicality," sifu Wong notes. "There are close-range techniques, hair and wrist grabs, elbow and knee strikes, and a continuous flow of punch, kick-grab combinations. Also, the phoenix eye punch is used throughout the routines."

There are five solo fist routines named after the five elements of nature: wood, fire, water, metal, and earth. There are two-person fist routines and an arsenal of practical short weapons. These weapons include the walking cane, single and double daggers, double needles, the machete, and the double crutch.

Combining the Systems

Learning three different martial art systems can be quite challenging. However, sifu Wong feels fortunate that he has been able to learn and preserve these systems over the years.

"Yes, it's true that learning three different styles at the same time can be confusing," he admits. "However, I learned these arts one step at a time. I was young at the time and my brain and body were fresh and eager to learn. At some point, I learned up to 140 routines (forms). I had a good aptitude for learning the martial arts and I was eager. I could learn movements and duplicate them just by observing. I used to be able to learn an entire routine in a couple of hours. Of course, I do not teach 140 routines today as many are either too basic, repetitive, or are not practical. Now I teach about 80 routines that I think are more practical and I am still trying to cut away as I know that people are too busy to learn so many routines."

While varied and based on different concepts, these system still complement each other.

"I'm very happy about learning and being able to add these three styles together," sifu Wong states. "And the three styles seem to connect and flow together very well. The mah jong law horn is a good style with long-range jumping, kicking, punching, and grabbing techniques. The praying mantis is more medium-range and the dao gah is more close range. The three, together, interconnect smoothly."

Sifu Wong adds that the flaws of one system may be compensated by the strengths of another.

"For example, in the grabbing technique, the my jong law horn grabs tight like an eagle," he says. "But, there is no follow through after the grab; also, it uses a one-strike approach, hoping to get a one-strike knockdown. Typical long fist style. But, in the dao gah, you continue with more techniques to maintain control. The praying mantis is very similar to the dao gah in the techniques, as well as close-in fighting with hair grabs, elbow strikes, shin kicks. The dao gah stylist is in a continuous flow of punching and attacking until the opponent goes down."

Sifu Wong's journey into the world of three different martial arts has been filled with dedication, persistence, focus, tradition, and effort. It is not one that many today would be willing to experience. However, there are those that would find such a challenge inviting and could appreciate the curriculum that sifu Wong has to offer. The paths through the three doors can be long and grueling, but a higher plateau is accessible. This plateau is finally achieved when one realizes that the three pathways traveled have in its finality evolved into becoming one. This oneness can be known as the Three Doors of sifu Raymond Wong.

Ron Quan is an instructor in Northern China my jong law horn, flying eagle hapkido and American boxing in Los Angeles' Chinatown. He can be reached at sifuron@earthlink.net

MARTIAL ARTS

Andy Kimura—The Sum of All Parts

The son of legendary Taky Kimura is trying to follow in the big footsteps of two martial arts icons.

David Tadman

The definition of legacy is "anything handed down from an ancestor." When we think of the legacy Bruce Lee left to his students, specifically Taky Kimura, we think of the holy grail of martial arts instruction. The years Taky Kimura spent alongside Bruce Lee learning the physical and the philosophy of Bruce's jeet kune do was invaluable. Today, there are students throughout the world teaching Bruce's art, but maybe no one has enjoyed a better education than Andrew Kimura, Taky's son. Andy has benefited from learning from the teacher who learned from the master. There may have been no one closer to Bruce Lee than Taky Kimura, and it is through his father than Andrew Kimura is doing his part to keep Bruce's legacy alive.

INSIDE KUNG-FU: Can you tell us about your martial arts background?

ANDY KIMURA: I have studied Jun Fan gung-fu and jeet kune do under my father Taky Kimura, who was an appointed instructor and close friend of the late Bruce Lee. My father has taught me since my childhood. I have studied judo, jiu-jitsu, Western boxing, kali, jeet kune do, wing chun, Thai boxing and shoot wrestling. I have been exposed to all of these disciplines. Some of my instructors have been sifu Dan Inosanto, Eric Paulson, Wally Jay and Yori Nakamura, and many more that had shared their time and donated their talents through the Jun Fan Jeet Kune Do Nucleus. I have been studying about 15 years now.

IKF: Your father was the student of the legendary Bruce Lee. Can you tell us what it was like to be your father's student?

AK: My father and I share a very unique relationship. We are best friends. He is my father, best friend and sifu. That's a very unique relationship. It's an honor to know the man and to be his son has made me humble. The wealth of knowledge my father has does not stop at the physical; it carries into

Up Close
Name: Andrew Kimura
Birthdate: Sept. 17, 1971
Birthplace: Seattle, Wash.
Current Residence: Woodinville, Wash.
Martial Arts Studied: Jun Fan gung-fu, jeet kune do, muay Thai, shoot wrestling
Contact: Andykimura.com

Andrew works out on the wing chun dummy.

Andrew throws a side kick in the Seattle Jun Fan Gung Fu Club.

Andrew poses next to the graves of his sigung, Bruce Lee, and Bruce's son, Brandon.

the philosophical and spiritual. I would have to say being my father's student has taught me more than martial arts. He has taught me how to be a good human being. He is my mentor.

IKF: What's your training like with your father?

AK: At times it's great fun and at other times he can be extremely demanding. Bruce Lee would never take anything that was not 100-percent effort and my father is the same way. My father always told me if you are not going to do it right, then don't do it at all. You can say my father knows what each individual needs and he pushes them until that's accomplished.

IKF: What's the greatest lesson you've learned from your father?

AK: He always stresses to me that you have to believe in yourself and follow your heart. Many people come to my father for help and my father always says, "It was Bruce that helped me to help you." There is a lot of truth to this, because sometimes you have to look outside yourself for help, be it a higher power, friend, etc. In his own way, my father is still influenced by Bruce Lee to this day, and it helps my father help others in many different ways. My father has taught that the spiritual and philosophical are more important than the physical aspects of martial art.

IKF: Do you and your father teach classes together?

AK: Yes we do. My father has had me teaching for the last six-to-eight years now. As I have gotten older my father has pushed me to the forefront to help him. It's been very enjoyable to work side by side with him. I have learned and continue to learn many things.

Sifu Dan Inosanto, Andrew Kimura and sifu Taky Kimura at the Inosanto Academy.

Andrew and his father, sifu Taky Kimura, work out together.

IKF: Do you and your father train together?

AK: I am truly fortunate to be able to train with him whenever I like. There is only a certain amount of time in one's life that he or she is at their physical best. I am fortunate to have a father/sifu who has preached and shown me the spiritual and philosophical aspect of martial art. He has often told me that, "When one is old or cannot move like they did in their youth, then they have to rely more on timing and rhythm, not strength and speed." I have learned through my father that martial art is life and it is an endless journey I look forward to.

IKF: I know you teach the art of Jun Fan gung-fu. How are your classes structured?

AK: The classes are loosely structured just like Bruce used to teach, but we do have a curriculum that was left behind from him that we follow. We stay true to that curriculum and as one gets more proficient we then introduce the student to the concepts of jeet kune do. When Bruce was in Oakland and then on to Los Angeles he would frequently call my father to update him on the new strides he was making in his jeet kune do. He constantly told my father that he would show him new techniques in jeet kune do when he came back up to Seattle for business, etc. We slowly show our students what Bruce taught my father, but we do it when we feel that particular student is ready for the next step.

In a group picture with the Seattle chapter Jun Fan Gung Fu School, Bruce Lee is top row, sixth from the left and Taky Kimura is bottom row, second from the left.

IKF: In your opinion, what separated the way Bruce taught in Seattle to the way he taught in Oakland and Los Angeles?

AK: I feel his mental attitude was always the same. Bruce was an innovator from the beginning. He was constantly changing and inventing new ways to better himself and continually evolving as a human being. I feel Seattle to Oakland and then Los Angeles should be looked at as a progression time for Bruce. He was young and changing his way every day. Bruce did have his foundations, but they did not bind him, and as he got older and wiser, he discovered what worked best for him. He felt that in the process of learning jeet kune do it must be tailored to one's individuality. Bruce was simply evolving from place to place, which is the natural progression of life. There are many that learned their piece of the pie, so to speak. In Seattle Bruce taught my father many things and in Oakland he taught James Lee many things. In Los Angeles sifu Dan Inosanto was taught many things as well. Bruce shared what he knew with people he felt close to and the closest people were certified to teach by him. There is much to learn from Seattle, Oakland and Los Angeles.

Bruce Lee and Taky Kimura work out at the Seattle class.

"I want my students to know that they belong to a great lineage that goes back to the Shaolin Temple, Yip Man and Bruce Lee."

IKF: How many students attend your classes?

AK: My father and I have around 40-to-45 students right now. We do not have a "school"; it is like a club, and we do not charge.

IKF: Is there a selective process one goes through before being accepted into your classes?

AK: We are very selective and look for individuals that have had some type of martial arts training previously, but this does not mean we would not accept an individual who has no prior training. My father interviews the individual to see what that person's goals are and if it meets what we are trying to accomplish in our school, then we will accept that person. We have many individuals from many walks of life, and they all have needs. We try to meet everyone's needs by helping them express their self through our training.

IKF: Do you cater to each individual's physical and philosophical make-up?

AK: I feel we do. Some people will excel in punching when others do it in kicking. There are people that want to dive right into sparring, etc. We are all different and we should be taught that way. I must say that we do have our foundation and we do teach a certain curriculum, but each individual will be taught in a way that helps him excel.

IKF: What do you try to stress most to your students?

AK: I want my students to know when they walk out of the class that they belong to a great lineage that goes back to the Shaolin Temple, Yip Man and Bruce Lee. This is very important. I want the students to take with them a sense of pride. If they leave feeling good about themselves and their accomplishments, and if they are happy with where they are in their lives, then I am doing my job right.

IKF: What does Jun Fan jeet kune do mean to you?

AK: It is and has been a path for me in finding myself. It is a spiritual and philosophical quest. It starts out being physical, but ends up being a search for one's self. I have learned much, but I am still following that path. To me Jun Fan jeet kune do represents the truth of expressing yourself.

IKF: Do you feel an obligation to keep the art of Jun Fan jeet kune do alive?

AK: My loyalty lies with my father and the memory of Bruce Lee and his teachings. I do have an obligation to share my knowledge and preach Bruce's word, so to speak. The art must go on for generation to generation and I am obligated to help this happen. It is an honor for me.

David Tadman is a frequent contributor to Inside Kung-Fu.

MARTIAL ARTS

Internal Power

How to cultivate Ki in Aikido

Rev. Kensho Furuya

Ki (life force or vital energy of life) is, I believe, one of the most commonly used but most commonly misunderstood words in the martial arts today. For example, *aikidoists* speak of ki all the time. We also hear about chi (ki) in *chi gong*. Chi, as you know, is the Chinese pronunciation. It seems that just 20 or 30 years ago ki was a rather mysterious, exotic word. Today it is a common term in our English language, and we use it in acupuncture, alternative medicine and sports, as well as in almost all of our martial arts.

The ancient Chinese created the character for ki using the radical for "gas" or "steam" and the radical for "rice." Noticing the steam rising up from the boiling rice inspired the notion of something material out of this world and something really not there. Today, we think of ki in terms of something psychic or telekinetic, but ki, as you will see, comes from something much more ancient and profound.

HARMONY, PEACE

When referring to ki, especially in training, we are not talking about something that "we will" or something that we order around by our thought process. Ki, instead, refers to something much greater than ourselves and how we blend into or harmonize with nature itself.

The 11th century Sung philosopher, Chu Hsi, concluded that ki is "ri," and ri is "reason, measure, order, law" ... as in order of the universe or nature. As ri is the order of nature, ki is the energy that expresses this order. Ki is not self-willed, psychic power. It is more the energy we are endowed with as we harmonize with the laws of nature itself. This is why, in aikido, ki fits so well with and is so compatible to the principles of harmony and peace.

In aikido training, it is important for the beginning student to understand the technique through big, circular movements, never clashing with but deflecting, evading and blending with the opponent's movement, attack and energy. It is through strong, circular movements from a strong balance and well-centered posture that we begin to feel the emergence of ki energy without ourselves.

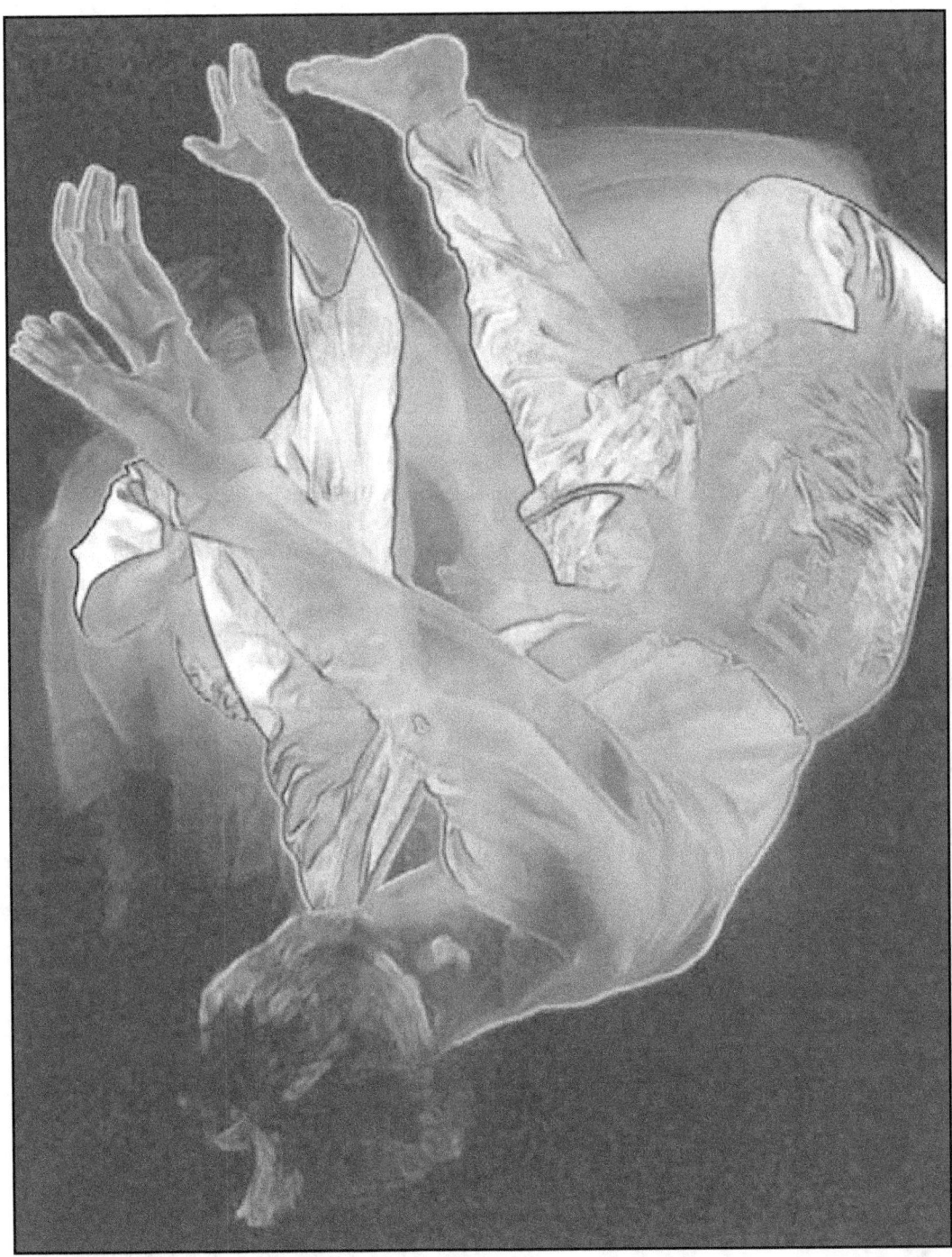

Becoming too stiff, hard, inflexible and always clashing with the opponent causes the ki to stop or become blocked.

In Japanese, the word that means "stuck," "stopped up" or "stale" ki is *byoki*, which also, by the way, means sickness or disease. When the ki gets stuck or stopped in our bodies, we become sick.

MARTIAL ARTS

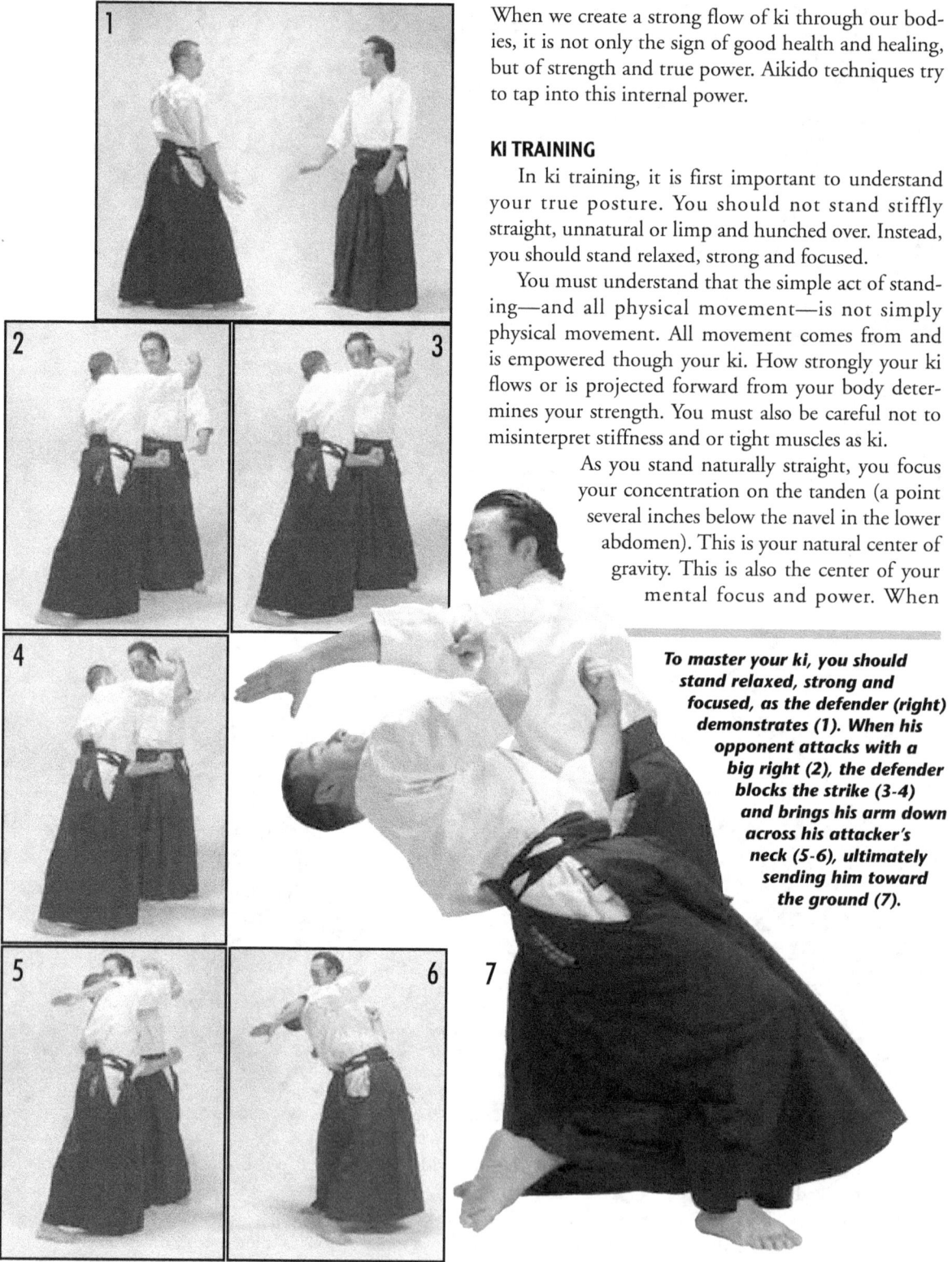

When we create a strong flow of ki through our bodies, it is not only the sign of good health and healing, but of strength and true power. Aikido techniques try to tap into this internal power.

KI TRAINING

In ki training, it is first important to understand your true posture. You should not stand stiffly straight, unnatural or limp and hunched over. Instead, you should stand relaxed, strong and focused.

You must understand that the simple act of standing—and all physical movement—is not simply physical movement. All movement comes from and is empowered though your ki. How strongly your ki flows or is projected forward from your body determines your strength. You must also be careful not to misinterpret stiffness and or tight muscles as ki.

As you stand naturally straight, you focus your concentration on the tanden (a point several inches below the navel in the lower abdomen). This is your natural center of gravity. This is also the center of your mental focus and power. When

To master your ki, you should stand relaxed, strong and focused, as the defender (right) demonstrates (1). When his opponent attacks with a big right (2), the defender blocks the strike (3-4) and brings his arm down across his attacker's neck (5-6), ultimately sending him toward the ground (7).

When you have a strong sense of ki through your body, it is a sign of good health, healing, strength and true power. Here, one of Kensho Furuya's students easily disposes of an attacker.

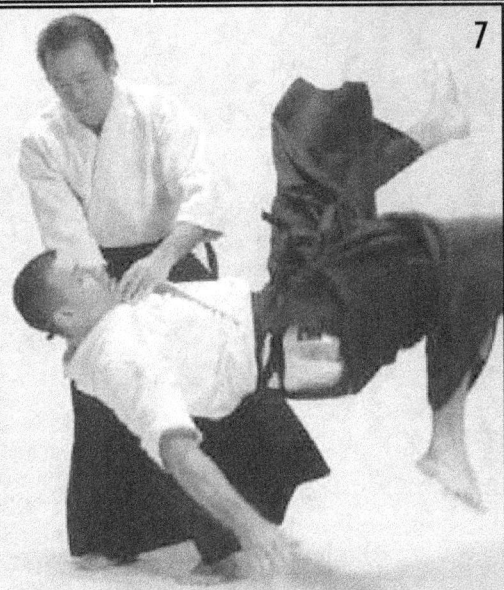

you are properly focused, centered and standing naturally straight, you do not necessarily feel well-balanced and centered. You will, however, feel mentally alert and active. This is the same posture as in zazen or in Zen meditation.

If you are doing this wrong, you will feel stiffness in your back, neck and muscles, your legs will not feel comfortable and, after a few seconds, you will begin to sway or lose your balance. You will not be able to focus clearly and may lose your mental connection with your opponent. This is most dangerous in a

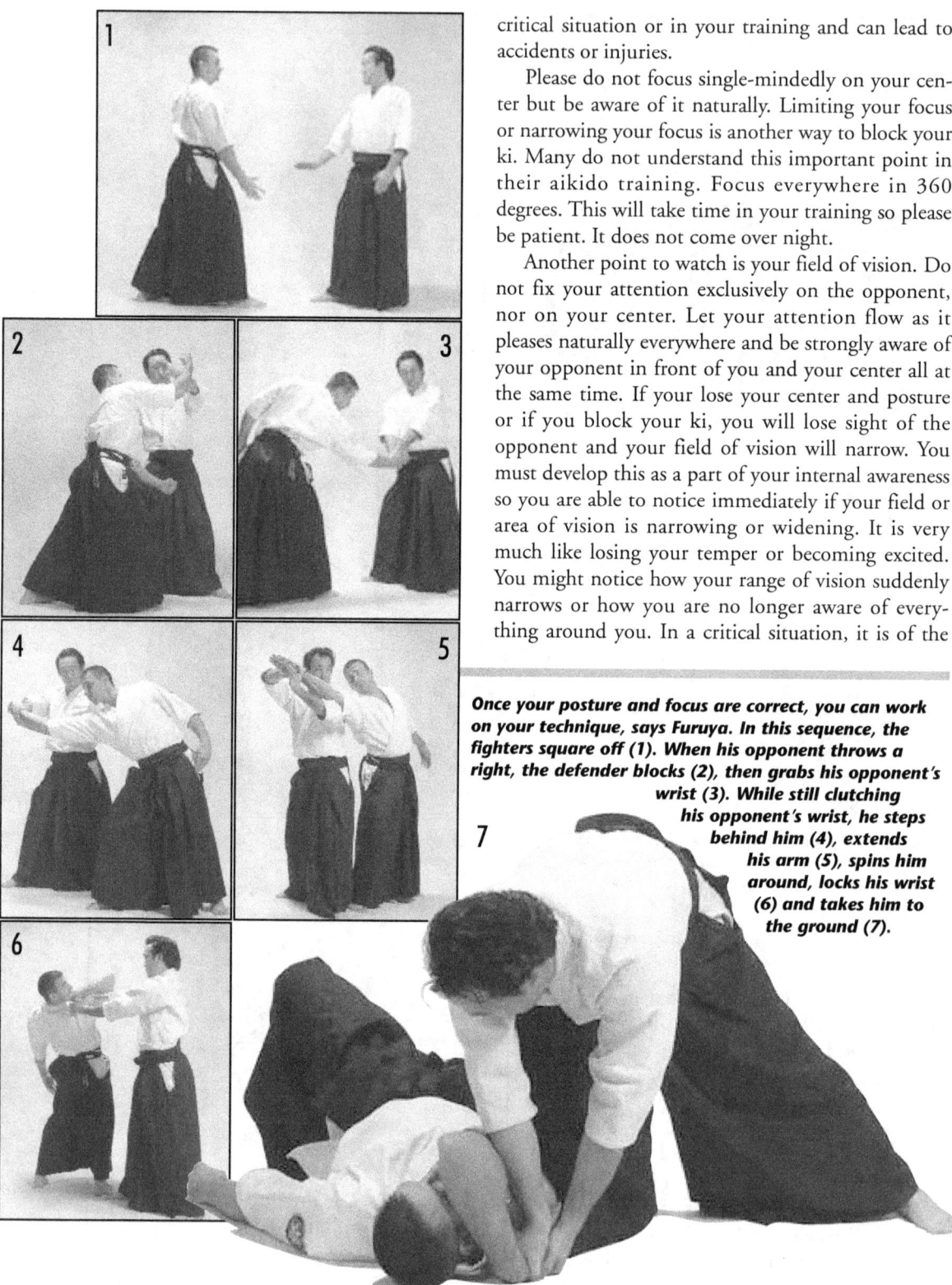

critical situation or in your training and can lead to accidents or injuries.

Please do not focus single-mindedly on your center but be aware of it naturally. Limiting your focus or narrowing your focus is another way to block your ki. Many do not understand this important point in their aikido training. Focus everywhere in 360 degrees. This will take time in your training so please be patient. It does not come over night.

Another point to watch is your field of vision. Do not fix your attention exclusively on the opponent, nor on your center. Let your attention flow as it pleases naturally everywhere and be strongly aware of your opponent in front of you and your center all at the same time. If your lose your center and posture or if you block your ki, you will lose sight of the opponent and your field of vision will narrow. You must develop this as a part of your internal awareness so you are able to notice immediately if your field or area of vision is narrowing or widening. It is very much like losing your temper or becoming excited. You might notice how your range of vision suddenly narrows or how you are no longer aware of everything around you. In a critical situation, it is of the

Once your posture and focus are correct, you can work on your technique, says Furuya. In this sequence, the fighters square off (1). When his opponent throws a right, the defender blocks (2), then grabs his opponent's wrist (3). While still clutching his opponent's wrist, he steps behind him (4), extends his arm (5), spins him around, locks his wrist (6) and takes him to the ground (7).

utmost importance to remain calm and well centered. It is not only your mental posture but your physical abilities are greatly affected.

It is appropriate to develop the proper posture, center of gravity, mental focus and vision through your training. One well-known aikidoist once said that he could maintain this posture for one minute, totally concentrated and balanced. This was the result of many years of training. Very few of us can develop such powers of concentration in our practice.

Once you have the correct posture and focus, you can discover the beginning of good technique. Although one may imitate moves and techniques, if you cannot develop the proper balance in every movement with the correct projection ki, it is not real aikido technique.

DEVOTED TO TRAINING

While many want instant gratification, you can only develop your ki through devoted training. But it is is worth the time, effort and sacrifice, says Kensho Furuya.

In the ancient East, the masters valued movements that are in tune with nature and in harmony with the principles of moving this energy. In most cases, we look at only the physical technique. In aikido training, it is important to master both the physical skills and the fundamentals as it is to fully understand the principles of ki. Many times, we are in danger of simply using our imagination or trying to convince ourselves this is ki we are using. This is why these subtle principles should be learned under the strict eye of a competent teacher.

In my own experience, most students can catch the basic movements but fail to completely understand the importance of good posture and balance. As you develop strength and speed against the opponent's attack, you begin to appreciate how critical it is.

These principles can only be developed through devoted training. Today, we are obsessed with instant gratification. Nothing, truly worth learning, can be learned in an instant. Take time, make sacrifices, develop priorities and take the time and energy to practice correctly and you will find sold rewards for your efforts. The other side of the instant gratification coin is easy come, easy go.

About the writer: Kensho Furuya operates the Aikido Center of Los Angeles.

The Secret Behind Tiger Iron Palm

Whoever said every iron palm technique was the same never experienced the challenge of tiger iron palm.

Wing Lam and Chet Braun

Tiger iron palm comes from the hasayfu hung gar lineage and introduces a unique twist to the shaolin lineage popularized by the noted Gu Ru Zhang. Tiger iron palm uses a unique set-up requiring a special table and demanding more overall body movement during practice.

The most distinguishing features of tiger iron palm are the addition of a sliding bag and a fifth strike—a combination heel-hand with tiger claw pull. The sliding bag arrangement requires a table with a hardwood base that's designed to tilt forward and backward to provide resistance, either when pushing the bag away (tilted forward) or when drawing it back (tilted backward).

The warm-up routine for the tiger iron palm is different from the warm-up routine for shaolin iron palm. Instead of swinging your arms to bring energy to your hands, you'll immerse them in a type of herbal soak called sai si fong to achieve the same results. Before you start training, soak your hands in the sai si fong for ten-to-15 minutes and then allow them to dry.

Use the same hand positions when practicing tiger iron palm as when practicing shaolin iron palm—a palm slap, a backhand slap, a knife-edge strike, and a fingertip strike—with one important addition and modification: Insert a heel-hand strike before the final fingertip strike to push the bag away, and then modify the fingertip strike into a tiger claw to pull the bag toward you again.

Just before the bag hits the forward stop, sink both the heel of your hand and your elbow to stop

MARTIAL ARTS

Excerpted with permission from Ultimate Iron Palm © 2002 by Wing Lam & Chet Braun.

it. The complete sequence of strikes is palm, back, edge, forward thrust heel-hand, fingertip, tiger claw drawback, and heel-hand sink.

While the stances in shaolin iron palm training are basically static, the tiger iron palm method has specific movements into and out of stances designed to accommodate the new hand strikes. Stand in a horse stance during the first three strikes (palm, backhand, and knife edge). After the knife-edge hand, and as you position your hand for the heel-hand strike, step forward into a bow stance with the same foot as the striking hand. Step back into a horse stance as you drag the bag back, completing the motion into the horse as you sink your wrist and elbow to stop the bag. The

MARTIAL ARTS

This is the front view of a traditional tiger iron palm table. Made of solid teakwood, it could withstand the tremendous forces generated by the old iron palm masters. This kind of table would often last many generations. Teakwood is now extremely expensive, so pine, fir, or oak is often used. The design of this table is true to tradition.

Different Bags
Your tiger iron palm training will involve different levels of steel bags. Begin by using a steel bag weighing about 30 pounds, and then increase the weight of the bag by about ten pounds each time you're ready to advance. In ancient times, iron palm masters used bags that weighed up to 200 pounds.

"The most distinguishing features of tiger iron palm are the addition of a sliding bag and a fifth strike."

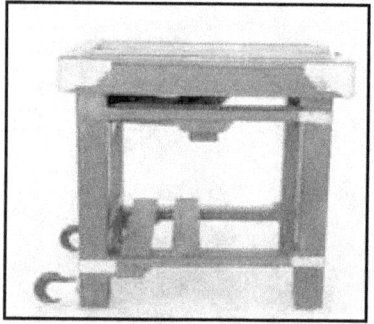  

This is the side view of a traditional tiger iron palm table. For this table, wheels have been added to the back of the rear legs so the table can be moved by tilting and rolling it backward.

This view shows the table's inclined setting, used when you want to focus on the pushing power of the heel strike.

This view shows the table's declined setting, used when you want to focus on the pulling power of the final tiger claw. In general these angles are set from eight-to-12 degrees. You can customize a table to allow for a steeper incline or decline to focus more on these two strikes.

Here is a view showing an advanced steel bag. As with shaolin iron palm, begin your training on a bag filled with mung beans, move to a gravel-filled bag, and finally to a bag filled with steel shot. This close-up view shows how the bag sets into the track on the table.

MARTIAL ARTS

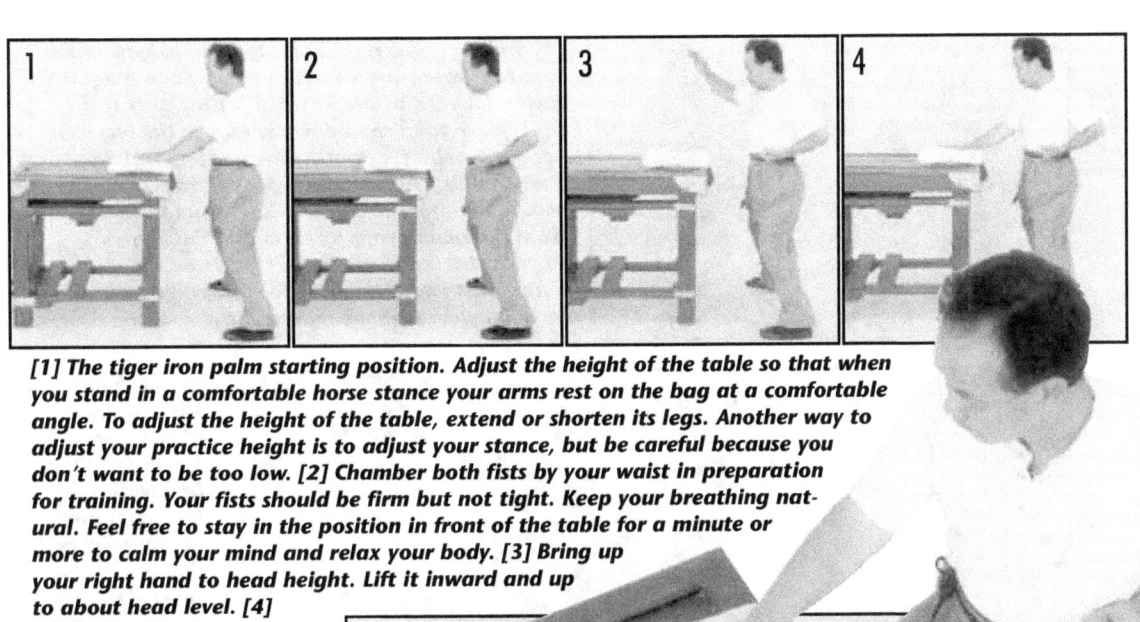

[1] The tiger iron palm starting position. Adjust the height of the table so that when you stand in a comfortable horse stance your arms rest on the bag at a comfortable angle. To adjust the height of the table, extend or shorten its legs. Another way to adjust your practice height is to adjust your stance, but be careful because you don't want to be too low. [2] Chamber both fists by your waist in preparation for training. Your fists should be firm but not tight. Keep your breathing natural. Feel free to stay in the position in front of the table for a minute or more to calm your mind and relax your body. [3] Bring up your right hand to head height. Lift it inward and up to about head level. [4] Bring your hand down in a palm strike to the right center of the bag. Hold your fingers firmly together and form your palm into a shallow cup. Focus on transferring your energy deep into the table. One way to tell if you are doing this correctly is to listen to the sound of the strikes. The tiger iron palm table acts in some ways like a drum. If you are penetrating with your strikes, you will hear the sounds of your strikes being amplified and coming from deep within the table. [4 Top] This view shows a palm strike from the top. Note the hand position at the right center of the bag, away from its edges.

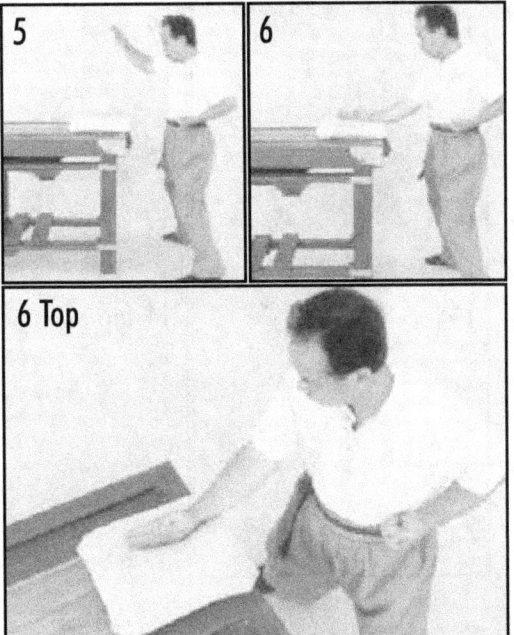

[5] Bring your right hand up to head height. Lift it inward and up to about head level. [6] Drop the back of your hand down onto the bag, focusing on the area from the fingernails to about halfway down your hand. Do not use muscle power. Simply let your hand drop with a whipping motion. Do not use your body or strength from your shoulder to create this whipping power. [6 Top] Your thumb does not fully touch the bag. Your wrist hits the bag, but the focus is on the striking point mentioned above and not on the wrist.

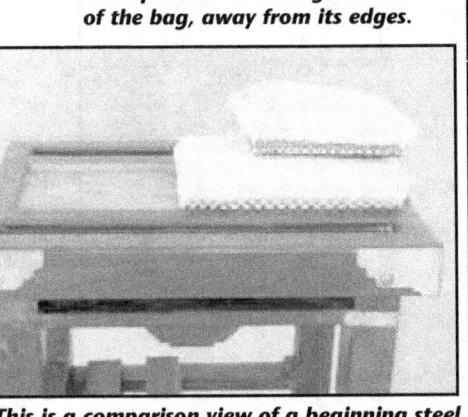

This is a comparison view of a beginning steel shot bag and an advanced steel shot bag.

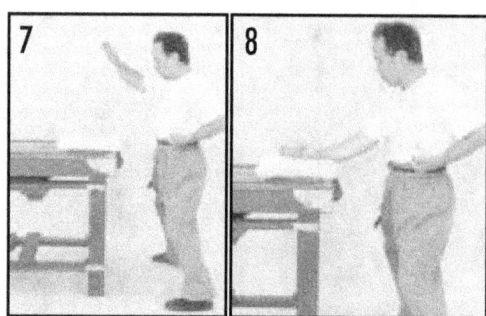

[7] Bring up your right hand to head height. Make sure to rotate your forearm so your palm is again facing forward as preparation for the next strike. [8] Willow palm chop downward into the bag. Stack your fingers tightly together and tuck in your thumb. This strike is more external so you should use more strength, which should come from tightening your forearm and the fingers of your striking hand. Do not generate the external strength required for this strike with your shoulder or body movements.

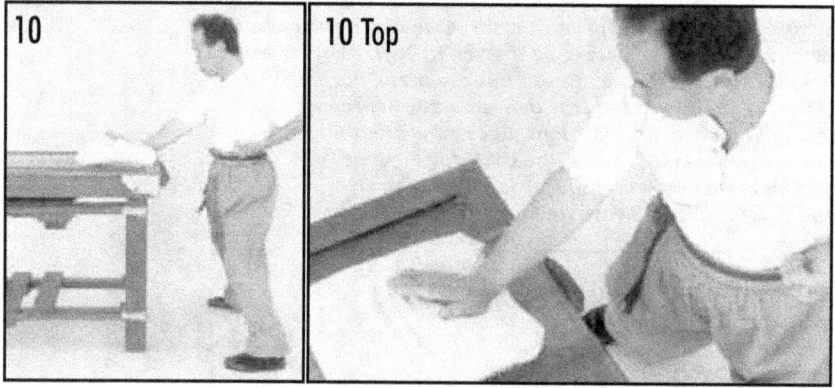

[9 not shown] Lift your hand about four inches from the bag with your fingertips pointing forward and 45 degrees down toward the bag. Cock your wrist tightly and focus your power in the heel of your hand below the thumb. Don't let tension enter the wrist. [10] Snap your wrist forward and strike with the heel of your hand directly into the center of the bag about two inches above the bag's lower edge. Do not strike the wood or just above the wood. At the end of the strike add pushing power to drive the bag forward. [10 Top] (Note that Lam sifu's right shoulder drives forward. For this push, generate power by twisting the waist.)

[11] The bag should travel forward but don't follow with your striking hand. [12] As the bag reaches the end of the table, step in under the table with your right leg and into a high bow stance. Leave your left leg in place. [13] Bring your right hand down and claw into the bag. Dig in deeply with your fingers and start to pull back. [14] Pull back simultaneously with your right leg and hand. As you pull, don't let your wrist touch the bag. You should return to a horse stance with your hand back in a comfortable position on the bag. [14 Top] During the claw, focus on squeezing and digging into the bag.

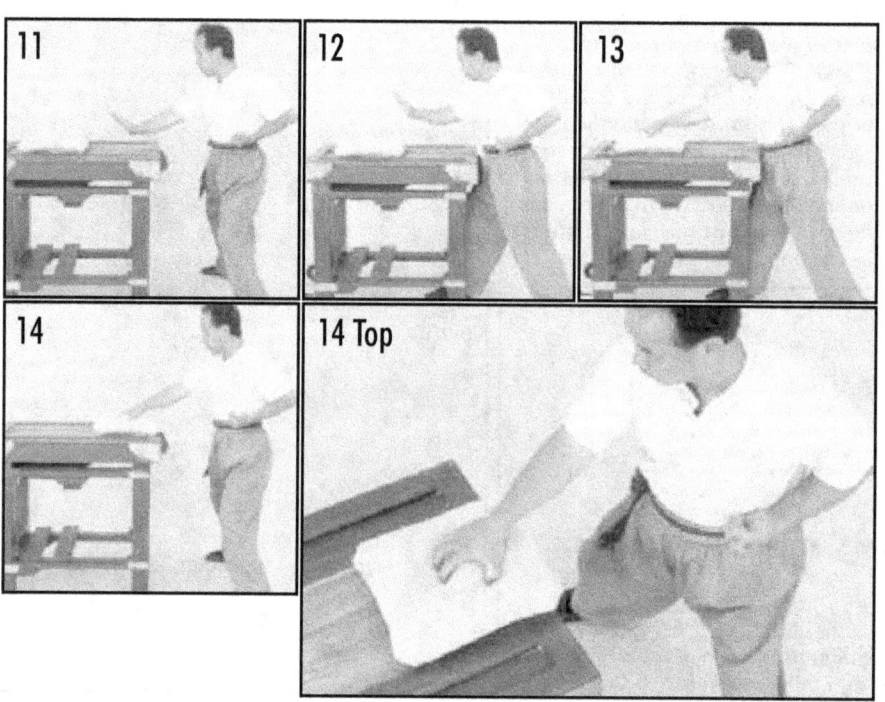

[15] As the bag approaches the front edge of the table, press downward with your heel and wrist to control the bag's movement. The power in this press comes from sinking the elbow, shoulder, right hip, and knee. [15 Top] As you execute the heel press, completely relax your fingers. This completes the first repetition with your right hand.

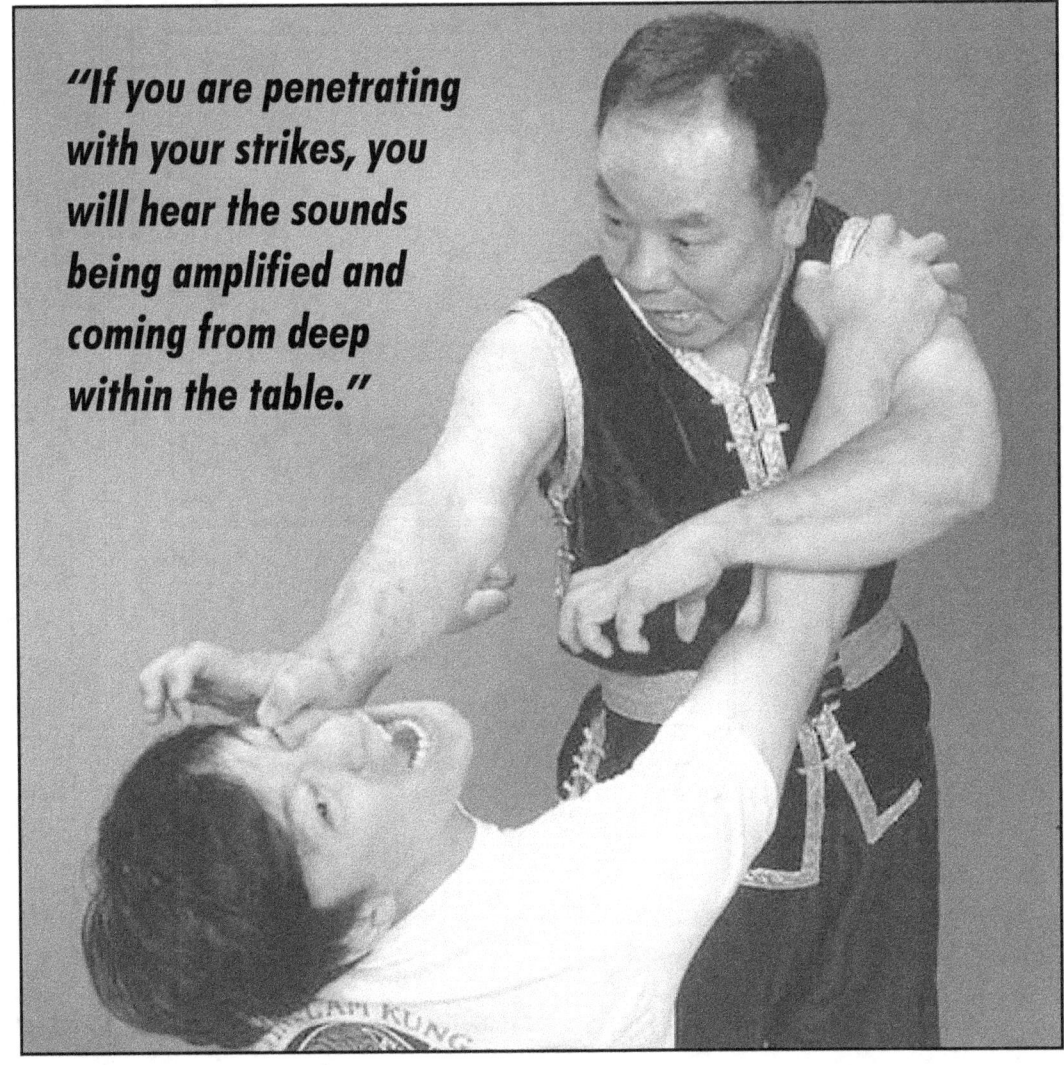

"If you are penetrating with your strikes, you will hear the sounds being amplified and coming from deep within the table."

[16-22] Repeat with your left hand. Continue to alternate hands.

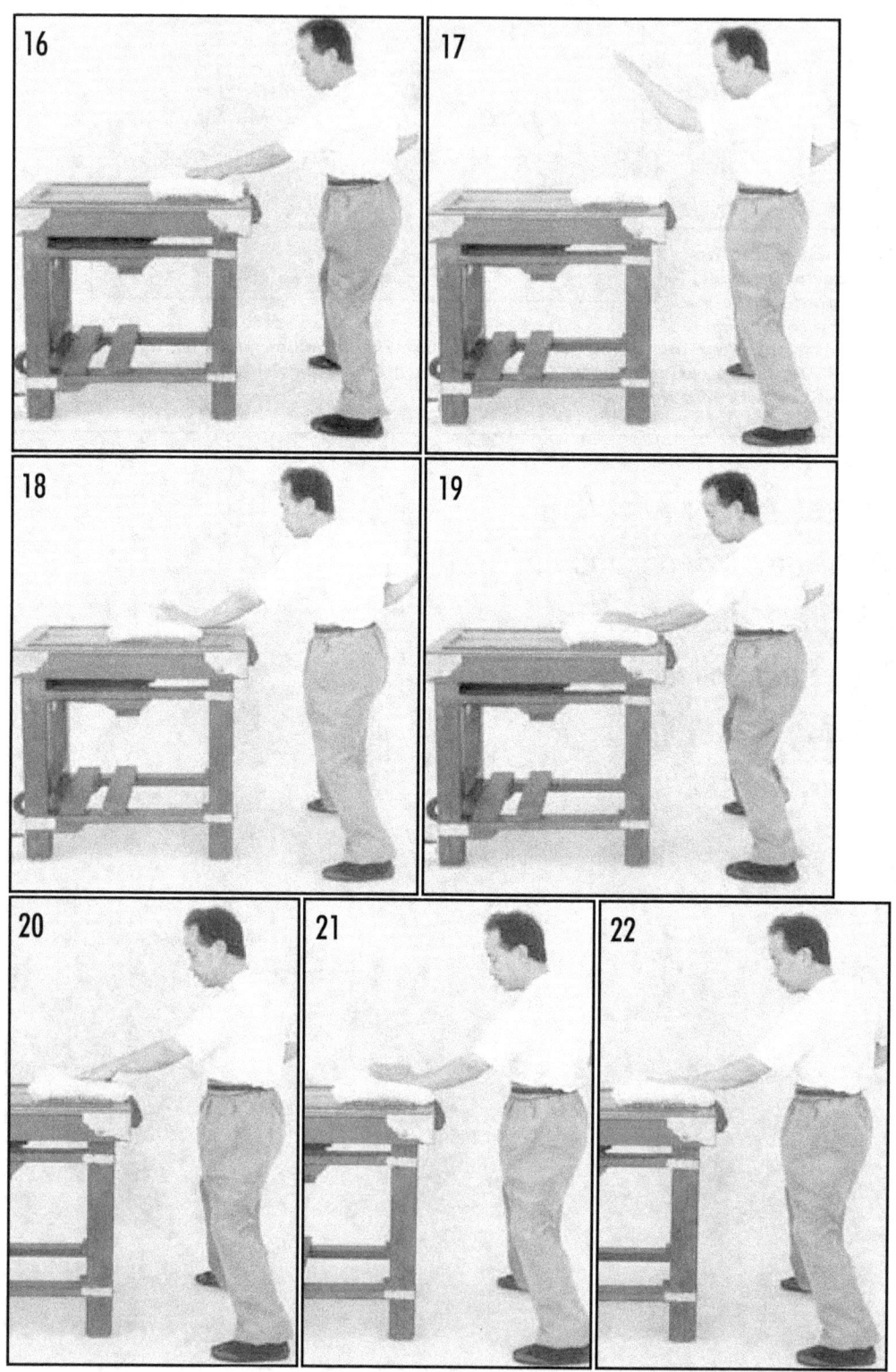

heel-hand strike should be a short, powerful strike with no drawback, driven by the movement of your body into a bow stance. The same is true for the tiger-claw pull; your arm motion should be short, and the pull should be powered by your return to a horse stance.

Tiger iron palm also requires you to strike the bag in a different location. In shaolin iron palm training the bag is struck four times on the right side by the right hand and then four times on the left side by the left hand to mix the contents of the bag and spread them out evenly. In tiger iron palm all strikes are delivered to the center of the bag.

While the bag's contents must be distributed evenly for the heel-hand strike and the tiger-claw pull, the violent forward and back motion of the bag effectively mixes, loosens, and evens out its contents.

MARTIAL ARTS

Karate Hand Strikes

Shito-Ryu stylist Fumio Demura explains how to throw 6 vicious techniques.

Doug Jeffrey

If you want to learn how to write, you read Jim Murray, the former sports columnist for the "*Los Angeles Times.*" If you want to learn how to paint, you study Vincent van Gogh. If you want to learn how to throw karate hand techniques, you train with Fumio Demura.

In the following story, Demura, the chief instructor of Shito-ryu Karate-do Genbu-kai, explains how to throw backhands, reverse punches, chops, palm strikes, finger thrusts and elbows. You'll learn all about the mechanics and he'll point out common errors.

WHY THE HANDS?

To begin, let's look at the benefits of throwing hand techniques.

First, although your legs are stronger and longer [thus you can strike from a greater distance] than your arms, kicking has its disadvantages, he says.

"When you kick, you have to use one leg at a time," notes Demura.

Unlike your feet, you can use both hands at the same time, he says.

"If someone grabs one arm, you can use your other arm to respond [to the attack]," says Demura.

Not only that, but your legs (and kicks) aren't worth a whole lot if you're so close to your opponent that you can't extend them and put a little power into the technique. Your hands, however, are a different story. When you're in tight, you've got a variety of techniques you can unleash on your adversary because you're in the perfect spot to hammer him.

When you talk about angles, the hands also have the advantage over [some] kicks. Take the knees, for example. When you throw a knee, it's going to "go this way or that," says Demura. On the other side of the coin, your hands provide a little more diversity as to which direction they can go.

"You can throw an elbow up, down, to the side and back," says Demura. "You have more and different angles."

278 Best of CFW Enterprises, 2002

MARTIAL ARTS

The Demura Scoop
Name: Fumio Demura
Age: 64
Years Training: 55
Favorite Technique: reverse punch
Styles: shito-ryu and shotokan
Occupation: President and chief instructor of Shito-ryu Karate-do Genbu-kai
Contact: www.genbu-kai.com or (714) 543-5550

FUNDAMENTAL MECHANICS

Everyone has seen different shots of a batter hitting a home run in baseball. In the shot from behind home plate, you see the batter clearly step into the pitch. From the outfield camera, you can see him watch the ball all the way in, turn his hips into the pitch, turn his wrists over and swing. Things aren't a whole lot different in the martial arts. You watch your target, you step toward your opponent, you turn your hips into the technique and, hopefully, you'll "hit a home run."

"When you punch, you have to twist your body just like a baseball player or golfer does," he says.

Similarly, if you're dropping an elbow onto an unsuspecting opponent, you have to put all of your weight into the move, he says.

"You need that body weight for full power," he says. "You don't just want to use your hands."

OTHER ESSENTIALS

If you take these mechanics and blend them with the following four characteristics, you've really got a winning technique.

Backhand
Fumio Demura (right) squares off with Dave Hines (1). When Hines throws a left, Demura slaps his hand away (2-3). This also breaks his concentration, says Demura, who then snaps his arm back (4) and unleashes a backhand to the face (5). Afterward, he brings his arm back to the starting position (not shown). Here, Demura shows the wrong way to throw a backhand (6) and the correct way (7).

MARTIAL ARTS

Reverse Punch
The fighters square off (1). Demura blocks his opponent's punch (2) and counters with a reverse punch (3). In this shot, Demura shows the wrong form (4). Note his back leg. A close-up of the strike (5).

Power

When you throw these techniques, you want to have a little oomph behind them. You know ... good, old-fashioned power. One way to accomplish that is to train and train and train.

"You have to do these moves hundreds of times over and over until the moves are natural," says Demura. "You want your techniques to be natural. You want to move automatically. Besides, in a fight, you don't have time to think."

Kime, which is the ability to think single-mindedly about an objective, is also important. This will help you to generate additional power. For even more power, tighten your wrist and arm just before you make contact.

"This will give you the perfect punch," he says.

Of course, you should mix a little strength training into your routine. To develop power, you can hit a *makiwara* or a heavy bag. The idea, Demura says, is to strengthen your muscles so your wrists are strong when you strike an opponent. If your wrist bends when you hit somebody, you'll lose all of your power, he adds. Finally, you can boost your power by working with weapons because this will strengthen your wrists.

The strength training, regardless of which form you choose, should be done two to three times per week for 30 to 60 minutes, says Demura. You don't want to do it more often because your muscles need time to recover.

Speed

Speed is another essential element in hand techniques. To be fast, you need strength and you need to relax. Everyone is going to have his own ways to relax. Some use music.

"I've never done this, but some do," says Demura. "Maybe it's a good idea."

To understand the importance of relaxing, think of a baseball pitcher, he says. If he's real stiff, he won't be able to throw the ball fast. He has to be relaxed.

There are also sparring drills you can do to enhance your relaxation skills. Demura has his students pair off, stand about three feet away from each other, move in and out and throw punches at

MARTIAL ARTS

each other. In this drill, they do not strike each other. Instead, it's strictly designed to get them more relaxed in a sparring situation.

Another way to develop speed is through the use of kendo steps. Again, the students pair off. One takes a deep step toward his opponent and then several short-burst steps to reach his opponent quickly. When you're doing this, keep your weight on the balls of your feet.

Accuracy

One-point sparring (*ippon kumite*) is a great way to develop accuracy. When Demura has his students do this drill, the students throw a punch (or kick), block and counter. This drill enables them to control their body movement, the distance between themselves and their opponent, and hone their focusing skills, he says.

Conditioning

You can also do some conditioning drills. Demura's students make a fist and repeatedly pound various surfaces of their body. They do this to get used to getting hit, he notes.

"If you hit your arm all the time, the little strikes will not hurt anymore," he notes.

THE TECHNIQUES
The Backhand

How To Do It: Stand with your legs slightly wider than shoulder-width. Your front leg, which should face your opponent, should be slightly bent. Your rear foot should be perpendicular to your front foot and also slightly bent. Hold your hands in the fighting position. Draw your front arm back toward your chest and then whip it out toward your opponent's face. Strike your opponent with the top of your knuckles.

Keys: Get close to your opponent, keep your fist tight when you throw the technique and make sure your shoulder is

Palm Strike
The fighters square off (1). When his opponent starts to strike, Demura slides back and snaps his adversary's wrist down (2-3). Note how Demura drops his body to get more power in the technique. Demura then slides back in and throws the strike to his opponent's chin (4-5). Here, Demura shows the wrong technique (6) and a close-up of two targets (7-8).

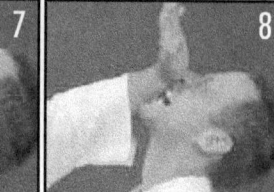

MARTIAL ARTS

Chop
The fighters square off (1). When his opponent prepares to kick, Demura steps back and grabs his opponent's leg (2-3). He then raises his arm and throws a chop to his opponent's neck (4-5). An example of the wrong way (6) and a close-up of the action (7).

Elbow
The fighters square off (1). As his opponent begins to strike, Demura catches his arm and starts to turn (2-3). He brings his arm out in front of him (4) and then drives his elbow into Hines' back (5). An example of the wrong way to hold your fist (6).

relaxed so you can snap the technique out and back fast.

Errors: Attempting to strike from too far away and not clenching your fist.

Reverse Punch

How To Do It: Assume a horse stance. Hold your arms in the ready position. Step forward with your left leg, turn your right hip toward your opponent and throw the punch with your right arm. You should be straight and upright when you connect. Of course, you can throw the technique with either arm.

Keys: To generate twice the power, move in toward your opponent while he is moving toward you. Make sure your wrist is straight, and make contact with the first two knuckles of your fist.

Errors: Bending your rear knee when you punch. This will change the impact point of the punch.

Chop

How To Do It: Assume a horse stance. Raise your right arm to head level, turn your right hip toward your opponent, twist your body and strike the neck. Keep your thumb bent and your fingers tight.

Key: Twist your hips just like a hitter. This will build power.

Errors: Poor balance and loose fingers.

Palm Strike

How To Do It: Stand with your left foot slightly in front of your right. Keep your right arm at your waist, step toward your opponent and throw the strike with your left arm to his chin or nose.

Key: Tighten your palm and make sure you keep your fingers way back when you make contact.

MARTIAL ARTS

Finger Thrust

The pair squares off (1). When his opponent prepares to strike, Demura steps back and makes contact with his arm (2-3). Demura then turns his hip into the technique, which nullifies his opponent's strike, and thrusts his fingers to the eyes (4). A close-up of the strike (5) and an example of how not to do it (6). Note how Demura hasn't twisted his body enough. Therefore, his opponent's strike can still reach him.

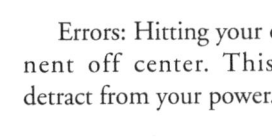

Errors: Hitting your opponent off center. This will detract from your power.

Finger Thrust

How To Do It: Stand with your left foot slightly in front of your right. Turn your hips to the right and thrust your fingers [on your left hand] at your opponent's eyes.

Keys: Make sure your fingers are tight. You can also use fewer fingers, but four fingers make the technique more powerful. Be sure to turn your hip into the technique. You can simultaneously block your opponent's strike [with your arm] when you thrust your fingers into his face.

Errors: Not twisting your body into the technique. This leaves you open to your opponent's strikes.

Elbow

How To Do It: Assume a horse stance. Bring your striking arm out in front of you at head level and then quickly drive it into your opponent's back.

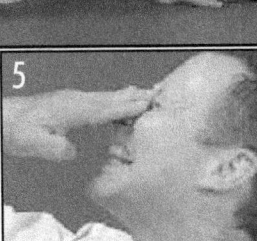

Key: Keep your knuckles up.

Errors: Holding your knuckles any which way but up. If they are not up and your target is behind you and you're aiming for his back, your strike will not be accurate.

SIMPLY A MASTER

These are six techniques that you should add to your repertoire. Without a doubt, you'll have some awesome artillery and be one formidable fighter. So get off your butt, practice them and refine them. And make sure you study Demura's form. You can search high and low or far and wide, but you won't find a better instructor than Demura. He's Murray with a reverse punch. He's van Gogh with an elbow strike. He's simply a master, and his techniques are flawless.

www.ingramcontent.com/pod-product-compliance
Lightning Source LLC
Chambersburg PA
CBHW081441070526
44586CB00019B/2192